THE LAND OF TRUTH

DELPHI PUBLIC LIBRARY

222 East Main Street
Delphi, Indiana 46923
765-564-2929

University of Nebraska Press | LINCOLN

The Land of Truth

Talmud Tales, Timeless Teachings

JEFFREY L. RUBENSTEIN

The Jewish Publication Society | PHILADELPHIA

© 2018 by Jeffrey L. Rubenstein. All rights reserved.
Published by the University of Nebraska Press as a
Jewish Publication Society book.
Manufactured in the United States of America. ∞

Library of Congress Cataloging-in-Publication Data
Names: Rubenstein, Jeffrey L., author.
Title: The land of truth: Talmud tales, timeless
teachings / Jeffrey L. Rubenstein.
Description: [Lincoln]: University of Nebraska Press,
[2018] | Includes bibliographical references and index.
| "Published by the University of Nebraska Press as a
Jewish Publication Society book."
Identifiers: LCCN 2017058299
ISBN 9780827613089 (pbk: alk. paper)
ISBN 9780827614352 (epub)
ISBN 9780827614369 (mobi)
ISBN 9780827614376 (pdf)
Subjects: LCSH: Aggada—History and criticism. |
Rabbinical literature—Translations into English.
Classification: LCC BM516.5 .R818 2018 | DDC 296.1/9—
dc23 LC record available at
https://lccn.loc.gov/2017058299

Set in Vesper by Mikala R. Kolander.

In memory of Dr. Maureen Hack

מנוחה בת שרגא יהא זכרה ברוך

May her memory be for a blessing

Contents

Acknowledgments

I am grateful to teachers, colleagues, and friends who have contributed to my education and thinking. This book draws on the work of many excellent scholars of Talmud and ancient Jewish literature, and I thank them and the general academic community in which I work. Thanks to those who read drafts of chapters and made valuable suggestions: Burton Appel, Tamar Appel, Michael Friedland, Thomas Friedman, Beth Kissileff, Barry Holtz, and Lawrence Solomon. I thank Rabbi Barry Schwartz, director of the Jewish Publication Society (JPS), for supporting this project from the beginning; Joy Weinberg, JPS managing editor, and Judith Sandman for their meticulous editing; and the University of Nebraska Press, for publishing the book.

I am grateful to my extended family for their constant support: Arthur, Denise, Errol, Sarah, Evelyn, Milton, Ronald, Miriam, Shulie, Dan, Rena, Jeff, Talia, Yaron, and Sarah. My wife, Mishaela Rubin, has been a constant source of love and devotion, as have my children, Ayelet, Maya, Adam, and Noah. Thank you for helping me stay focused on the important aspects of life.

I also wish to acknowledge my maternal aunt, Dr. Maureen Hack (1937–2015), to whose memory this book is dedicated. Born and educated in Pretoria, South Africa, Maureen moved to Israel in 1960 and worked as a doctor in the Israeli army. Settling in Cleveland in 1977, she became one of the world's leading neonatologists, carrying out important studies on the development of low-birth-weight babies. Maureen did not have children of her own, but she contributed to the life and development of thousands of children in her practice and research. She was extremely generous, cultured, kind, thoughtful, and devoted to her family. May her memory be for a blessing.

Introduction   *Of Stones and Stories*

Once a man was removing stones from his field [and putting them] into the public domain. A certain Holy Man came upon him and said, "Scoundrel! Why do you remove stones from a domain that does not belong to you [and put them] into your domain?"

The man laughed at him.

After some time that man was in need, and he sold his field. He was walking in that very place, and he stumbled on those very stones.

He said, "That Holy Man spoke well to me when he said, 'Why do you remove stones from a domain that does not belong to you [and put them into] your domain.'"

(Babylonian Talmud, *Bava Qamma* 50b)

When first reading this story from the Babylonian Talmud, most of us probably react to the Holy Man's words much like the owner of the field. "Wait just a minute!" we think. "That is *not* at all what he did. This man took the stones *out* of his field and threw them *into* the street. He got rid of the stones from his backyard and tossed them over the fence into some public area. He wanted a smooth, grassy, flat lawn and didn't care about littering. What was that Holy Man talking about?"

Only after reading the end of the story and reflecting for a moment do we readers, like the protagonist, understand the truth of the Holy Man's charge. The homeowner suffered a reversal of fortune; financial pressures evidently forced him to sell his house and yard; one day when walking down the street near his former property he stumbled and fell on the same stones he had discarded. The combination of dramatic irony (sometimes called Sophoclean irony) with the measure-for-measure principle provides a beautiful illustration of the moral. Seeking to avoid a certain situation—stumbling on stones in his (apparent) domain—he ends up bringing it about—stumbling on stones in his (true) domain. Measure for measure, effect meets cause, reaction follows action, and punishment fits crime. The hazard he recklessly inflicted on others boomeranged. At this point he repeats the Holy Man's words, now with enlightenment, comprehension, self-realization: "That Holy Man spoke well to me."

This story teaches many lessons. On a basic level, one should not disrespect public property, litter, or debase the environment, for it belongs to us all. "What goes around, comes around," as we sometimes say, or "Don't do unto others as you would not want done to you." We also learn the importance of humility, of not laughing at the words of others we fail to understand, for these may possess valuable wisdom. Most significant is the core message, which the Holy Man articulates and the protagonist repeats at the end. While we human beings naturally feel that our lawfully acquired property—our possessions, our house, and especially our land—belongs to us and cannot be taken away, in truth, all material wealth is subject to changing circumstances. Acquisitions can easily be lost: by theft or cheat, by swindlers and strongmen, by the arbitrary vagaries of fate. The only goods we truly possess are those we share with all others: public spaces, including libraries, museums, public beaches, public gardens, national parks. Paradoxically, we do not eternally possess that which legally belongs to us, while we can never be deprived of many things that we do not own.

The talmudic storyteller communicates his lessons through a sophisticated narrative art, including dramatic irony, a measure-for-measure principle, and deliberate repetition. He has also chosen his language very carefully. Astute readers will note that the selection of the word "stumble" evokes the "stumbling block" of the biblical commandment, "You shall not place a stumbling block before the blind" (Lev. 19:14). Our protagonist literally stumbles over the "blocks"/stones he had callously cast into the path of others, a result of his figurative blindness both to the repercussions of his actions and to the deeper structure of reality. The use of the verb for "removing stones," *mesaqel*, is also evocative as the word also means "to stone" or to "execute by stoning." Ironically, intending to remove the stones, he ends up "stoning" himself; his lack of understanding is contained within the double meaning of the word. And we might also interpret the word for scoundrel, *reiqa*, from the root *reiq*, for "empty" or "void," as alluding to the man's efforts to empty or clear his field—an endeavor that reveals he is empty or void of understanding.

The protagonist in fact experiences a double fall: a figurative fall from prosperity, which ultimately causes his literal fall over the stones. What provoked his fall from prosperity the storyteller does not tell us. We are probably meant to analogize the answer from the literal fall—the same shortsightedness, self-centeredness, and lack of concern for others. In this way the storyteller tries to move us to embrace the Rabbinic worldview in its wider sense: to always act with sensitivity, forethought, and understanding.

Like many talmudic narratives, this brief story teaches us a deeper perspective on reality in contrast with superficial appearances. The Holy Man, a type of Rabbinic figure on the one hand,

and the stone thrower, on the other, look at the world through different eyes. The protagonist sees things for what they are—no more, no less. He does not ponder the consequences of his behavior or consider the implications if everyone acted as he does. He fails to understand the precariousness of his situation, the uncertainty of all of life's circumstances, and how his nonchalant discarding of stones into a public area may harm himself or others. The Holy Man, on the other hand, sees through the apparent nature of things to a deeper truth—to the way the world works, to the possibilities entailed in any given choice.

The stories in this book provide an entry into this Rabbinic world and its deeper perspectives on life. They try to move us to think beyond the world of experience to matters of ultimate concern. To study them involves a journey back in time to sources of ancient wisdom and then forward again to our own time. This ancient wisdom on matters of fundamental meaning is surprisingly and deeply relevant to us today.

The Talmud and Its Tales

The Babylonian Talmud, the great compendium of Jewish law from late antiquity (ca. 200–700 CE), is usually thought of as a legal textbook, a collection of legal discussions, and the foundational source of Jewish law or *halakhah*. Yet the Talmud is as much an anthology or encyclopedia as a law book and includes a great deal of *aggadah* or lore—nonlegal material including biblical interpretation, historical memories, prayers and liturgical formulas, wise sayings and proverbs, poems, interpretations of dreams, and more.

The Talmud is also one of the great repositories of Jewish tales. No one has attempted a complete inventory of talmudic stories, but there are probably more than one thousand. Additional stories are found in the other Rabbinic texts, including the Mishnah, the earliest Rabbinic law book (edited ca. 200 CE); the Babylonian Talmud's "sister," known as the Jerusalem Talmud or Talmud Yerushalmi (ca. 400 CE); and the many books of midrash or biblical interpretation (ca. 250–700 CE).

Most talmudic tales take the form of biographical anecdotes, brief accounts of an event or deed in the life of a particular Sage. Some function narrowly as legal precedents, relating how a Rabbi acted on the Sabbath, conducted himself in prayer, or carried out one of the commandments. Others address Rabbinic social and cultural life, relationships among the Rabbis, tensions between masters and disciples, the Rabbinic hierarchy, and competition for status. A great many stories speak of mundane affairs, ordinary life, the difficulties and struggles we all face as we try to make our way in the world. Pick an issue or problem and odds are that you will find a relevant talmudic tale.

The talmudic Sages employed stories as a crucial pedagogical tool. While knowledge of Jewish law was fundamental to becoming a Rabbi, wisdom and character were equally important. Legal discussions and analyses, no matter how extensive, could not teach an aspiring student everything he needed to know about becoming a Sage. Filling in some of those gaps, talmudic stories engage other dimensions of religious life, such as the development of spiritual sensibility and ethical character. They address the world beyond the Rabbinic academy in all its complexity, including the struggle with one's evil inclination, the difficulties of earning a living, and relationships with wives and children.

Many of these Rabbinic concerns are shared by all Jews, and to a certain extent by all human beings. The tales thus provide a means to bridge the gap between the professional and technical knowledge expected of the talmudic Rabbis and the life of piety required of the laity. They teach how to summon spiritual values as we look at the world, and how to act justly and righteously in diverse arenas of life.

Many of these stories were excerpted from the Talmud and retold throughout the Middle Ages and into modern times, pointing to their enduring meaning throughout the generations. Like the great narratives of classical literature, Talmud tales grapple with the tensions, contradictions, and struggles of human existence. To be sure, as we read, study, and contemplate them, we may encounter some outdated or alien tales of a premodern culture, but overall our search will yield fabulous narratives that address constants of Jewish and human life, even if the particulars have to be translated into modern terms. A story about a Rabbi who encounters a hostile Persian or Roman government official may have much to teach about confrontations with unsympathetic, bureaucratic government functionaries today. A story about misunderstandings between husbands and wives in talmudic times can still shed light on the difficulties and importance of communication between spouses in our era (see chapter 4).

By today's standards, Talmud tales are extremely brief, rarely exceeding a few hundred words. The story of the stone thrower, for example, numbers about fifty words in the original Hebrew. This brevity results from the Talmud's original oral form: since oral literature requires memorization, texts had to be formulated with maximum economy to facilitate the mnemonic process. Storytellers omitted introductions, backgrounds, detailed descriptions, and aftermaths, only providing the information critical to understanding the plot. A proportionately large amount of dialogue appears, but this, too, advances the story's essential needs; there are no superfluous interchanges or digressions. As in folktales, children's stories, and other genres of oral literature, these stories also offer immediate characterizations of the protagonists through descriptive names such as "Joseph the Sabbath Honorer," "Mr. Five Sins," "Ḥoni the Circle Drawer."

Because of their terseness, many Talmud tales contain interpretive gaps. Often we wish the storytellers had supplied us with more information so we could make better sense of the story. For example, in the story of the stone thrower, we do not know either the protagonist or the Holy Man's name, where the incident took place, why the Holy Man happened to be walking near the offender's property, or whether they had a prior relationship.

As a pedagogical strategy as well, storytellers rarely explicitly spell out the morals or lessons they hope to convey; instead, they invite their audience to study, analyze, reflect upon, and make sense of the story for themselves. Nor can most talmudic stories necessarily be reduced to a single, simple message, any more than the best novels and poems. Depending on how we as interpreters fill the gaps, the stories can be understood on multiple levels and in different ways. This is yet another reason why talmudic stories still have much to teach us today: modern readers inevitably fill the interpretive gaps in relevant, meaningful ways for their times.

Narrative Worlds

To study the stories of the Talmud is to enter the Talmud's narrative world. To study the stories of the Talmud with an open mind and an open heart renders the Talmud's narrative world a part of oneself.

Every human being inhabits a narrative world. To answer any substantive question about our lives we inevitably tell a story: How did you come to live in Philadelphia (Chicago/Paris/Albany)? Why did you become a teacher (electrician/nurse/computer programmer)? How did you meet your spouse (partner/best friend)? Timewise, we never think of ourselves in terms of the present alone but also of the past: how we arrived at this point of time and space. Inevitably we imagine ourselves in the future too: Where do we hope to be one year (five years / ten years) from now? If we choose to take a particular course of action now, how will it impact us tomorrow (next week /next month / next year)? Moreover, those who profess to "live in the present" cannot sustain the feeling for more than a short time. Almost everyone who sets a goal, formulates a desire, or pursues an objective has in mind a narrative of why that goal, desire, or objective should be attained. And how many human beings live without goals, desires, and objectives? We make significant plans and take all-important actions because they are parts of a story we tell ourselves. Thus ethicist and philosopher Alasdair MacIntyre writes: "Man is in his actions and practices, as well as in his fictions, essentially a story-telling animal . . . . I can only answer the question 'What am I to do?' if I can answer the prior question 'Of what story or stories do I find myself a part?'"[1]

Similarly, we make sense of other people by framing their lives in narrative terms. Rather than isolate whatever others do or say, we conceptualize it in the context of stories that explain how and why people came to act or speak that way. Behind the query "What's his story?"—sometimes uttered in genuine curiosity, other times expressed derogatorily—lies this truth: we cannot begin to understand other human beings until and unless we learn their personal narratives. Daniel Kahneman, the Nobel Prize-winning psychologist, abandoned the promising field of "decision analysis," which attempted to remove irrational personal biases from decisions by translating them into more objective probabilities, because people could not forgo narrative thinking even when confronted by clear evidence to the contrary. "No one ever made a decision because of a number," Kahneman reportedly said. "They need a story."[2] If many people make up stories, stories also, and always, make people.[3]

Most of us have a crude narrative, a story-sketch, in mind according to which we attempt to pattern our lives. Something like: "I will go to college and graduate school, become an engineer, marry, have children, and buy a house in such and such a suburb." Or: "I will travel the world after high school, working odd jobs as I go, and settle down when I find a congenial place." Or again: "I will finish business school, work for a company to get some experience, then open my own business and build it up until I am a millionaire." Narratives inevitably change due to unpredictable and uncontrollable events: an unexpected opportunity, the failure of one's business, the birth of twins, the untimely death of a relative. Experiences may cause us to reject the narratives we had adopted, as we discover, say, that a career in law is not fulfilling, that life as a bachelor is lonelier than anticipated, or that we hate living on a farm. In such cases we search for a different narrative, a new narrative, and begin to pattern our lives accordingly. The smaller goals, desires, and objectives we pursue are mostly those we believe will help us transform our internal narratives into lived reality. But at root, our self-conceptions, our identities, devolve less from what we do, less from our behavior, than from the underlying narratives we tell ourselves.

Where do these narratives come from? What gives us the idea that certain life stories are valuable and worth living while others must be avoided? What makes some life narratives viable and compelling and others incomprehensible to us?

Traditional premodern societies possessed sets of narratives by which their members defined themselves and navigated their lives. The Greek myths, for example, not only offered the Greeks accounts of the gods and heroes, but a sense of collective identity and a vision of how life should be led, of what ends should be pursued and how to achieve them. Stories of successes and tragedies enabled individuals to make sense of their personal situations. Why had they suffered or prospered, sickened or recovered, married happily or miserably, sired healthy children or remained barren? Where had they come from and to what should they aspire?

Life in premodern times was typically much harsher than ours today, as bloodshed, violence, war, plagues, starvation, and social oppression were more often the norm than the exception. Despite upheavals and the concomitant uncertainties, possessing shared stories gave men and women in traditional societies a deep root-edness in time and place, a profound sense that they led meaningful lives. Their behavior, beliefs, and sense of belonging were anchored in the stories they received from their ancestors and would pass on to their descendants.

The sets of narratives or myths of traditional societies were never fixed in either scope or wording. Over the course of time new stories responding to novel circumstances joined the corpus while other stories ceased being told and were gradually forgotten. Different storytellers altered and embellished stories according to their individual proclivities and the needs of the hour. Plots, conflicts, and narrative details metamorphosed as a new generation encountered the stories of their ancestors and shaped them for their age. Paradoxically, such variations were both accepted and undetected: accepted, because the concept of an original or "authentic" version did not exist; undetected, because premodern culture changed so slowly that the process by which storytellers updated the stories they had received occurred at a subconscious level. In this way stories remained relevant even as political, social, and economic circumstances changed.

Fulfilling these functions for generations of the Jewish people, talmudic stories, together with biblical stories, essentially constituted a traditional mythology. Rabbis stood with the biblical patriarchs, prophets, heroes, and kings as role models, both positive and negative, for patterning behavior and negotiating life's challenges. These stories comprised a narrative world through which Jews structured their lives and understood their place in the cosmos. On the national scale talmudic stories told of the post-biblical fortunes of the Jewish people, their triumphs and defeats, the destruction of the Jerusalem Temple, the Roman and Persian Empires and individual emperors, kings, and governors; and of Rabbinic martyrs and heroes. On the individual plane, stories related to every aspect of life: birth, marriage, and death; suffering and illness; relatives, friends, acquaintances, and enemies; love and loss. Jewish religious life, in particular, is a constant theme: the commandments, Torah study, prayer, and charity. Hearing, telling, repeating, and thinking over these stories enabled their audiences to answer fundamental and existential questions: Where had they come from? Where did they wish to be? How could they get there? Why were they to live their lives a certain way? Traditional Jewish life had its share of suffering, but because of its rich narrative tradition it was never devoid of meaning.

The Crisis of Modernity

The challenge, even crisis, of modernity can be understood, in part, as the shattering of narrative worlds formed by the stories shared by members of traditional societies. The causes of this rupture include: the Enlightenment and loss of faith in the presumptive authority of the past, scientific and technological progress, historical self-consciousness, and the rise of individualism and autonomy. Modernity involves a sense of distance, a feeling of alienation from the traditional world of our ancestors. We no longer believe their stories.

The different sense of the term "myth" illuminates this shift. The Greek word *mythos,* meaning "word" or "story," was used to characterize traditional stories about gods, heroes, or origins. Today "myth" can mean a false belief, a widely held but fictitious idea, a misrepresentation of the truth. Our ancestors' myths have become myths. Their truths—for them, nothing could be truer than the ancient myths they received from the distant past—have become our falsehoods.

Yet more pernicious than the loss of belief in the contemporary age is the loss of knowledge: we no longer know the stories of our ancestors. We cannot tell their stories, let alone ours. In place of the cohesive and dependable corpus of stories our forefathers and foremothers possessed, we moderns have received scattered, disjointed, and often incoherent fragments. A Hasidic story from early modern times recounted by author Elie Wiesel beautifully captures the awareness of the loss of traditional knowledge and rupture from the past:

> When the great Rabbi Israel Baal Shem-tov saw misfortune threatening the Jews, it was his custom to go into a certain part of the forest to meditate. There he would light a fire, say a special prayer, and the miracle would be accomplished and the misfortune averted.
>
> Later, when his disciple, the celebrated Magid of Mezritch, had occasion, for the same reason, to intercede with heaven, he would go to the same place in the forest and say: "Master of the Universe, listen! I do not know how to light the fire, but I am still able to say the prayer." And again the miracle would be accomplished.
>
> Still later, Rabbi Moshe-Leib of Sasov, in order to save his people once more, would go into the forest and say: "I do not know how to light the fire, I do not know the prayer, but I know the place and this must be sufficient." It was sufficient and the miracle was accomplished.
>
> Then it fell to Rabbi Israel of Rizhyn to overcome misfortune. Sitting in his armchair, his head in his hands, he spoke to God: "I am unable to light the fire and I do not know the prayer; I cannot even find the place in the forest. All I can do is to tell the story, and this must be sufficient." And it was suffifficient.[4]

The Ba'al Shem Tov, the founder of Hasidism, died in 1760, and Rabbi Israel of Ruzhyn died in 1850. Already the remarkably self-aware storyteller recognizes how much traditional knowledge has been lost with each generation in the modern age. Despite his guardedly optimistic conclusion, one wonders whether he would say the same of successive generations: How much continued to be lost after 1850, and would whatever remained suffice? Rabbi Israel of Ruzhyn still can tell the story; are his descendants capable even of that?

However unfortunate the loss of knowledge of tradition, few of us would want to return to the Middle Ages or antiquity. We would never give up our rights to be freed from the coercive political, religious, and social institutions of the past, nor sacrifice modern technological and medical progress and the meteoric rise in our standards of living. In any case, there is no way to turn back the clock, even if we so desired, any more than we can return to jungles or caves in pursuit of a more natural existence. Even to decide to live in an ultra-religious or fundamentalist community, to shut oneself off from the modern world, is for most of us a free choice, an autonomous decision that can always be undone.

Our modern freedoms come at a steep price. The foundational stories our ancestors inherited and believed provided a limited set of models for orienting one's life and for fashioning oneself, for better or for worse. In our multicultural, global societies of today, we now have many narratives from which to choose, all equally possible—which is to say, all equally inauthentic. Scholars accordingly write of modernity as characterized by the fragmentation of a previously unified worldview: "In a post-traditional order . . . an indefinite range of possibilities present themselves, not just in respect of options for behaviour, but in respect also of the 'openness of the world' to the individual."[5] As a result, the story fragments we have received from our ancestors compete with hundreds of others that derive from permeable and jumbled modern cultures. We have the freedom to choose our personal narrative in a way that could not have been imagined in traditional society, but without any clear understanding of what to choose or why. What should you be when you grow up? Should you marry? What pursuits are most important? Such basic questions never arose in ages past as the responses were taken for granted. Today we must ask and answer these and countless other questions. Without an inherited narrative world, we are poorly equipped to do so.

The result is a sense of alienation, rootlessness, and meaninglessness that many experience today: the feeling that we muddle through life without a clear sense of direction, not completely understanding the path we have chosen, why we have chosen it, or what it leads to. Observing that such rootlessness is the great failing of modernity, the philosopher Simone Weil averred that "to be rooted is perhaps the most important and least recognized need of the human soul . . . . A human being has roots by virtue of his real, active, and natural participation in the life of a community which preserves in living shape certain particular treasures of the past and certain particular expectations for the future."[6]

Without these deep roots in tradition and the vision of a future oriented to defined goals, many feel that they have somehow fallen into a course of life by default, not having made a choice at all, perhaps pushed into it by parents and general societal expectations or having a path of life choose them in some mysterious way. Sometimes this discontent produces a full-blown midlife crisis and a radical restructuring of one's priorities, though often, after a short time, the new course proves little better than the old. Sometimes it manifests as "restless mobility, consumerism, frenzied sexuality, substance abuse, therapy, and boredom."[7] More often it leaves a gnawing sense of dissatisfaction, an awareness that something is missing, that there must be more to life than material possessions and modern comforts. As keenly observed by Rabbi Harold Kushner: "[I]t is not dying that people are afraid of . . . . We are afraid of never having lived, of coming to the end of our days with the sense that we were never really alive, that we never figured out what life was for."[8] To put this in slightly different terms: many understand that they are living out a story but realize that this story is not, never was, and never can be their own.

There are no easy answers to this problem, and in some respects it cannot be solved completely, as it inheres in the modern condition, a symptom of self-determination and freedom. Yet partial reparation is possible. Those willing to embrace a tradition, whether religious, philosophical, or cultural, and to internalize its narrative world, may discover a path to a richer and more centered life. Ancient traditions offer what modernity lacks— interconnected collections of stories to help structure a meaningful existence. Even if our commitments to these sources are necessarily less than the total identification of former generations, they can help us to answer some of life's deepest questions and find a meaningful path through the emptiness.

For those of us who desire a deeper connection to the past, a narrative world infused with ancient values and perspectives, I believe there is no better path than to immerse oneself in the stories of the Talmud.

Let us begin the journey.

Understanding the Structure and Organization of the Talmud

We travel back to the great ancient repositories of Jewish tradition: the Babylonian and Jerusalem Talmuds.

The Babylonian Talmud, or Bavli, is a commentary to the earliest text compiled by the Rabbis: a law code known as the Mishnah, edited around 200 CE. Most of the Rabbis whose traditions appear in the Mishnah lived from 70 CE, when the Romans destroyed the Jerusalem Temple, until 200 CE, although there are a few traditions from Sages who lived in previous centuries.

While we speak of the Mishnah and Talmud as texts, they were studied and compiled orally throughout late antiquity, and only written down in the Middle Ages. For the Rabbis, the Mishnah and Talmud were the "Oral Torah," which they believed was revealed on Mount Sinai together with the "Written Torah," the Five Books of Moses. "Mishnah" in fact means "repetition" or "repeated tradition," after the manner of studying an oral text by repeating it until it is memorized. "Talmud" means "learning," from the Hebrew root *l-m-d*, "to learn" or "to teach." The Mishnah was composed in Hebrew, while the Talmud is a mixture of Aramaic and Hebrew.

The Mishnah is divided into sixty-three tractates, short books organized by content and named for their principal topic. Some of these tractates include *Berakhot* (Blessings), *Ketubot* (Marriage Contracts), *Nedarim* (Vows), *Yoma* (The Day of Atonement), and *Avodah Zarah* (Idolatry). Any given tractate, however, may include a variety of laws not strictly related to its main topic.

In subsequent centuries, the Rabbis living in two centers, the Land of Israel and Babylonia, continued to study, analyze, discuss, supplement, and interpret the Mishnah. These discussions were collected and edited into a commentary on the Mishnah known as the Gemara or Talmud. Both words mean "learning": the former is Aramaic, the latter Hebrew. The words are synonymous, although some use Gemara when referring to the commentary to the Mishnah alone and Talmud for the book that includes both Mishnah and Gemara.

The Rabbis produced two Talmuds: the Jerusalem Talmud, edited around 400 CE, and the Babylonian Talmud, edited around 600 CE. The name "Jerusalem Talmud" is something of a misnomer, as this Talmud was actually compiled in the cities of Sepphoris and Tiberias in the Galilee; at the time, the Romans did not allow Jews to live in Jerusalem. Some scholars refer to this Talmud as the "Palestinian Talmud," after the Roman name for the province, Palestine, or as the "Talmud of the Land of Israel."

The Babylonian Talmud was compiled in Mesopotamia, a region of the Persian Empire and site of the ancient city of Babylon. Longer and more complex than the Jerusalem Talmud, it became the canonical source of Jewish law in the Middle Ages and until the present day.

The Babylonian Talmud, as commentary to the Mishnah, is divided into the same tractates as the Mishnah. However, this Talmud appears on only thirty-seven of the Mishnah's sixty-three tractates. Tractates of the Mishnah that deal primarily with agricultural laws, which only applied to the Land of Israel, were not studied intensively by the Babylonian Rabbis and therefore did not generate Talmud commentary. Likewise there is no Babylonian Talmud commentary to tractates that focus on laws of purity, which essentially ceased to function when the Temple was destroyed. Similarly, the Jerusalem Talmud contains only thirty-nine of the Mishnah's sixty-three tractates. All talmudic citations in this book are to the Babylonian Talmud unless otherwise specified.

When the Talmud was printed at the end of the fifteenth and beginning of the sixteenth century, it was paginated by the printers. References to the Talmud follow the pagination of these early printings. Thus "*Berakhot* 5a" refers to tractate *Berakhot* (Blessings), page 5, side a; that is, the front side of page 5 in the standard printing. "*Ta'anit* 16b" refers to tractate *Ta'anit* (Fasts), page 16, side b; that is, the back side of page 16.

The "Rabbis," or the "Sages," is a collective term referring to the Rabbis who lived throughout the first seven centuries CE, whose traditions appear in these classical Rabbinic texts—the Mishnah, the Talmuds, and books of midrash. "Rabbi" literally means "master"—that is, a master of Torah. Babylonian Sages typically use "Rav" (e.g., Rav Ze'eira), which also means "master," while the Sages of the Land of Israel employ "Rabbi" (e.g., Rabbi Elazar). These different terms simply reflect different dialectical pronunciations.

The versions of the Talmud tales in this book sometimes follow the readings of Talmud manuscripts, which tend to be more accurate, and not the standard printed edition.

Transliterations of Hebrew and Aramaic employ *q* for *qof* (ק), *ḥ* for *ḥet* (ח), *k* for *kaf* (כ), and *kh* for *khaf* (כ), and is otherwise phonetic.

Using This Book

This book is intended for all those interested in exploring the Babylonian Talmud and understanding how its stories engage the full range of human experience.

Part One, "The Human Condition," focuses on aging, both our own and that of others; relationships with parents and spouses, as well as the emotions and ethical obligations involved; and suffering and illness, those great equalizers, which impact the great and the lowly, the strong and the weak, the most brilliant and the least educated alike.

Part Two explores stories of "Virtue, Character, and the Life of Piety." How do we fashion ourselves into moral, pious, and self-respecting individuals? Talmud tales provide instruction through both positive and negative role models. The five stories here explore humility, dignity, and remorse; compassion and disgust; truth and lies; Torah study, the Talmud's highest ideal; and heroism and humor.

Part Three considers "The Individual, Society, and Power." These stories grapple with such questions as: How and when should one confront political powers? What makes a virtuous ruler and a moral social order? What causes the breakdown of society? Who is ultimately responsible?

The book can be used for individual and group study: supplementary questions and resources for each chapter can be found on the book's JPS website, jps.org/books/thelandoftruth. To fully appreciate Talmud tales and to achieve maximum personal growth, it is well worth wrestling with the texts on one's own with the aid of the online study guide or discussing the questions together with a partner.

A famous Rabbinic tradition states: "You are not required to finish the work, but neither are you free to desist from it" (*Mishnah Avot* 2:21). Interpreting this "work" as the search for wisdom, a later commentator explains that just because it is impossible to attain complete wisdom, we are not to think that whatever we achieve is futile and false. Rather, every bit of knowledge we acquire has independent value and bestows its own reward.

Similarly, the Talmud contains hundreds of tales, and it is difficult to master them all. But each and every narrative has copious wisdom to impart to those of us ready to devote ourselves to its study and contemplation.

THE LAND OF TRUTH

Part 1 The Human Condition

1 The Surreal Sleeper

Among the most popular characters in talmudic stories is Ḥoni the Circle Drawer, a mercurial figure who has enjoyed a long after-life in Jewish folklore and still features today in legends and children's literature. The famous story that accounts for his nick-name relates that, during a time of drought, Ḥoni drew a circle in the ground and refused to move until God granted rain (*Mishnah Ta'anit* 3:8). For this reason he developed a reputation as a special type of "miracle worker," a divine favorite whose prayers—or demands—received immediate attention.

Though many Rabbis perform miracles of all sorts in numerous talmudic sources, the following Ḥoni story stands out for its surreal quality.

Rabbi Yoḥhanan said: All his life that righteous man [Ḥoni the Circle Drawer] was troubled by the Scripture, "When the Lord restored those who returned to Zion we were like dreamers" [Ps.126:1]. Ḥoni said [to himself], "[How could they be] in a dream for seventy years?"

One day he was walking along his way when he saw a certain man planting a carob tree. [Ḥoni] said to him, "Now a carob tree does not bear [fruit] for seventy years. Are you sure that you will live seventy years and will eat from it?" He said to him, "I found the world with carob trees. Just as my ancestors planted for me, so I plant for my offspring."

[Honi] sat down to eat his meal. Sleep [*sheinta*] came upon him. While he slept, a mound of earth [*meshunita*] encircled him and he was concealed from sight. He slept for seventy years.

When he awoke he saw a man gathering carobs from that carob tree. He said to him, "Do you know who planted that carob tree?" He said to him, "My father's father."

He said [to himself], "Certainly seventy years [passed] in a dream!"

He went to his house. He said to them, "Does the son of Honi the Circle Drawer yet live?" They said to him, "He is no more, but his grandson lives." He said to them, "I am he [Honi]." They did not believe him.

Honi went to the study house. He heard the Sages saying, "Our traditions are as clear today as in the years of Honi the Circle Drawer. For when he entered the study house, he solved every difficulty of the Sages." He said to them, "I am he." They did not believe him, and they did not treat him with the honor that he deserved. He prayed for mercy and his soul departed.

Rava said, "Thus people say, 'Either fellowship or death.'"

(*Ta'anit* 23a)

Rabbi Yoḥanan, the storyteller, begins this story in a somewhat unusual manner: Honi has difficulty understanding a biblical verse, "When the Lord restored those who returned to Zion we were like dreamers" (Ps. 126:1). While the Talmud and the books of midrash are filled with interpretations of verses—the term "midrash" essentially means "interpretation"—few stories feature the characters struggling to make sense of Scripture, especially stories not explicitly situated within the Rabbinic academy. One question to bear in mind is the function of this narrative opening.

Psalm 126 is among the better-known psalms today because of its prominent place in the Jewish liturgy. This psalm traditionally is recited prior to the *Birkat ha-Mazon* (Grace after Meals) on Sabbaths and festivals, on account of its joyous sensibility, and often sung to an upbeat melody. According to kabbalistic-mystical tradition, a copy of the psalm should be placed in the delivery room at birth or in a baby's crib, as these holy words stimulate God's mercy. In its biblical context, the psalm is part of a group of fifteen psalms (120–134) that all begin "A Song of Ascents"; these may have been sung by pilgrims when they came up to the Jerusalem Temple on the *Shalosh Regalim* (three pilgrimage festivals) in the Second Temple period. The talmudic Sages believed that the psalm was originally composed and sung by the Jews who returned to the Land of Israel in 516 BCE, after the first exile, as it mentions "those who returned to Zion." Having lived in Babylonia for seventy years after the Babylonians destroyed the First Temple in 586 BCE and deported much of the population there, the Jewish returnees ecstatically sung the psalms as they journeyed home.

Ḥoni's problem stems from his awareness of this historical setting coupled with an overly literal understanding of the psalm's figurative language. The singers describe themselves with a poignant simile: "We were like dreamers." In context they mean that the experience of returning to Zion, to the Land of Israel, felt like a dream coming true. Is this wondrous event, for which they had hoped and prayed, really happening, or is it rather a delusion or a fancy, the type of incredible vision that only takes place in dreams?

Ḥoni, however, takes the simile literally. How can the singers compare themselves to dreamers when a dream takes place during a single night's sleep but the return from exile occurred after seventy years? For the literal-minded Ḥoni, the verse seems to imply that they must have been sleeping and (literally) dreaming for seventy years.

In the second part of the story Ḥoni confronts a different sort of puzzle, not an enigmatic text but enigmatic behavior. A peasant plants trees that take so long to grow that he cannot hope to enjoy their fruits. Ḥoni cannot understand such a selfless act— why someone would expend the time and effort in an enterprise that will bring him no personal benefit. The only explanation Ḥoni can imagine is that the fellow believes he will live another seventy years—a rare event in antiquity, when life expectancies were much shorter than today. But the farmer gives Ḥoni an unexpected answer: he plants for his descendants, for future generations, not for personal profit. His work, however, is not completely altruistic, as he benefited from the same contributions of his ancestors. The generations of humankind are thus linked together, participating in a type of "generational economy" in which they give and receive equally, only not from the same people. This becomes a beautiful lesson about the interconnectedness of human generations: our debts to the past and obligations to the future.

The story now enters the realm of the surreal. In talmudic stories, the Rabbis, like other Holy Men and Women in antiquity, routinely perform miracles and display the ability to summon divine intervention. In this case, nature itself spontaneously responds so as to teach Ḥoni a lesson, although we should probably assume that God works behind the scenes. Ḥoni sleeps for seventy years in an underground cocoon while two generations pass. He wakes up to a new age in a new world: the carob tree has grown to maturity, just as the farmer foresaw—and here in flesh and blood Ḥoni beholds the grandson consuming its fruit! This child too knows the source of his sustenance; he tells Ḥoni that his grandfather planted the tree, and presumably he in turn plans to continue the tradition by planting trees for his grandchildren. Ḥoni thus witnesses and experiences in real life what most of us understand abstractly and take on faith: our present actions can create a better life for our grandchildren and grandchildren's children many years in the future.

Surprisingly, Ḥoni remarks not about the continuity of human generations, but about the passage of time—that seventy years passed by while he slept and dreamed. This observation, of course, returns to the story's opening. Ḥoni now understands the verse— that it is in fact possible to sleep and dream for seventy years, which justifies the simile "like dreamers." His (sur)real life thus exemplifies the truth of Scripture. The storyteller has invented a playful and entertaining plot by taking the figurative language of the verse literally.

Now, we can conceive of the opening section as a strategy to Judaize or "Rabbinize" a folktale that otherwise has little distinctly Jewish content. The account of Ḥoni and his seventy-year sleep, which calls to mind stories of Rip Van Winkle and other famous "super sleepers" (discussed later), relates to a truth of common human experience, not to Jewish beliefs and practices. In fact we might have expected Ḥoni himself to articulate the solution to the human behavior he is unable to comprehend. Couldn't he have realized, "Certainly it is crucial to provide for the generations to come!" or, "How true the farmer's words: just as he found the world full of fruit trees thanks to his ancestors, so his grandchildren enjoy a world full of all good things thanks to him."

Rather, Ḥoni returns to the Scripture he did not understand and expresses his satisfaction that the verse indeed makes sense. This may imply that Ḥoni has not appreciated the lesson about the interconnectedness of the generations and that his education remains incomplete. At the same time, the omission draws the audience into the world of the story, requiring us to decipher the moral of the "folktale" for ourselves.

The storyteller may also be inviting us to draw a connection between the farmer and the exiles who returned to Jerusalem. That generation dreamed of returning to the land of their forefathers—land that epitomized their connection to their ancestors and the traditions that their parents and grandparents had fostered over seventy years. Like the farmer who perpetuated the groves of carob trees for future generations, the Jews deported to Babylonia perpetuated Jewish traditions, customs, hopes, and dreams to sustain their posterity. Both were successful—the farmer in providing for his grandchildren and the exiles in maintaining a sense of peoplehood such that their descendants could return to the Land of Israel, rebuild the Temple, and reestablish the community. By this means both Ḥoni and we the audience learn an important lesson about Jewish continuity.

Now the story takes a darker turn, a dramatic shift from success to failure: after the seventy-year interruption, Ḥoni makes a futile attempt to resume his life. He tries to return to two houses, his family house and the house of study, but in both cases his efforts to identify himself ("I am he!") are met—understandably—with skepticism. Members of the two most important societies for a Rabbi, the domestic society of his wife and children, and the academic society of rabbinic colleagues and disciples, cannot believe that the Ḥoni who has been neither seen nor heard from in seventy years has stepped out of a time warp and stands before them in flesh and blood.

In particular, Ḥoni's inability to resume his former position and status in the house of study proves disastrous. The current occupants of the Rabbinic academy do remember Ḥoni's brilliant insights, the Torah he mastered, and specifically his talent for resolving difficulties, which the Babylonian Talmud regularly portrays as the highest form of Torah. From other stories we know that the Babylonian academy was a hierarchically structured institution where the Rabbis competed for honor and status by displaying their knowledge of Torah, propounding questions, and expertly parrying objections in the course of lively, and often contentious, dialectical debate. Ḥoni was apparently so brilliant a Sage that his disciples' disciples, or possibly even "third-generation" disciples, still remember his dialectical skills a full seventy years after he dazzled his colleagues. Alas, because these contemporary Sages do not recognize Ḥoni for who he is, they do not honor or defer to him as would befit a Sage of such status. Ḥoni consequently experiences unbearable, unspecified humiliation—perhaps students and other Rabbis not rising in his presence, not offering him a choice seat near the front of the academy, not granting him liturgical honors during daily prayers. He cannot endure this constant affront to his dignity, the persistent feeling of loneliness and shame. He prays to die.

Ḥoni's unfortunate death teaches a variation of the lesson of the first half of the story in reverse. In this account, Ḥoni cannot establish a connection to the succeeding generations, both of his family—his genetic or biological children—and of his students—his intellectual or spiritual "children" who pass on his traditions to posterity. The channels of continuity have been severed; he now stands alone and apart.

And so it is that memories of Ḥoni nurture his grandchildren and "grandstudents" and anchor them in the tradition of their forefathers, while the confidence that the coming generations, many years in the future, will benefit from his efforts sustains the farmer. But neither the satisfaction that Ḥoni's line continues nor the knowledge of his intellectual legacy can replace real human connection. A fulfilling life requires both vertical relationships with the past and horizontal relationships with fellow members of one's community.

In this respect, Ḥoni's predicament proves surprisingly modern. Many today have lost connection to their families, parents and grandparents, friends, and even to the wider society. Dr. John Cacioppo, a professor of social psychology at the University of Chicago, quoted in an ominously titled article "Chronic Loneliness Is a Modern-Day Epidemic," notes that 40 to 45 percent of Americans report feelings of loneliness today compared to 11 to 20 percent as recently as the 1970s. He observes: "We aren't as closely bound. We no longer live in the same village for generations, which means we don't have the same generational connections. That releases social constraints—relationships are formed and replaced more easily today."[1] The psychologist Rebecca Harris explains that "changes in modern society" are the cause of contemporary loneliness: "We live in nuclear family units, often living large distances away from our extended family and friends, and our growing reliance on social technology rather than face to face interaction is thought to be making us feel more isolated."[2] A review essay of seventy studies on the effects of loneliness concluded that social isolation can increase mortality risk by 30 percent.[3] As Rava states in conclusion, "Either fellowship or death."

Aging and Indignity

Like Ḥoni, many senior citizens feel themselves lost and adrift in a foreign world they do not know and that knows them not. Changing manners, fashions, values, speech, ideas, and beliefs can produce a sense of alienation and disconnection from one's own world, a feeling that one has unknowingly stepped through a looking glass and emerged in a bizarre age of the future. Today, the accelerated pace of technological development and innovation causes many to feel further removed from the way of life they once knew. While the "generation gap" is acutely felt on both sides, time inevitably sides with the young and skews the world in their favor.

The loss of dignity that accompanies growing older can be particularly distressing. In many cultures, the aging process in and of itself is associated with diminished self-worth. As a founder of a care center for the elderly put it: "There's so much shame in our culture around aging and death. When they're aging people feel that there's something wrong with them and they're losing value."[4] Former patriarchs and matriarchs of a family, providers and care-takers, become dependent on their children and grandchildren in an uncanny reversal of hierarchies and roles. Former doctors, CEOs, business owners, directors, and other professionals, retired or removed from their positions, no longer receive the deference and respect they once enjoyed. Elsewhere the Talmud teaches that God instructed Moses to put the fragments of the broken tablets of the commandments in the Ark of the Covenant together with the new tablets, offering this striking lesson: "A scholar who for-gets his learning due to unpreventable causes should not be dis-respected" (*Menaḥot* 99b). In other words, although he no longer possesses wisdom and Torah, such a scholar retains his worth, just as the shattered fragments of the tablets retained their holiness. So too the prayers for the Day of Atonement invoke Psalms 71:9: "Do not reject me in my old age." When facing a respected human being now weakened or destroyed by mental decline, we are to show the respect he or she once deserved lest we compound this individual's suffering with demoralizing humiliation.

Aging always involves loss. As family, friends, and loved ones die, the world seems to be inhabited mostly by younger people. Those who reach extreme old age may outlive not only most of their spouses, siblings, and contemporaries, but also their children, nieces, and nephews. This is the world to which Ḥoni awakens: his son is no more, and his colleagues in the academy have long passed away too. Precisely this lack of friendship, of collegiality, often causes the elderly to lose the will to live: "Either fellowship or death." The tragedy of Ḥoni is the tragedy of human mortality; all of us may become "Ḥoni" in the passing of the years.[5]

Talmudic Environmentalists

Environmental ethics has largely developed in modern times as a response to pollution, industrial waste, toxic chemicals, and the devastation of nature. Ancient peoples simply could not have imagined these technological "advances" that give us the ability to destroy the earth on such a scale. For the ancients, the earth was a goddess—awesome, vast, infinite—whom neither humans nor human artifacts could integrally damage.

However, some keen observers commented upon the negative impact of human farming, logging, and building on their local environment. Plato noted that the city of Athens and its immediate surroundings had been denuded of trees that had once grown in abundance but in his day could be found only in building beams. Too much grazing by goats and other animals also contributed to deforestation and lack of vegetation; as a result, the rains were not retained by forests but poured down to the Aegean Sea, causing the land to erode and springs to dry up.[6] He lamented that Athens now resembled "the skeleton of a sick body with barely any flesh on it." Both Plato and Aristotle made various suggestions as to how to prevent further decline and preserve the soil, shrubbery, and trees. These philosophers and other ancient authors were thus focused on what we might call "environmental sustainability," supporting long-term ecological balance in part by not depleting natural resources.

The lesson the farmer teaches Ḥoni, "I found the world with carob trees. Just as my ancestors planted for me, so I plant for my offspring," is in keeping with this ancient perspective. He understands that to harvest carobs without replacing the trees is unsustainable in the long term, as future generations will encounter a world bereft of the resources they need to survive. Only concern for the needs of those generations and a commitment to the exertions necessary to sustain a fertile habitat will ensure that human life continues to flourish "just as" in one's own time.

In biblical and Rabbinic theology, humans do not really own land, even the land that law recognizes as our private domain. All the earth belongs to God, and humans serve as tenants, temporary occupants, stewards caring for the property of the true Owner. Thus Leviticus 25:23 states, "The land is Mine; you are but strangers and residents with Me." As a temporary resident, the farmer acknowledges the responsibility to replace what he consumes so as to leave the natural world intact, "just as" he found it, for the next tenant.

This perspective has much in common with currents of thought found in indigenous cultures today. Native Americans, for example, express their concern for environmental sustainability in terms of "The Seventh Generation Principle"—that decisions must be made with considerations for the well-being of the seventh generation to come. As expressed by one Native American chief: "How will this affect the seventh generation . . . Respect the proper manner so that the seventh generation will have a place to live in . . . . Where are you taking them? What will they have?"[7] Similarly, the "Constitution of the Iroquois Nations" instructs: "Look and listen for the welfare of the whole people and have always in view not only the present but also the coming generations, even those whose faces are yet beneath the surface of the ground." The horror Native American tribes expressed at the irresponsible development or exploitation of their ancestral lands and natural habitat was often based on this sentiment: "Though tribes did not describe their laws in Western legal terms, their governing sovereign mandate was essentially a trust concept. Native peoples' understanding of their traditional role as stewards of the land—a gift from the Creator—was that the Earth should be protected in perpetuity for the sake of future generations."[8] Sam Penny, of the Nez Percé tribe, explains, "For generations our ancestors were the caretakers of the Pacific Northwest's salmon runs and treated them as part of the world that our creator had entrusted to us."[9]

As trustees, his tribe understood they were morally obligated to preserve natural resources intact for their descendants. Similarly, a saying associated with Native American folk wisdom—though sometimes attributed to traditional African cultures—insists: "We do not inherit the Earth from our ancestors—we borrow it from our children."[10] Consequently, like the motivated farmer in the story, we are to take pains to ensure that we leave the earth for our progeny the precise way we found it.

The most acute matter of sustainability confronting humanity today is global warming. Despite the growing body of scientific evidence, the issue can feel remote and irrelevant because many people do not see the direct effects of climate change on their immediate surroundings and each individual's role is so miniscule in the global arena as to undermine a sense of personal responsibility. Nevertheless, the shrinking polar ice caps, receding glaciers, rising seacoasts, and other large-scale changes proceed now at such a rate that they certainly will impact the next generation, let alone the seventh. Will we be able to paraphrase the farmer with good conscience: "I found the world with polar ice caps. Just as my ancestors preserved them for me, so I preserved them for my offspring"? Or again: "I found the world with polar bears / emperor penguins / intact coastlines / robust glaciers / coral reefs."

Cross-Cultural Super Sleepers

The literature of many cultures—German, Chinese, Japanese, Dutch, and Arabian, among others—features the motif of a multidecade sleep and reemergence to a changed world.[11] Rip Van Winkle, protagonist of "the most famous American short story," falls asleep for twenty years in the Appalachian Mountains and awakens to find the sleepy village he left transformed into a bustling town.[12] In one ancient Greek legend, a young boy, Epimenides, who has been sent by his father to look for a lost sheep, enters a cave and falls asleep for fifty-seven years. In an early Christian story, "Seven Sleepers of Ephesus," seven young Christian men take refuge in a cave to escape persecution by the Roman emperor Decius and sleep for two hundred years. In our era, the possibility of living in a future time has become a staple of fantasy and science fiction, from H. G. Wells's *The Time Machine* to *Planet of the Apes*, from *Star Trek* and *The Time Traveler's Wife* to dozens of other books, television shows, and films.

Inasmuch as change is necessary and unavoidable, all of these narratives grapple with the paradox of continuity amidst the rupture of the past. In fact, many of these stories associate the passage of time with progress and a better life. Having slept through the American Revolution, Rip van Winkle now finds himself in a nascent country seeking to expand with a new identity and spirit: colonists have become citizens and British sympathizers a relic of the past. The "Seven Sleepers of Ephesus" wake up to a better world: there are churches and crosses adorning buildings as the pagan Roman Empire has converted to Christianity. The story of Ḥoni also seems guardedly optimistic: carobs planted for the coming generations flourish as intended, and the house of study continues to thrive. In these narratives, human society, in the aggregate, finds effective strategies to preserve continuity within the inexorable passage of time. These strategies, however, work on a general level—not for the individual.

As prisoners of this time, we human beings are apt to wonder: What would it be like to live in the age of our children and descendants? What will become of our legacy—our family, generations in the future; our contributions to society? If we woke up to a new reality far in the future, would our lives be much better, or easier? Ḥoni's story suggests that for all the seeming appeal of living in the future, the actual experience would be decidedly more ambivalent.

Planting and Planning

The motif of planting for future generations appears in another rabbinic story that reveals both parallels and differences to our story of Ḥoni. This story is found in the midrash *Qohelet Rabbah* (Ecclesiastes Rabbah), a compilation of Rabbinic interpretations of the biblical book of Ecclesiastes, Qohelet.

Hadrian (may his bones be ground to dust) was passing by the road to Tiberias when he saw an old man digging furrows to plant shoots. He said to him, "Old man! Old man! How old are you this day?" He said to him, "One hundred years old." He said to him, "You are one hundred years old!? Yet you dig furrows to plant shoots? Do you think you will eat from them?" He said to him, "If I merit it, I will eat. But if not—just as my forefathers labored for me, so I labor for my children." Hadrian said to him, "By your life! If you merit and eat from them, be sure to let me know."

After some time the shoots produced figs. He thought, "Now is the time to let the emperor know." What did he do? He filled a basket with figs and went up and stood at the gate of the palace. [The guards] said to him, "What is your business?" He said to them, "Go and say to the emperor, 'The old Jewish man that you passed by has come to greet you.'" They went and said to the emperor, "An old Jewish man wishes to greet you." He said to them, "Bring him in."

When he came in, Hadrian said to him, "What do you want?" He said to him, "I am the old man you passed by while I was digging furrows to plant shoots, and you said to me, 'If you merit to eat from them, be sure to let me know.' Behold, I have merited and eaten from them, and these figs come from their produce." Hadrian said [to his servants], "I command that you empty that basket and fill it with gold coins." His servants said to him, "You give all this honor to an old Jewish man?" He said to him, "His Creator honored him. Shall I not honor him?"

(*Qohelet Rabbah* 2:20)

The Roman emperor Hadrian questions the old man about whether planting at his advanced age makes any sense. Historically, Hadrian led the Romans to victory against the "Second Jewish Revolt," namely the Bar Kokhba revolt of 132–35 CE, and so talmudic stories typically portray him as the consummate villain, as evidenced by the parenthetic curse, "may his bones be ground to dust." Here, though, the storyteller presents a comparatively benign view of the emperor, having Hadrian ultimately reward the old man and recognize his merit. Still, the choice of an evil Roman emperor to articulate the question creates an opposition between a shortsighted, superficial, pagan view and a deeper, spiritual, rabbinic understanding of the nature of reality. The emperor's initial question should therefore be understood as ridicule, as if to say: "You foolish old man! Why do you bother working so hard to plant shoots when you will probably not live long enough to benefit from your labor?"

In antiquity, if a person reached age one hundred, death was expected imminently; there would have been no reason to provide for the future—or at least for one's own future. Thus we have a variation of the question Ḥoni posed: Ḥoni asked a young man about planting a type of tree that takes so long to bear fruit that he cannot hope to eat it; Hadrian asks a very old man why he should bother to plant at all when he is knocking at death's door.

The old man answers with two possible scenarios. He himself may in fact benefit from these very fruits of his labors—his pious life may continue to "merit" reward from God in continued exceptional longevity. But—similar to the carob planter's explanation—even if he dies as expected, his efforts will not have gone for naught, as his descendants will enjoy the fruits.

As it turns out, the old man lives to harvest figs from the sprigs he planted and receives a much greater reward too: Hadrian remunerates him with their weight in gold. To his incredulous servants the emperor reveals the logic underpinning his munificence: God has rewarded the old man with extreme longevity, hence the emperor should do no less.

Of course there is a little more to it than this, as the emperor does not go about showering every senior citizen with gold. The old man respectfully answers the emperor's query and later travels to the palace to generously offer the emperor figs—proof of his ethic and obedience to the emperor's wish to be apprised of a successful harvest. In these ways, the old man has taught Hadrian valuable lessons.

In contrast to the story of Ḥoni, the insight about the interconnectedness of the generations is diluted, or even obscured, into a fallback contingency rendered unnecessary by the old man's longevity ("If I merit it, I will eat. But if not . . ."). This raises the question of the basis of this merit, namely, Why, exactly, has the old man merited this divine blessing of extreme age? Perhaps we are to infer that divine favor stems, at least in part, from this man's unflagging concern for future generations, as this sensibility provides a substantial motivation never to desist from planting. Paradoxically, however, his very dedication to this responsibility ends up benefitting him personally, thereby blurring the lesson for the audience, or at least transforming it from practice to theory.

The differences between planting figs as opposed to carobs and benefiting personally as opposed to vicariously through one's offspring lead to the key contrast between the stories in the natural versus supernatural dimension. The story of the old man and Hadrian lacks any supernatural element; his old age is unusual but not miraculous. However, Ḥoni's witnessing the truth of the farmer's claim that his descendants two generations later enjoy the fruits of his labor requires a supernatural seventy-year sleep. Since miracles and other supernatural phenomena are not uncommon in talmudic stories, Ḥoni's multidecade sleep is not troubling in and of itself. Yet still, it marks the story as fictional—as a didactic narrative rather than an ostensibly true tale featuring a realistic role model whom we can emulate. The character Ḥoni can provide general insight into the human condition. The unnamed old man, by contrast, can serve as a real-life example to imitate (and if we do, the story implies we might be blessed with a similar reward).

More important, the two stories have very different perspectives on aging. The story of the old man and Hadrian treats old age as a blessing, a divine reward. His longevity in and of itself provides Hadrian the proof that the old man has received divine favor. He seems to be in good health, being physically capable of digging, planting, and traveling with a (heavyish?) basket of figs to the emperor's palace, presumably at some distance from Tiberias.

This perspective of old age is consistent with the dominant biblical and rabbinic view. Various biblical commandments promise old age as a reward. The fifth of the Ten Commandments instructs: "Honor your mother and your father, that you may long endure on the land that the Lord your God is assigning to you" (Exod. 20:12). The book of Proverbs states: "Gray hair is a crown of glory; it is attained by the way of righteousness" (16:31). For this reason we are enjoined to respect the elderly: "You shall rise before the aged and show deference to the old" (Lev. 19:32).

Similarly, the Talmud contains accounts of disciples asking their teachers, "To what do you attribute your longevity?" in hopes of learning the secret to long life. Rav Adda bar Ahavah replied to this question with a list of his pious practices:

> I never became angry within my house . . . nor have I walked four cubits without thinking of Torah or without wearing tefillin [phylacteries], nor have I ever fallen asleep in the house of study . . . nor have I rejoiced at the disgrace of my friends. (*Ta'anit* 20b)

The Talmud's story of Ḥoni, by contrast, offers what is often a more realistic view of the aging process. The brilliant talmudic storytellers move us to consider a deeper view of reality beyond superficial appearances. Is this a case of "Be careful what you wish for"? Is it possible that the "blessings" of extreme old age could bring someone to the most tragic of circumstances such that he or she prays for death? Ḥoni's heartbreaking prayer for death provoked robust discussion in Rabbinic law codes and medieval literature about whether such prayers are permitted and, if so, under what circumstances, as Jewish tradition strongly prohibits suicide. Given modern medicine's capability of prolonging life despite the most debilitating of conditions and today's need for "Do Not Resuscitate" directives and health care proxies to *avoid* being kept alive against one's will only to suffer miserably—the story of Ḥoni seems ahead of its time.

2 What to Do with an Aged (and Annoying) Mother?

"Honor your father and your mother!" (Exod. 20:12). Not only was parental honor deemed sufficiently significant to be included among the Ten Commandments, but its location as the Fifth Commandment is instructive.[1] When arrayed in two columns of five commandments each upon the two "Tablets of the Covenant," the Fifth Commandment falls on the first tablet along with the commandments "between humans and God" ("You shall have no other gods besides me. You shall not make for yourself a sculptured image"), and not on the second tablet, beside the commandments "between humans and humans" ("You shall not murder," "You shall not steal"). Rabbinic interpreters understood this placement to mean that honor of parents was equal in importance to the honor of God and that it served as a bridge between earthly and heavenly relationships. Similarly, to the Rabbis, the commandment in Leviticus 19:3, as phrased "You shall each revere his mother and his father, and keep My Sabbaths: I the Lord am your God," taught the fundamental equivalence of fear of parents and fear of heaven. The juxtaposition of parental and divine reverence, as expressed through observance of God's Sabbath, establishes both precepts on the same level. Indeed, many traditional societies, past and present, grant parents a level of esteem unfathomable to more modern societies.

How exactly does one carry out the commandment? While some aspects of "honor" and "reverence" may be straightforward and matters of common sense, the precise parameters of the precept prove difficult to pinpoint. The Talmud defines "honor" as providing food, drink, and clothing, and leading a parent in and out; and "reverence" as prohibiting the child from standing or sitting in a parent's place, from contradicting a parent, and from "tipping the scales" against a parent—that is, from siding with another party in an argument or legal matter. "Honor" thus encompasses a few essential positive duties toward a parent, while reverence forbids blatant expressions of disrespect.

Yet even these elaborations on the biblical commandment offer only very basic guidelines and are not meant as an exhaustive description of the commandment's scope.[2] Nor do they address more complex issues, including conflicts between honor of parents and other values. Must one obey absolutely everything a parent requests, even if it violates the law of God or of human society? Are there any limits to obedience? What if a parent makes degrading or humiliating demands? To provide some perspectives on these questions, if not absolute answers, the Talmud includes a long series of stories of children and parents with some comments and discussion. In the course of this passage we find the following story:

Rav Assi—he had this elderly mother.

She said to him: "I want jewels."

He got them for her.

[She said to him:] "I want a husband."

[He said to her:] "I will look into it for you."

[She said to him:] "I want a husband who is as handsome as you."

He left her and went to the Land of Israel.

He heard that she was following after him.

He came before Rabbi Yoḥanan.

He said to him, "Is it permitted to go out of the Land [of Israel] to [areas] outside of the land?"

Rabbi Yoḥanan said to him, "It is forbidden."

Rav Assi said to him, "To greet one's mother—is it permitted?"

Rabbi Yoḥanan said to him, "I do not know."

Rav Assi waited [itaraḥ] a little while. He came again [to Rabbi Yoḥanan].

Rabbi Yoḥanan said to him: "Assi, have you reconciled yourself to go? May God [Hamakom] bring you back safely."

Rav Assi went before Rabbi Elazar. He said to him, "God forbid, perhaps Rabbi Yoḥanan became angry [mirtaḥ rataḥ]?"

Rabbi Elazar said to him, "What did he say to you?"

Rav Assi said to him, "'May God bring you back safely.'"

He said to him, "Had he been angry [rataḥ], he would not have blessed you."

In the meantime, Rav Assi heard that her coffin was coming.

He said [to himself], "Had I known, I would not have left."

(Qiddushin 31b)

Let's review the basic contours of the story as the laconic talmudic style can be difficult to grasp. Rav Assi's aging mother imposes increasingly burdensome demands upon him. She may be entering senility or suffering from what we might call the early stages of dementia or Alzheimer's. Or perhaps she is simply a very disagreeable, crotchety person. Still, Rav Assi does his best to honor her by fulfilling her requests, procuring the jewelry she desires and agreeing to try to find her a new husband (as evidently she has been widowed recently). When she insists the husband be "as handsome as you," Rav Assi understands that she will never be satisfied. Her demands have become unreasonable, unobtainable. He will be trapped forever in an increasingly onerous and unhealthy cycle. To refuse her outright or to reprimand her, however, risks disrespect, a violation of the commandment "to honor your father and mother." Rav Assi feels he has no choice but to flee so that she can no longer put him in an impossible situation. He "leaves her" in Babylonia and makes *aliyah* (immigrates) to the Land of Israel. (Freudians presumably will find intimations of an incestuous desire in her final demand and take the interpretation in that direction.)

Alas, Rav Assi has underestimated his mother: apparently she is not only extremely annoying but extremely persistent. He soon learns that she will be undertaking a dangerous journey of several weeks or even months in order to reunite with him in the Land of Israel. This places Rav Assi in a quandary. To honor his mother, he feels obligated to immediately go forth to meet, escort, and assist her. He may be neither able nor willing to find her a husband, but to greet and escort a parent are fundamental aspects of parental honor. To wait until she arrives at his locale would show lack of concern and respect. Yet to intercept her along the way would also entail leaving the borders of the Land of Israel, and a Rabbinic precept prohibits leaving the Holy Land except for a few critical purposes, such as to study Torah or find a wife. In this way the

Rabbis give legal thrust to the theological idea of the value and holiness of God's special and chosen territory.

When Rav Assi asks Rabbi Yoḥanan, among the leading Sages of the Land of Israel, if he might leave the land—not specifying a reason—the elder Sage predictably answers in the negative. Rav Assi responds with the real question: Does the commandment to honor one's parents supersede the prohibition against leaving the Land of Israel? Which value takes precedence? There also is irony in Rav Assi's question, as he hardly moved to the Land of Israel in order to fulfill the dream of living a life of piety in the Holy Land. For him the Land of Israel has provided a haven, a means of escape, and there may be something disingenuous about his worries about leaving its confines.

In any case, Rabbi Yoḥanan does not know. So Rav Assi waits a little while. Perhaps the great Rabbi Yoḥanan will ruminate on the issue and determine the answer. Perhaps Rav Assi had caught Rabbi Yoḥanan at a bad time when he had temporarily forgotten the tradition. When Rav Assi returns, Rabbi Yoḥanan offers a curious response: part question, part blessing, no real answer. "Have you have reconciled yourself to go?" That is, "Have you made your peace with going? Then have a great trip!"

Understandably, Rav Assi is perplexed by Rabbi Yoḥanan's answer. Did Rabbi Yoḥanan mean: "I see you have made up your mind to go even though I told you before I was not sure of the law and therefore withheld my approbation. But if you plan to go anyway, rightly or wrongly, you may as well have a safe trip." Or did he mean: "It's a gray area. Because you feel strongly, you should definitely go, and God bless you and pious children like you!" Were we able to observe Rabbi Yoḥanan's mannerisms or body language, we might be able to answer this question. Did he respond with an exasperated and irritated demeanor, suggesting he did not approve of Rav Assi's leaving given that he cannot find explicit legal permission for the journey? Or did he express his response with an accepting smile and friendly tone, suggesting that, given the lack of clarity on the legal point, he supports Rav Assi's wish to proceed?

Alas, the audience cannot see beyond the storyteller's words, and Rav Assi does not seem to be able to interpret those cues. He therefore consults another colleague, Rabbi Elazar, a student of Rabbi Yoḥanan, relating his conversations with the master. Rabbi Elazar displays much more self-confidence than Rav Assi in decoding the ambiguous utterance. Without hesitation, Rabbi Elazar reassures him: "If Rabbi Yoḥanan blessed you with a prayer that God protect you in your endeavor, clearly he approved. Go to your mother in peace!"

"In the meantime," a little later, Rav Assi receives another message: his mother is arriving in the Land of Israel—as a corpse, for burial. Either the first communication he received was garbled or incomplete—a frequent occurrence in antiquity— or the new message reports a secondary development: she has died along the way and her coffin will complete the journey.

Rav Assi's concluding, rueful reflection, "Had I known, I would not have left," is ambiguous, allowing for two very different interpretations of the story. To which place does "I would not have left" refer: The Land of Israel or Babylonia? Does he mean, "Had I known of her death, I would not have left the Land of Israel to honor my mother? I may have violated the prohibition against leaving the land for naught, as I can no longer show her honor." In this case the implication is that Rav Assi set forth to meet his mother, crossing beyond the borders of the Land of Israel, when he heard along the way that his mother had died. Or does he mean: "Had I known before I left that she would die and that I would never see her again, I would not have left Babylonia in the first place?" In this case, Rav Assi may not have left the Land of Israel: he might have received the news of her death while still trying to decide whether to go, rendering his question to Rabbi Yoḥanan moot.

There may be yet a third way of interpreting his statement. Perhaps the first words, "had I known," do not refer to knowledge of his mother's death but to "knowledge" in the sense of "understanding" his mother's feelings toward him. His mother's death after a futile quest to see her beloved son again may have led Rav Assi to reevaluate his attitude toward her. Could he mean: "Had I known how profoundly she actually loved me, as evidenced by her efforts to reunite with me, I never would have left my home. Her demand for a husband as handsome as I, though vexing, was perhaps fundamentally an expression of her devotion to me, and I should have been more tolerant." We know from Ḥoni's experience that connections to one's family are critical for human well-being (see chapter 1). In the end, Rav Assi may have realized that his mother was trying to maintain those very connections with him after his father's death.

Cornell gerontologist Karl Pillemer solicited life lessons from senior citizens in his book *Thirty Lessons for Living: Tried and True Advice from the Wisest Americans*. Many of his subjects emphasized this lesson: "Avoid a rift at all costs." Those who had spent years or even decades not speaking to siblings, children, or parents almost universally regretted the ruptures in their relationships. The breach in the parent-child relationship was particularly devastating: "Among the saddest people I met were those living with such a situation," Pillemer writes. "No matter how long it had gone on or what the specific circumstances were, the destruction of the parent-child bond was a persistent source of melancholy, a feeling of incompleteness that weighed down the soul."[3] By fleeing, Rav Assi severs his relationship with his mother such that he never speaks to or sees her again. He may have regretted his escape and wished he had responded otherwise.[4]

A Good and Anxious Boy

Despite the story's brevity, the storyteller has crafted Rav Assi's character masterfully enough for the audience to attain a fine appreciation of his personality. Although ordained as a Rabbi, *Rav Assi* still has much to learn. (In the Talmuds, "Rav" designates Babylonian Rabbis; "Rabbi" refers to those from the Land of Israel.) While he is a good son who tries his utmost to "do right" by his mother, catering even to her inappropriate demands, his decision to escape to the Land of Israel shows a degree of immaturity.[5] The storyteller narrates his departure by adding the verb "he left" her (from the root *sh-v-q*)—which can be understood as "he abandoned" her—rather than simply stating "he went to the Land of Israel" or employing the more neutral "he went out," as Rav Assi does when he questions Rabbi Yoḥanan. Certainly Rav Assi finds himself in an awkward and difficult situation, but to run away from one's problems rarely works out in the long run. As the saying goes, your "problems follow you wherever you go," and here Rav Assi's problem literally follows him across the Asian continent.

Rav Assi's interaction with the other Sages suggests he suffers from a lack of self-confidence as well. When he first approaches Rabbi Yoḥanan, he skirts the true issue; rather than asking the real question, he makes a more general inquiry, one he himself should have known how to answer. When Rabbi Yoḥanan declares that he cannot answer that follow-up inquiry, Rav Assi fails to appreciate that his predicament lacks a simple solution and he needs to solve it himself. Instead he waits and repeats his question, thereby avoiding having to make a decision.

Rabbi Yoḥanan's third response, by contrast, displays the wisdom of a true Sage. He understands that Rav Assi seeks approval, that deep down his younger colleague believes he must go to his mother but lacks the confidence to rely on his own judgment. He gives voice to Rav Assi's psychological condition, perhaps attempting, in a quasi-therapeutic manner, to manifest to Rav Assi the choice he has subconsciously made, such that Rav Assi can confront it himself. And, with the blessing, he expresses the approval Rav Assi seeks. While Rabbi Yoḥanan cannot say "yes" to a question beyond his knowledge, he can try to relieve his colleague's self-doubts.

Unfortunately, Rav Assi's lack of self-confidence not only prevents him from understanding Rabbi Yoḥanan's message and experiencing relief, but produces an additional anxiety: that he has angered the great Rabbi by his pestering. The storyteller underscores Rav Assi's proliferating worries with a fine wordplay on "waited," *itaraḥ,* and "angry," *mirtaḥ rataḥ,* revealing that the strategy of waiting in the hope that Rabbi Yoḥanan will solve his problem for him has the opposite effect, exacerbating his angst. Perhaps we are even to recognize an ironic parallel between his mother's badgering in the first part of the story and his own irksome queries in the second—the storyteller expresses both in a series of three questions—like mother like son.

To address his new concern Rav Assi now consults another colleague, again seeking reassurance from others rather than relying on his own judgment. We do not know how long Rav Assi waits before approaching Rabbi Elazar and whether, had he set out immediately, he might have reached his mother before her death.

This, in any event, is not the point. The storyteller does not conclude with a moral about seizing the moment but a counterfactual self-reflection—"Had I known . . . I would not . . ."—that points to the precise lesson Rav Assi needs to learn. Life is full of uncertainly. We need to be confident enough to trust our own judgment and instincts, and make decisions with less than complete information. Hopefully one makes wise and balanced decisions that produce satisfactory results. Even well-considered choices, however, do not always work out optimally; sometimes they may even lead to disasters. Such is the human condition, and one must embrace it and struggle within its limitations.

Fortunate Is One Who Never Saw His Parents!

Rav Assi's struggle to develop the self-confidence necessary to support both his professional and nonprofessional life is a familiar challenge for many of us today. At a certain point in their careers, doctors, lawyers, electricians, teachers, and many other professionals must cease relying on their mentors and make independent judgments about their work. When a medical student becomes a doctor, he or she needs to overcome feelings of self-doubt and insecurity to be able to take responsibility for a patient's treatment. So too a lawyer who drafts her first contract for a client, an architect who designs his first house, and so on. Similarly, it takes maturity and confidence to negotiate complex family relationships—to find creative and noble ways to get along with difficult relatives. Although many young men and women choose to attend colleges and graduate schools far from home, moving far away rarely proves a viable solution in the long haul. Any real issue tends to catch up with you sooner or later, as it did with Rav Assi.

In particular, the burden of responsibility for aging parents that drove Rav Assi to flee his homeland has become a challenging contemporary ethical dilemma. As lifespans increase due to advances in medicine and healthcare, adult children are often faced with taking care of parents who experience years of steady mental and physical decline. And, as the years pass, the costs of nursing homes or other such facilities, medical care, and prescription drugs may also fall to children as their parents' resources become depleted. While most children accept this responsibility as an act of filial piety, some even nobly and happily, the disruption and pressures on daily life over the course of years can lead to untenable situations. Many find their lives put on hold, almost held hostage to the constant demands of parental care. Where are the limits to the honor demanded of us?

The section of Talmud that contains our story (*Qiddushin* 31b) proposes exactly this question: "How far does the commandment of honoring one's father and mother extend?" In answer, the Talmud offers a series of narrative traditions modelling an extremely high standard. We are told of a man who refused to disturb his father's sleep to retrieve a key under the father's pillow, even when offered a business deal that would have netted the son a six-hundred-thousand-coin profit. Another tradition relates that Rabbi Abbahu once asked his son Avimi to bring him a drink but then dozed off in his chair, so Avimi stood at that spot and stooped over him with the cup poised above his lips until his father awoke. Rabbi Tarfon was known to bend down and allow his mother to step on him to ascend to her bed; likewise he would prostrate himself for her to tread upon him as she got out of bed.

But after these and other such anecdotes the Talmud quotes an astonishing statement of Rabbi Yoḥanan, who was orphaned at birth: "Fortunate is the one who never saw them [parents]"! In other words, if we must aspire to the standards modelled in these traditions, we will almost certainly fail and end up violating the Fifth Commandment—better not to have the obligation in the first place. Notably, the Talmud places the story of Rav Assi immediately after Rabbi Yoḥanan's declaration.

Now Rabbi Yoḥanan's statement need not be taken literally. It may be an expression of the difficulties and frustrations inherent in trying to fulfil the commandment. In this context, the story of Rav Assi offers a sharp contrast to the unrealistic expectations in the accounts of Avimi, Rabbi Tarfon, and the others. It provides some solace to all those trying nobly to honor their parents despite the hardships and strains. Perhaps the story affords a measure of comic relief. "That's exactly how I feel," we might say to ourselves. "I too would run away if only I could."

In this long passage, then, the Talmud attempts to address two dimensions of the commandment: the potentially infinite demands entailed in an ethical obligation of this type on the one hand, and the concomitant practical difficulties and psychological stresses on the other. That said, the Talmud does not provide a more concrete answer to its own question regarding the extent of the commandment. How could it really, given the complexities of human life and interpersonal relationships?

Instead, the Talmud challenges us to work out our own solutions—to develop the self-confidence and maturity Rav Assi struggled to attain, and to aspire to the highest levels of parental honor while recognizing the intricacy and potential fragility of human interactions.

3 Forbidden Fruit, or How Not to Seduce Your Husband

Rabbinic Judaism is often characterized as "this worldly" religion, meaning that it has a positive view of life in the present world, and does not focus exclusively on one's posthumous fate in heaven or hell. Pleasure and bodily enjoyment are recognized as legitimate, even holy and mandatory, dimensions of life, not inherently evil temptations that divert attention from the soul and its quest for holiness. Jewish views on sex, likewise, tend to be portrayed as affirming bodily and sexual desires as "healthy" and "favorable" forces of good. As the contemporary Jewish philosopher Rabbi Elliot Dorff writes: "Judaism has a distinctly positive view of sexuality as the gift of God and it articulates values and rules that make sex the pleasurable yet holy activity it was meant to be."[1] Another ethicist, Rabbi David Feldman, notes that Judaism mandates sex and marriage for their "intrinsic joys independent of the procreational ideal" and that "the attitude to marital sex is uniformly affirmative and joyous."[2]

While there is much truth to such depictions of Jewish views of sex and the body, they tend to oversimplify matters. Rabbinic Judaism includes countervailing voices suspicious of sexuality and troubled by its immense power to corrupt. Were sex easily limited to the "holy activity it was meant to be," all would be well. But how often is this the case? Like many other religions and philosophies in antiquity, Rabbinic Judaism *also* saw sex, and more exactly sexual desire, as an enormously disruptive and destructive force often directed, against one's will, at illegitimate objects. Sexual urges devolved from the machinations of the "evil inclination" or of demonic powers that attempted to corrupt the righteous. As such, sexual activity had to be strictly controlled and regulated lest it burst forth in problematic, sinful ways. Yet controlling the "evil inclination" was no easy task. In the following story a Rabbi miscalculates and comes to a tragic end.

Rabbi Ḥiyya bar [son of] Ashi regularly would fall on his face [in prayer] and say, "May the Merciful One save me from the evil inclination."

One day his wife heard him. She thought, "Since it has been many years since he has separated from me, what is the reason he speaks thus?"

One day he was repeating traditions in the garden. She adorned herself and passed back and forth in front of him.

He said to her, "Who are you?"

She said, "I am a courtesan who has arrived at this place just now."

He propositioned her.

She said to him, "Bring me the pomegranate from the top of the branch."

He jumped up, went, and brought it to her.

When he returned to his house, his wife was lighting the oven.

He went up and sat inside it.

She said to him, "What is this?"

He told her, "Such and such happened."

She said to him, "It was I!"

He said to her, "Nevertheless, I intended to sin."

(*Qiddushin* 81b)³

Rabbi Ḥiyya bar Ashi's daily prayer implies that he wages a daily battle against "the evil inclination," which he seems to identify with any and all sex. For this reason he has separated from his wife for several years and has not had sexual relations with her even once. Unaware of his daily affirmation, his wife assumes he is too old or too weak for intimacy. When she happens to overhear his prayer one day, she realizes it is a matter of choice not ability. It is not the case that her husband is willing but unable; rather he is able but unwilling—so she sets out to seduce him, dressing up like a courtesan and parading before him. At first her plan works brilliantly; she even makes sure to have evidence of the encounter by demanding a fruit as payment for the tryst.

When he returns home later that day, however, the plan backfires. The Rabbi proceeds directly to the oven and starts to burn himself to death, confessing his "sin". His wife discloses that in fact she was the courtesan, and presumably shows him the fruit as proof. That the sex was technically licit, however, fails to assuage his guilt or stop his suicidal path. Rabbi Ḥiyya bar Ashi explains that he intended to sin by engaging in forbidden intercourse. He apparently remains in the oven and dies of his self-inflicted wounds.

Sex and Sin

The story begins in a straightforward manner . . . and then immediately takes a dramatic, shocking shift. The image of a Rabbi prostrate on the ground in prayer entreating the "Merciful One" for divine assistance to resist the "evil inclination" is not uncommon. The traditional daily liturgy includes numerous petitions asking God to spare us both from sin in general and specific offenses. "Falling on the face" can be a technical term for a section of the morning service known as the "Supplication" (*Taḥanun*), which includes silent and individual prayers during which the worshiper might add personal requests such as this. The phrase can also refer to a passionate and sincere spontaneous prayer uttered in response to deep yearnings at any point in the day. So we initially form the impression that Rabbi Ḥiyya bar Ashi acts much like other pious Rabbis in praying that his "good inclination" triumphs over the "evil inclination" that tempts him to sin.

His wife's perplexity at his prayer forces us to completely revise our understanding. She cannot make sense of his words: he has ceased all sexual relations with her for years, while his prayer indicates that he struggles each day to refrain from capitulating to carnal temptation. To her surprise, his abandonment of conjugal sex is voluntary, not involuntary, a freely chosen celibacy. While his body is potent, he resolves to suppress his carnal desire and abstain. We now understand that the "evil inclination" for Rabbi Ḥiyya bar Ashi does not pertain to sin in general, nor even to sexual sins such as adultery, extramarital sex, and prostitution, in keeping with the standard meaning, but to sex itself. Jewish tradition not only permits marital intercourse but requires it, and the talmudic Rabbis viewed marriage as a crucial means to prevent sexual sins by providing a licit sexual outlet. For Rabbi Ḥiyya bar Ashi, however, sex in and of itself has become associated with base urges and sinful passions. Contrary to initial impressions, our protagonist's daily prostrations are anything but typical.

Nor has Rabbi Ḥiyya bar Ashi shared this apparently misguided struggle for spiritual purity with his wife, despite her obvious personal stake in the endeavor. (That the storyteller does not even provide her with a name underscores the lack of concern for her perspective.) She has presumably interpreted his separation as a function of illness, old age, or infirmity. For many years she has had to suppress her own passions and desire for intimacy. Perhaps, as sometimes happens, she has also suffered from guilt and self-recrimination, mistakenly blaming some imperfection of her own for her husband's withdrawal. We do not know how long Rabbi Ḥiyya bar Ashi maintained a normal sex life before embarking on this quest for holiness, nor his exact age when this story takes place—details the storyteller does not consider necessary to supply. Possibly, some years have passed since their marriage; hence his wife has aged, perhaps lost some of her former beauty, and she may see those changes as the cause of her husband's apparent loss of sexual potency. She may have noticed that he averts his eyes when she dresses each morning, does not look at her body as he once did, or even rushes out of the bedroom when she starts to unbutton her outer garments.

Now, she realizes, these modest gestures do not reflect the pain he experiences—or serve as a defense mechanism to avoid feelings of inadequacy—at being incapable of the intimacy he desperately desires. His actions, rather, are deliberate tactics, strategic moves in a constant battle to keep the stirrings of desire at bay—sublimation of the libido, in Freudian terms. If so, she may well resent his unilateral choice for a celibate life without so much as deigning to let his devoted wife know the true cause, so as to spare her feelings of self-blame.

Understanding how she prepares for and carries out the seduction requires some of our own imagination, details we might find fascinating to consider, as again the storyteller omits such information that is not strictly required to achieve his didactic point. But let us try again to fill in this narrative gap. We might conjecture that she mulls over her discovery for a few days, not sure how to proceed, though pretty sure she doesn't like what she has learned. Then one day she notices that her husband has abruptly exited their house for the little garden accessed by a short path from their backyard. She used to think he retreated to this peaceful, quiet, pastoral space to memorize the Oral Torah without interruption—an endeavor that required hours of concentrated review each day. Now she recognizes the need for such an environment was less a function of the stillness of the garden than of her very presence in their house. His sudden departures served to quell distressing bodily stirrings before they could overpower his resolve, to sublimate his sexual feeling through intellectual and spiritual activity. Distance from his lawfully wedded wife, more than duty to his legal studies, motivated his movements. She feels a sudden rush of anger at this realization.

Hoping to teach her "holy" husband a lesson, she decides to put him to a test. She rummages in the bottom of her clothes chest and dredges up the attractive, colorful outfit she has not worn in years. (No doubt her husband has forgotten about it—it's likely he hardly noticed her clothes during their early years of marriage when he was dutifully amorous). She forgoes her stockings, hikes up the skirt, adjusts the blouse to show maximum cleavage. She loosens the hair from the tight bun she has worn for years, brushes it out, and arranges it to dangle down and partially cover her eyes: an exotic and provocative look. She ties a bright, colorful scarf around her neck to distract her husband from studying her features too intently. Satisfied that if she can hardly recognize herself, her husband will not recognize her either, she takes a roundabout way to the garden, approaching it from the opposite direction. Sure enough, there sits Rabbi Ḥiyya bar Ashi cross-legged under a shady tree, eyes closed, lips moving in the dogged and relentless repetition of Rabbinic teachings.

The Rabbi's wife does not know exactly how a wanton woman operates, though she has sometimes heard men talk and joke of the prostitutes they have encountered at inns when traveling or at the margins of city markets. She ascertains it's probably best to be subtle, to plant a seed and let her husband take the initiative. She walks slowly across the garden—but he barely notices. A quick look and then his eyes close, back to his recitation. Undeterred, she walks back across, then in a circuitous route, as if to smell and study each flower and plant. Now he starts to track her movements. When their eyes meet momentarily, she cocks her head slightly, smiles flirtatiously, and winks. Then it's time for another few slow circuits around the garden. When she wanders close by his tree, he calls out: "Who are you? What are you doing in this garden?" and her answer is ready: "I am a courtesan and have arrived at this place just now." Slowly she walks toward him, swinging her hips, tossing her hair back, passing in front of him, close enough to reach out and touch . . . then abruptly turns aside toward a pomegranate tree. Pressing her back up against the tree, she reaches back with her hands to grip the trunk, raises one knee, and places the sole of that foot on the roots. This time she senses his eyes are glued to her, studying her figure with great intensity. "What is . . . your . . . fee?" he asks, barely audible. "Ten *dinars*"—she states a sum, somewhat arbitrarily. "I have no money with me," he replies, a mixture of disappointment and relief. She does not care about the money, but the ruse must be plausible. "Then just bring me that pomegranate from the top of this branch," she replies, lifting her eyes skyward. Near the top of the tree a brilliant, large, red pomegranate hangs splendidly from the vine. Her husband takes the bait. Methodically he strides toward the tree, grabs a branch, hoists himself up, and with surprising speed and agility ascends to the top branch, picks the fruit, and shimmies back down. More evidence that she has underestimated his potency. She takes the fruit from his extended hand, careful to brush her fingers delicately across his wrist in the process. Then she sinks to the ground, pulling him down on the soft grass beneath the pomegranate tree . . . .

I leave it to each reader to fill in the rest of the narrative gap. (Was it amazing sex, a function of the extended period of celibacy, the repressed passions of both husband and wife/courtesan bursting forth in an incredibly satisfying mutual experience? Was it disappointing sex, a function of the extended period of celibacy, the repressed passions of both husband and wife/courtesan bursting forth in an incredibly unsatisfying mutual experience? Something in between . . . ?)

The story's semicomedic elements—the tree-climbing Rabbi, the husband who does not recognize his wife during copulation—become tragic in the final scene. Returning home after the encounter, the wife has resumed her mundane tasks, presumably planning to confront Rabbi Ḥiyya bar Ashi with the pomegranate when he next "falls on his face" in prayer, or even that night in bed. She fires up the oven to prepare dinner.

But when Rabbi Ḥiyya bar Ashi returns home a short time later, without so much as a word, he clambers up the oven to commit suicide by burning himself inside it. Talmudic ovens, made from clay, were large and cylindrically shaped, with a wide opening at the top and an aperture in the front for a pan laden with food to be inserted and removed. The Rabbi's short climb to the oven top parallels his climb to the top of the tree, a type of measure-for-measure (self-inflicted) punishment for his "sin." His wife queries, "What is this?"— "What are you doing?"—though she undoubtedly realizes what motivates him. When he confesses his sin, she divulges that she was in fact the "courtesan" and presents him the pomegranate as evidence. Alas, this disclosure does not deter Rabbi Ḥiyya bar Ashi, who descends into the interior of the oven.

The wife has underestimated her husband's radical views on sex and sin. Because he intended to have extramarital sex—because he could not restrain himself from what he believed to be a sin—he judges himself guilty. That he in fact slept with his lawfully wedded wife is a "technicality," irrelevant. After all, he had "separated" for years from the marital bed, so the fact that he had sex with his rightful spouse in the end is of marginal comfort. For him, it is all the same—a lost battle against the sexual urge itself. And so both the Rabbi's pursuit of celibacy in the name of holiness and his wife's plan to test him end in tragedy.

Among the lessons in this story is the imperative for clear communication between partners. Had Rabbi Ḥiyya bar Ashi spoken candidly about his views of sexuality and sin, had his wife revealed to him what she had overheard, and had they talked it out, this tragic ending would have been averted. To speak to a spouse or partner about intimate matters can be awkward and frightening, but the consequences of silence can be devastating.[4]

The Garden of Eden and the Garden of Ḥiyya

Our sad story evokes two biblical narratives. First, Adam and Eve's sin in the Garden of Eden lurks in the background, especially since some Rabbinic traditions identify the pomegranate as the biblical fruit. (The apple is a much later interpretation, mainly found in the medieval Christian tradition.) In the Bible, Eve picks the fruit and gives it to Adam to eat in order to acquire knowledge of good and evil, whereas in our story "Adam" picks the fruit and gives it to his "Eve" in order to "know" her. The biblical story, strictly speaking, has little to do with sex. Knowledge, not sexual satisfaction, is the protagonists' goal, and disobedience or rebellion is their sin. The Jewish interpretation (and one line of Christian interpretation) holds that Adam and Eve engaged in sexual relations before their sin and expulsion from Eden (after all, how could there be paradise without sex?). Nevertheless, the fact that they hide to cover their nakedness after eating the fruit suggests some relationship between sin, knowledge, and sexuality, the precise dimensions of which have received considerable interpretation through the ages. In postbiblical tradition sexuality often takes on some association with sin, but this is largely a function of the potential for illicit types of sex. In the talmudic story, by contrast, Rabbi Ḥiyya bar Ashi has clearly identified sex per se with sin, such that all sex is ipso facto sinful.

Both stories feature temptation: in the biblical story the snake tempts Eve, who in turn tempts Adam, whereas in the Rabbinic story the wife turns to disguise to tempt her husband. However, since Rabbi Ḥiyya bar Ashi prays to be saved from the "evil inclination," from his point of view the "snake," often identified with the evil inclination in Rabbinic sources, plays a key role in his demise too. Like Adam and Eve, he succumbs to the tempter's wiles and accordingly must suffer the consequences. In this respect, the account of Rabbi Ḥiyya bar Ashi lives up to the "original" story better than the biblical narrative itself. After all, God warns Adam and Eve, "On the day that you eat of it you shall surely die" (Gen. 2:17)—but then only expels them from the garden; God defers their deaths for hundreds of years. Rabbi Ḥiyya bar Ashi, however, dies on the very day he succumbs to temptation! Some Rabbinic sources expect sinners to burn in a kind of hell after their death, and Rabbi Ḥiyya bar Ashi apparently hastens to bring such a punishment upon himself.

These parallels to the biblical story create a powerful irony. God imposes a prohibition on Adam and Eve, but Rabbi Ḥiyya bar Ashi imposes the prohibition upon himself. His own quest for an exaggerated holiness, not his failure to observe a commandment from the Almighty, leads to his "downfall." Even more so, unlike Adam and Eve, he never violates a prohibition and yet inflicts upon himself a considerably harsher punishment. He surpasses God, both in prohibition and in punishment. In this respect, the storyteller teaches the dangers of self-imposed stringency, of aspiring to an excessive level of holiness beyond human nature.

This message dovetails with an important Rabbinic understanding of the dynamics of Eve's sin. The snake asserts to Eve, "You are not going to die" (Gen. 3:3). Why did Eve believe this creature? The Rabbis note that God warns Adam only that "you must not eat of" the Tree of Knowledge of Good and Evil, but Eve informs the snake, "God said: 'You shall not eat of it *or touch it*, lest you die'" (Gen. 3:2). At this point, the Rabbis teach, the snake pushed Eve against the tree so that she touched the fruit, and, receiving no punishment for the touch, she has no answer to the snake's assertion.

The lesson is, "Whoever adds, [ultimately] takes away." Because she added a stringency to the divine prohibition, Eve ultimately "took away" and violated it. Rabbi Ḥiyya bar Ashi added to the prohibition against forbidden sexual relationships, and ultimately (almost) violated it by having sex with a "courtesan."

The Harlot in Disguise

The second biblical text that informs our story is the story of Judah and Tamar (Gen. 38). In the middle of the long saga of Joseph and his brothers (Gen. 37–45), the Bible offers a brief narrative interlude, relating that Judah married his son Er to a woman named Tamar and that Er died before siring children. In biblical and Jewish law, when a man died without children, his brother was obligated to marry the widow and bear children "in his name," a type of legal fiction to ensure the continuity of his bloodline and also to protect the childless widow from poverty. This practice was known as "Levirate marriage" (*yibbum*), from the Latin *levir*, "the husband's brother." Judah accordingly marries his next son, Onan, to Tamar, but Onan dies too. At this point Judah is reluctant to marry his third son, Shelah, to Tamar, fearing that Tamar is jinxed or cursed and that Shelah will die like his brothers. Judah procrastinates. After some time passes, Tamar becomes tired of waiting for the marriage owed to her and decides to take action on her own behalf:

> (38:14) So she took off her widow's garb, covered her face with a veil, and, wrapping herself up, sat down at the entrance to

Enaim, which is on the road to Timnah; for she saw that Shelah was grown up, yet she had not been given to him as wife. (15) When Judah saw her, he took her for a harlot; for she had covered her face. (16) So he turned aside to her by the road and said, "Here, let me sleep with you"—for he did not know she was his daughter-in-law. "What," she asked, "will you pay for sleeping with me?" (17) He replied, "I will send a kid from my flock." But she said, "You must leave me a pledge until you have sent it." (18) And he said, "What pledge shall I give you?" She replied, "Your seal and cord, and the staff which you carry." So he gave them to her and slept with her, and she conceived by him.

When Judah subsequently learns that Tamar is pregnant, he orders that she be burned to death, since she was technically betrothed to Shelah, hence guilty of adultery. But when Tamar produces the evidence of his seal, cord, and staff, Judah concedes: "She is more righteous than I, in as much as I did not give her to my son Shelah." Their encounter was in fact licit, a type of endogamous Levirate marriage, with the father-in-law instead of the brother-in-law. Tamar gives birth to the twins Zerah and Perez, to whom the Book of Ruth traces King David's lineage, an unambiguous indication that Tamar was "righteous" (Ruth 4:18–22).

The parallels to the story of Rabbi Ḥiyya bar Ashi include the disguise as a prostitute, the lack of recognition, a proposition for sex, "payment" with an identifiable item, disclosure of true identity with the evidence, and the punishment—burning—for the sinner. The sharp contrast in the endings, however, underscores the tragic irony of the talmudic story. Judah recognizes that he has wronged Tamar by consigning her to a celibate widowhood, and therefore acknowledges that their liaison was in fact licit. Rabbi Ḥiyya bar Ashi, on the other hand, cares nothing for his wife or her needs, focuses exclusively on his failure, and insists that the union was illicit. Judah, upon realizing the "righteousness" of

Tamar's action, rescinds his decree that she be burned to death, whereas Rabbi Ḥiyya bar Ashi, upon realizing the courtesan was his wife, nevertheless burns himself to death. The story of Judah and Tamar ends with conception and the birth of the ancestor of the Davidic dynasty. The story of Rabbi Ḥiyya bar Ashi ends with shame and suicide.

Intention and Sin

In 1976, then U.S. presidential candidate Jimmy Carter confessed in a *Playboy* magazine interview: "I've looked on a lot of women with lust. I've committed adultery in my heart many times." Carter continued: "This is something God recognizes I will do—and I have done it—and God forgives me for it."[5] At the time, this frank admission of sexual lust disturbed many Americans, despite the fact that, as many pundits observed, just about all men would probably admit the same. Carter's theory that adultery "in the heart" required divine forgiveness also implied that such thoughts are sinful—a teaching Carter attributed to Jesus. In a long discourse known as the "Sermon on the Plain," Jesus proclaims:

> You have heard that it was said, "You shall not commit adultery"; but I say to you that everyone who looks at a woman with lustful intent has already committed adultery with her in his heart. If your right eye makes you stumble, tear it out and throw it from you; for it is better for you to lose one of the parts of your body, than for your whole body to be thrown into hell (Matt. 5:27–29).

"You have heard that it was said" refers to the Ten Commandments of the Hebrew Bible (Exod. 20:14). With the contrast "You have heard" / "But I say," Jesus emphasizes the higher level of morality to which he aspires, perhaps a standard for the Messianic Age or the new age of perfection (to the extent Jesus considered himself to be the Messiah, or at least that Matthew considered Jesus as such). Looking at a woman with "lustful intent" leads the man to imagine having sex with her—what we might call a sexual fantasy. In antiquity the heart, not the brain, was considered the locus of imagination as well as emotions, hence responsible for love and desire. Although no action has taken place, Jesus considers the lustful thought sinful in and of itself—so sinful that he suggests tearing out the eye lest it behold an object of desire. Loss of a body part is painful to be sure, but less painful than the expected punishment for sin, namely burning in the fires of hell.

Many commentaries claim, however, that this literal interpretation of Jesus's admonition is flawed. To them, Jesus is *not* claiming that thought and action are equivalent such that merely thinking of sex with another person makes one as guilty as having sex itself. The arousal someone experiences at the sight of an attractive man or woman is out of one's control and therefore cannot be considered sinful. Rather, Jesus means that one should not form the intent to commit adultery or sin, not slide from looking longingly upon a beautiful "object of desire" to contemplating and planning how one might possess that person. In other words, the "lustful intent" to which Jesus refers is not mere desire or sexual attraction but the deliberate cultivation of sexual fantasies about an illicit interaction with a base and dishonorable intent that may eventually result in taking action. We may not be able to stop ourselves from attraction, desire, even sexual fantasies, but as soon as we start thinking about how we can make those fantasies a reality, how we can consummate the desire in real life, we have crossed the line and committed the sin of adultery in the heart. In this light, Carter may have been too hard on himself.

Rabbinic Judaism, for the most part, does not consider mere intention to sin or thoughts of sin as equivalent to sin itself. The Talmud states: "A good thought, the Holy One conjoins with a deed. . . . Rav Assi said: even if a person thought to do a mitzvah [commandment] and he was prevented from doing so, Scripture considers him as if he did it. An evil thought, the Holy One does not conjoin with a deed" (*Qiddushin* 40a).[6] The exact meaning of "conjoin" here is not completely clear, but the basic idea seems to be that God facilitates the intention to do a good deed or fulfil a commandment such that the deed comes to fruition, helping the agent act on his thought. Some commentators understand "conjoin with" as "exchange for," meaning that God credits one who thinks of doing a good deed with the act itself. Rav Assi then adds that even if someone did not end up performing the deed due to circumstances beyond his or her control, the individual gets credit for carrying out the act. Not so an evil or sinful thought, including thoughts of an extramarital affair, which God does not reckon as an act itself and confers no guilt.

At the same time, the Rabbis considered sinful thoughts, especially lust, to be pernicious. Rabbi Elazar Haqappar stated, "Jealousy, lust, and ambition drive a person out of this world" (*Mishnah Avot* 4:21). More ominously, Rav Naḥman avowed: "Thoughts of [sexual] sin are more harmful than [sexual] sin. And your analogy is: the smell of meat" (*Yoma* 29a). The talmudic commentaries explain that the smell of meat stimulates hunger, which causes pain if not satisfied, whereas one does not suffer if he can eat the meat when he first smells it. Likewise, sinful sexual desires cause a feeling of weakness and frustration if not satisfied. Nevertheless, however harmful such thoughts are to the body, mind, and spirit, and however imperative to avoid them, they do not count as sins unless acted upon. For Judaism, "adultery in the heart" and "lustful intent" are not sins and therefore do not require divine forgiveness.

The status of intention in law and ethics is still very much relevant today. American law distinguishes premeditated murder from manslaughter and accidental homicide on the basis of intent. Likewise, an accountant who intentionally violates tax law to save his company money will generally receive a harsher penalty than one who does the same due to his ignorance of the law. The former is criminal, the latter incompetent. In personal ethics we often say, "It's the thought that counts" or, "She meant well." Yet many cases are tough to evaluate. Do we really believe this adage when we receive inappropriate gifts? Do we judge a parent who causes his child great unhappiness by sending him off to a harsh boarding school because he believes in the utility of strict discipline to be morally superior to a parent who sends his child there because he hates parenting and wants his children out of the home as much as possible? Are the Taliban any less odious because they destroy televisions and force women to wear modest clothing with the sincere intention of preventing decadence and promoting public modesty?

The case of Rabbi Ḥiyya bar Ashi has an added layer of complexity in that the Rabbi not only intended to sin but then acted on his intention. Unlike a man who thinks about another woman constantly but suppresses his desire, or even a man who goes about seducing a woman, arranges a place and time to meet, arrives to find her waiting for him, but suddenly has a change of heart and bolts—Rabbi Ḥiyya bar Ashi fulfilled his passion. For this reason he sentences himself to the flames of the oven, much as Jesus warns of the fires of hell. Yet in the final reckoning, because of his wife's deception, his act was completely lawful. This is a case of "harlotry in the heart" but not in deed.

Given the talmudic sources quoted above, do we as readers think that Rabbi Ḥiyya bar Ashi was excessively hard on himself as intentions, though evil, are not punishable? Or is his case different because he in fact committed an act on the basis of that sinful intention, even if the act turned out to be permitted?

On Celibacy and Sexuality

The cause of Rabbi Ḥiyya bar Ashi's downfall is his attempt to lead a celibate life. He withdraws from a sexual relationship with his own wife for years and prays daily for divine assistance to control his sexual urge—but ultimately fails. Why this attempt at "marital celibacy"?

The Rabbi's prayer points to his reasoning: "May the merciful one save me from the evil inclination." Rabbi Ḥiyya bar Ashi associates sex itself, including marital sex, with "the evil inclination," for reasons many of us can understand. Sexual impulses can be animalistic, irrational, and misdirected toward forbidden targets, leading to adultery or other illicit sexual activity. For some, the physical nature of sex can seem base compared with more "noble" spiritual pursuits such as Torah study, prayer, or contemplation of the divine. Still others shy away from sex due to other worries, such as performance anxiety and fear of the unknown, or because they have grown apart emotionally from their partner, or even because they have become bored with the routine. A recent study concluded that about 20 percent of married couples today have a no-sex relationship.[7] If the source of Rabbi Ḥiyya bar Ashi's aversion to marital sex devolves from the ancient context, the phenomenon itself—although extremely complex—is still widespread today.

The Rabbis, however, were suspicious of celibacy. Understanding God's words to humanity in Genesis 1:28, "God blessed them and God said to them, 'Be fertile and increase, fill the earth and master it,'" as a commandment, they considered it obligatory to marry and have children. A telling talmudic tradition relates: "Until the age of twenty, the Holy One sits and waits for a man to marry a woman. When he reaches twenty without marrying, God says 'Blast his bones!'" (a mild curse, expressing exasperation) (*Qiddushin* 29b). The Rabbis feared that sexual desire would get the better of even the most pious individuals. Thus a proximate talmudic tradition quotes Rav Huna as saying, somewhat hyperbolically: "A twenty-year-old man who has not married a woman spends all his days in sin." For the same reason the Talmud requires a widower to remarry even if he has fulfilled his obligation to bear children (*Qiddushin* 29b). More philosophically, Rabbi Elazar asserted: "A man without a wife is not [really] a man, as it is said, 'Male and female He [God] created them . . . and He called them 'man'" (Gen. 5:2) (*Yevamot* 63a). Without a wife, Rabbi Elazar is saying, a man is not completely whole and cannot live up to the purpose for which he was created, for only a man and woman together constitute the true image of God. Given contemporary understandings, we might equally apply these teachings to same-sex relationships: only with a marital partner does a human being achieve the state of wholeness God intended.

Celibacy, of course, was fundamental to the Catholic tradition and came to be required of priests and nuns. Scholars have long debated where Christianity derived this ideal, as its Jewish roots are hard to discern. The Essenes or "Dead Sea Sect"—the group associated with authorship of the Dead Sea Scrolls—seem to have adopted a type of celibacy, at least while studying in their desert retreat at Qumran near the Dead Sea. But the major influences on early Christianity were probably currents in Greco-Roman philosophy that influenced some pre-Rabbinic Jewish groups, including both the Essenes and the Jewish Christians. Plato and other philosophers distinguished the body from the soul in a strictly dualistic way that differed from the more complex, integrated relationship between the two found in the Bible (and Rabbinic Judaism); this, in turn, led to a devaluing of the body and of carnal love as inferior to love of the soul, or friendship, what we still call a "platonic relationship." Some philosophical systems subsequently considered bodily love (sex) not only as less noble than love of the soul but as evil and corrupt, necessitating asceticism and celibacy. Catholicism eventually distinguished the clergy, who were required to live up to the higher ideal of celibacy, from the laity, who, unable to achieve the exalted standard, were permitted to express bodily love within marriage.

Against this background, our story may be a polemic against Christianity and its ideal of celibacy. The storyteller suggests that celibacy is unrealistic; those who aspire to celibate life will inevitably surrender to their bodily desires.[8] Alternatively, the story may have been directed at Rabbis who were influenced by Greco-Roman or even Christian ideas about the body and had begun adopting similar ascetic practices. Some Rabbis may have attempted a type of celibate marriage in which they restricted sexual activity as much as possible, perhaps ceasing all marital relations after having children. Our storyteller expresses opposition to such practices by having Rabbi Ḥiyya bar Ashi fail and die a painful death.

At the same time—and more relevant for the modern context—the story reminds us of the unpredictable and explosive potential of sexual forces. Notably, a recent study of "purity pledges," teen vows to be sexually abstinent until marriage, revealed that those teens who break their vows are more likely to become pregnant and contract a sexually transmitted disease than those who never took the pledge in the first place.[9] The ostensibly noble effort to prevent unwanted teen pregnancies and improve reproductive health through temporary celibacy actually tends to backfire, as did Rabbi Ḥiyya bar Ashi's sexual ethic.

While Rabbi Ḥiyya bar Ashi severely misjudged his own situation and ignored his wife's needs and desires to both their peril, he was not altogether wrong in his insight that "the evil inclination" motivates much deleterious sexual activity. Elsewhere the Rabbis say of the sexual urge: "Let the left hand hold it off while the right hand draws it close" (*Semaḥot* 2:15). They advocate a middle course—but to negotiate between the Scylla of repression and the Charybdis of excessive overindulgence is no easy task.

4 Men Are from Babylonia, Women Are from the Land of Israel

The laws of betrothal, marriage, and divorce, as well as related issues such as dowries, adultery, spousal obligations, widowhood, and paternity, receive detailed treatment in the legal portions of the Talmud. Correspondingly, we find many aggadic (nonlegal) traditions—stories, proverbs, biblical interpretations—that focus on relationships between the sexes in all their dizzying complexity. These sources offer visions of marriage that cannot be expressed in legal terms, addressing such issues as what it means to be a good spouse, how to respond to the needs of the other, the character traits and virtues required to make a marriage work, and how to deal with mothers- and fathers-in-law. No utopian document, the Talmud realistically portrays the many challenges of sustaining a marriage. Some of these difficulties may seem to us somewhat dated, perhaps a product of a time when parents arranged marriages for financial and familial reasons, rather than the modern "romantic" ideal, where couples find each other and marry for love. Others seem surprisingly relevant today. Anyone who had trouble finding a spouse, or still searches, can appreciate the Talmud's comment, "To effect the union between husband and wife is as difficult as splitting the Reed Sea" (*Sotah* 2a). Consider the talmudic aphorism, "There is a replacement for all things except for the wife of one's youth" (by implication, a husband of one's youth too) (*Sanhedrin* 22a). Certain married couples can relate to the rueful observation: "When our love was strong, we could make our bed on the blade of a sword; now that it has weakened, a bed sixty cubits wide is not large enough for us" (*Sanhedrin* 7a). Indeed, many talmudic stories give you the sense that, when it comes to husbands and wives, the more things change, the more they stay the same:

A certain man from Babylonia went up to the Land of Israel, and he married a woman there.

He said to her, "Cook me two lentils." She cooked him two lentils.

He seethed with anger at her.

The next day he said to her, "Cook me a *geriva* [a very large measure] of lentils." She cooked him a *geriva*.

He said to her, "Go and bring me two *botsinei* [pumpkins].

She brought him two lamps [another meaning of *botsinei*].

[He said to her,] "Go and break them on the head of the gate [*bava*].

[Rabbi] Bava ben [son of] Buta was sitting at the gate [*bava*] and judging cases.

She went and broke them on his head.

He said to her, "What is this thing that you have done?"

She said to him, "Thus my husband commanded me."

He said to her, "You did your husband's will. May God bring forth from your belly two sons like Bava ben Buta."

(*Nedarim* 66b)

In this tragicomic tale, an emigrant from Babylonia moves to the Land of Israel and marries a native woman. At the time, the Jews both of Babylonia and the Land of Israel spoke Aramaic, but the dialects, idioms, and expressions were somewhat different. The husband first asks his wife to cook him a dinner of "two lentils"—in today's idiom, "a couple of lentils" or "a few lentils." She makes him exactly two lentils, adhering strictly to the literal meaning. Not surprisingly, he gets angry at her. The next day, wanting to make sure he has enough to eat, he asks her to make a *geriva* of lentils, a very large measure, between two and three gallons. This is tantamount to our saying today, "I'm so famished I could eat a horse" or "Give me a ton of soup." Again, she follows his directions literally and offers him a gigantic amount of food, more than he could ever eat.

The subsequent dialogue plays on the different Aramaic dialects. The husband asks for two *botsinei*, meaning two pumpkins or gourds to eat, although in Babylonian Aramaic the word can also mean "lamps." In the Aramaic of the Land of Israel, however, *botsinei* exclusively means "lamps" and not pumpkins, so she accordingly brings him two lamps. Exasperated, he commands her to break the lamps on the "head of the gate," the top of the town gate, perhaps to humiliate her. In Aramaic the word for gate is *bava*, which also happens to be the name of an early Rabbinic Sage, Bava ben Buta—and that Rabbi happens to be sitting at the town gate when she arrives, holding court. The wife, seeing "the head of *bava*" and again taking her husband's words hyperliterally, breaks the lamps over the Sage's head rather than over the gate as her husband had intended. Sensing that there is more to this unprovoked act than meets the eye, Bava ben Buta wants to know why she behaved in such a bizarre way. When she replies that she was carrying out her husband's orders, the Rabbi not only forgives her but blesses her. She should merit giving birth to two great Rabbis as sons, corresponding to the two lamps she broke over the Rabbi's head.

A Comedy of Errors

The story begins with all the "ingredients" for a marital comedy of errors: a newlywed "inter-marriage" of Jews from different ancient empires, raised with different cultures, who speak different dialects. What could possibly go right?

At first read, the story seems to poke fun at the wife by portraying her as a simpleton. She fails to understand the most basic rules of language use and slavishly clings to the literal meaning of words, ignoring the real-life context. After all, only the most smallminded and clueless individual would understand a request for "a couple of lentils" to mean literally "two lentils" rather than a small portion of beans. Likewise, it seems obvious that only a man the size of the Jolly Green Giant could eat more than two gallons of lentils for dinner; so when the husband says the equivalent of "a ton of food" (in our idiom) he does not literally mean a ton. The wife might also recall the previous day's misunderstanding that left the husband ravenous and "seething" (a nice choice of word for anger, considering the culinary context), and judge that he just wants an ample portion this time.

Even the third misinterpretation, which shifts from the literal meaning to a misunderstanding on account of dialect, does not completely exculpate the wife. She has probably ignored the contextual clues that would clarify that her husband wants food, not light. Is it not approaching mealtime, when he typically informs her of what he wants for dinner? Why, she might ask herself, does he want two lamps, when in all likelihood one is sufficient and two wasteful? Is he preparing, say, to clean out a dark corner of the storeroom or to do something that requires copious light, and if not, why does he solicit illumination? Given the unfortunate misunderstandings of the previous days, doesn't she bear some responsibility to be on the alert for any possible confusion now? Had she asked him, "Why do you need so much light?" the misinterpretation would have been avoided. Even using the same words, "Why do you need two *botsinei?*," would likely have obviated the problem, as he would have responded, "Because I'm hungry now" or "Because they taste good," thus making her aware that his request concerned his sustenance.

Her foolishness reaches a climax when she breaks the lamps over a Rabbi's head. The frustrated—and evidently immature— husband presumably had meant to exact some measure of revenge for her private incompetence by making a public spectacle of her. The town gate is public space, analogous to an agora or market- place, as we learn from the Rabbinic court's location there. Indeed, the storyteller undoubtedly would have set the scene in a mar- ket or public square except that he needed an ambiguous word, so he chose the less common "gate"/*bava* to allow for the farcical denouement. To break lamps gratuitously on the top of the public town gate is an immodest and wasteful, if not downright crazy, act, and most wives would have felt ashamed before the numer- ous bystanders. She, however, yet again misinterpreting her hus- band's words, behaves in an even more immodest, shameful, and crazy way. When here, too, she slavishly follows his literal mean- ing, it is a meaning that should only be possible in theory, as its practice overrides all norms of acceptable behavior.

Bava ben Buta's benign response to the woman's senseless attack derives from his Rabbinic wisdom. Her battering him with lamps was unlikely to have hurt him; in talmudic times, most lamps were molded from clay, small and easily breakable, hardly suited for real damage. As a judge who deals each day with personal con- flicts between various parties—business partners, employers and employees, heirs, buyers and sellers, husbands and wives—the Rabbi realizes there must be a backstory to her assault—especially given its strange method. Besides this brilliant inference, he also possesses exemplary Rabbinic virtues: patience, humility, self-control, and forbearance. He does not lose his temper or take offense but asks her politely to explain.

Another part of the reason for this humane response can be understood only by appreciating the story's context in Tractate *Nedarim* of the Babylonian Talmud. *Nedarim*, which means "vows," deals with oaths and vows, elaborating on the applicable laws found in various biblical passages. Oaths invoked God's name and were therefore extremely serious commitments that could not be violated under any circumstances. Hence the third of the Ten Commandments cautions, "Do not swear falsely by the name of the Lord your God" (Exod. 20:7)[1]; likewise, Leviticus 19:12 admonishes, "You shall not swear falsely by My name, profaning the name of your God." In talmudic times swearing oaths had become common practice, not unlike our use of expletives today. A man might become angry with his friend or brother and swear, "I will never speak to you again" or "You will never set foot in my house." Similarly a husband irate at his wife might swear, "I will not look at you again unless you punch your sister in the face." Or a wife might lose patience with her husband's criticism and swear, "I will never cook you another meal." This tendency to swear oaths in the heat of the moment often put people into unwanted predicaments. A little while later the swearers would calm down, make up, and regret they had made the oath— but could do little about it, as the oaths were binding; they had no choice but to fulfil them for fear of divine punishment. Some oaths would even require a husband and wife to divorce, as the couple could hardly sustain a marriage when one partner swore, for example, not to speak to, cook for, or look at the other.

To cope with this problem the Rabbis devised various legal fictions and strategies to free people from such oaths; a great many legal discussions grapple with these issues. Several stories in Tractate *Nedarim* describe Rabbis who went to extreme lengths to release people from precipitous oaths that threatened their marriages or otherwise left them in miserable situations. According to one story, a husband swore that his wife not benefit from him in any way unless she spit on a leading Rabbi, and the Rabbi arranged for her to do so for the sake of the marriage. These stories portray Rabbis as the ultimate marriage counselors, saving marriages from imminent self-destruction (e.g., forced divorce) and reuniting husbands and wives.

While our story does not deal with an oath per se, it shares with these stories the plot line of a husband whose verbal utterances place his wife in a very difficult position. His words have led her to club a Rabbi in the middle of a public court session. She could justifiably be arrested and ridiculed, and even suffer abuse at the hands of the Rabbi's followers, who would seek to protect their teacher or exact vengeance for his maltreatment. Yet in this case, too, the Rabbi considers it his duty to heal the rift between the couple. He does not criticize her, shame her, or impose any punishment. Rather, he justifies her unjust assault and the humiliation she caused him with the legal fiction that she was fulfilling her husband's command. Her battering was a mitzvah! In this way she can return to her husband and report that she carried out his orders exactly as instructed. Hopefully he has calmed down and now will ask again, this time more courteously, that she prepare the pumpkin dish he initially requested.

Bava ben Buta's forbearance of this egregious insult accomplishes a second purpose: modeling for the couple the virtues necessary for a successful marriage. He essentially says to them: "Look how I reacted to this offense. Not by retaliating in kind. Not by becoming angry. Patiently and humbly I overlooked this affront to my personal dignity in order to try to understand the cause of the problem and enable the relationship to continue. Both of you must act this way for the sake of your marriage. And you must communicate, like I did. Talk to each other. By speaking and conversing you will understand each other's needs and not have these kinds of misunderstandings."

In this context the two lamps are pregnant with symbolism, despite featuring in the story primarily for the linguistic possibilities—in theory the plot could have featured any other household object that was also the name of a food. The two lamps call to mind the two Sabbath lamps, which in turn evoke images of peace, calm, and domestic tranquility. The Talmud directs that lamps be lit in the house on the Sabbath specifically for the sake of "peace in the home" (*shelom bayyit*), as darkness can conjure a scary and tense environment. Thus the breaking of the lamps in our story denotes the shattering of domestic harmony and even the marital bond itself. And yet, in talmudic tradition a lamp also symbolizes the human soul, the "light" of the body, based on Proverbs 20:27, "The soul of man is the lamp of the Lord." To repair the broken marriage the Rabbi blesses her with two children, two divine lamp-souls, to shine light into their darkness.

The blessing thus functions as an odd play on, or inverse application of, the measure-for-measure principle of perfect justice and punishment. Bava ben Buta prays that the wife will have two sons (corresponding to the two lamps) like Bava himself (corresponding to the "gate"/ *bava*). The sons will issue forth from her belly, another skillful allusion to the cooking theme. Perhaps we are to understand that the husband soon will be thrilled that his wife has conceived, doubly thrilled to learn she carries twins, triply thrilled when she delivers sons, and quadruply thrilled as they grow up pious and learned like the great Rabbi. Ordinary Rabbis can apply their talmudic acumen to find a legal basis to annul a precipitous oath. But only the greatest of Rabbis, like Bava ben Buta, can put a marriage like this back on track!

A Very Clever Woman

This reading understands the comedy of errors to turn on misunderstandings of language that result primarily from the woman's obtuseness. While the storyteller pokes some fun at the husband too, as we picture his growing frustration at receiving the wrong responses to his straightforward requests, the wife comes off far worse. Perhaps, behind the scenes, this is a misogynistic story told by male Rabbis in the Rabbinic academy, a space mostly off-limits to women, where men bonded together in homosocial Torah study—the equivalent of an in-joke, similar to men's locker-room humor, where some men ridicule women as a means to express their annoyance at elements of the gender gap. Such stories that play on misinterpretations of words, typically by women, are attested in many cultures.

Is this the only possible reading? Would a woman really be so foolish as to cook just two lentils or break a lamp over a Rabbi's head, even in the twisted male imagination? Or, perhaps, she could indeed be that foolish—but only in the twisted male imagination, not in reality. Rudyard Kipling wrote, "The silliest woman can manage a clever man; but it needs a very clever woman to manage a fool."[2] Can we read the story in this opposite way, with the wife not naïve but deviously brilliant? Could she in fact be the trickster feigning ignorance so as to play a joke on her credulous husband? Let us try.

A man emigrates from Babylonia and marries a native woman from Israel. Why does he relocate? How does he find this woman? Like the storytellers in most talmudic tales, ours is frustratingly sparse with the details, so we must use our imaginations and background knowledge to fill in the gaps. The man may have been motivated by religious reasons to settle in the Holy Land, much like many who make *aliyah* today. Perhaps he also considered the women of the Land of Israel to be more holy and pious than those of Babylonia, or to be superior in other ways to the girls he grew up with, if only on account of their exoticism: he thought he was "marrying up." On the other hand, he may have felt himself to be superior to his wife, as some Babylonian Jews were known for a type of cultural chauvinism. And the wife? Presumably she had little say in her choice of marital partner, as fathers arranged their daughters' marriages in talmudic times (in fact in almost all premodern times). The man probably was wealthy, or wealthy enough in the father's judgment. The terseness of the story's introduction suggests the marriage took place immediately after the man arrived, else the storyteller might have related, "He settled there. After some years he married." In all likelihood the couple hardly knew each other before their wedding. It may even have been a long-distance agreement, a talmudic version of a mail-order bride, with the man having negotiated a marriage through his agents or contacts prior to setting forth from Babylonia.

Now the woman finds herself newly married to a foreigner, a man she hardly knows, who speaks a different dialect and with a strange accent. Like many men in premodern times, he expects her to cook and clean for him. He is the master of the house—the Hebrew and Aramaic words for "husband," *ba'al/ba'ala*, literally mean "master"—and he barks out orders: "Cook me this," "Cook me that," "Prepare my dinner," "Bring me this," "Get me a lamp." Perhaps that is how Babylonian Jewish men speak to their wives, as Eastern peoples were known to be far more restrictive of their women than was customary in the Roman Empire. But it is not how she was brought up. What is more, he often becomes angry, screaming and hurling insults at her. She is far from happy in this marriage but has no real option—a single, divorced woman would be considerably worse off in antiquity.

A contemporary Syrian poet, Mohja Kahf, writes: "All women speak two languages: the language of men and the language of silent suffering."[3] Confronting her husband will prove counterproductive, but she can make small yet significant gestures of "resistance." She looks for ways to assert her autonomy while simultaneously exacting a small measure of revenge for the demeaning treatment she endures. The little ways she expresses her resolve will then become, for her, crucial means of survival, a type of liberty. Of course these maneuvers must look completely innocent and unintentional or the punishment will be harsh. When her husband orders her to cook him "two lentils" in his typically irritating dictatorial voice, she seizes the opportunity. Obviously he means a relatively small portion. Sometimes she even thinks this formulation is a pathetic attempt at politeness in Babylonia, as if ordering but a "couple of lentils" gives her less work to do than would a normal portion. She smiles to herself as she plops exactly two lentils into the pot, cooks them well, and places them on his plate with the most innocent, puppy-dog look she can affect. The more he seethes in anger, the more she laughs inside, all the while profusely apologizing: "I'm so terribly sorry, my dear, for the misunderstanding. You did say you wanted 'two lentils,' didn't you? Let me cook you some more right away. They should be ready in a couple of [literally!] hours, so maybe you should grab something else to eat in the meantime."

The next day, as she has hoped, her husband hedges by demanding a *geriva* of those lentils. Remembering his unsatisfied hunger the previous day, he calculates that again she will produce much less than he desires. Another opportunity for revenge! Everybody knows that a *geriva* is an impossibly large amount. In fact, cooking a *geriva* of lentils requires extra effort, as she must use all the pots she has at once, balancing them awkwardly by the fire, and even running to a neighbor to borrow more lentils, as no one keeps that much on hand. But the payoff is well worth the extra effort. She can hardly wait to see her husband's face as she calls him to the table set with every plate and vessel they own heaped high with lentils. When he demands an explanation, she puts on a naïve expression and tries to appear on the verge of weeping: "I'm so sorry. I thought you asked for a *geriva*. I really tried to be a good wife and do exactly what you wanted since you became so angry yesterday."

The following day a different opportunity presents itself. As usual, close to dinner time, her bossy husband has imperiously demanded his dinner order. Never does he say, "Please be so kind as to cook me a" or "I hope it is not too much trouble for you to make your delicious . . ." Nor has he inquired what she would like to eat. He has ordered *botsinei*. This word usually refers to "lamps." But, having quickly become accustomed to her husband's unusual vocabulary, she also knows the word has another meaning in Babylonia: "pumpkins." With dinnertime approaching, he undoubtedly means "pumpkin." Pumpkins ripen right around this time of year; in fact, she is sick and tired of hearing how the pumpkins grown in his town in Babylonia are the largest and sweetest in the world and much better than the woeful specimens here in the Land of Israel. Like most families of modest means, they rarely use lamps; they rise with the sun at dawn and go to sleep at sunset. The oil to fuel lamps is expensive, and in any event the lamplight provides meager illumination. To call for *two* lamps would be impossibly extravagant.

But a light (or two) goes off in her head: her husband's order is the perfect setup for another prank. She calls to him that she will be right there, tarries as long as she dares so that his appetite increases, then innocently enters his room and extends to him (again, along with the most clueless of facial expressions) two small oil lamps. His initial surprise at the proffered lamps quickly turns into rage. The crafty wife can hardly suppress her glee as she sees her husband unsuccessfully trying to contain his fury. She takes additional satisfaction in not having to explain to him that she thought he meant "lamp"—her husband has figured it out himself this time. A genius.

"Take these lamps" he screams, "and break them on the head of the gate." He asserts that he will not let her back into the house until she does so. He says many other insulting things too, including that a pumpkin has more brains than she does.

Now she worries that she has gone too far, carried away as she has been with her little jokes. Her husband has not sworn an oath yet, but the wild look in his eyes indicates that he is dangerously close. To refuse to follow this order might push him to swear—and that could be disastrous. If the oath cannot be annulled they will have to divorce, which is the last thing she wants—divorce will quickly leave her stigmatized and in the most wretched and impoverished of conditions. She knows too that many of the men her friends marry are no kinder than her husband, even if they speak better Aramaic. All she wanted was a little payback, some satisfaction and retaliation for her husband's autocratic manner.

So she takes the lamps with a heavy heart and heads for the town gate. Certainly to smash them there will be humiliating. She will make a public spectacle of herself before the residents of her village, not unlike the lunatics and sick-in-the-head women who disturb the peace with their bizarre antics and provide entertainment for the men carrying on their business. But she has little choice. Walking slowly down the lane, she racks her brain to devise an excuse. Perhaps she can explain that the lamps didn't work and in the midst of her frustration at trying to light them she broke them into a million pieces. But if so, why go to the town gate and not just smash them in the backyard or outside the front door? What to do?

As she nears the gate she sees the Rabbinic court arrayed under the nearby grove of trees, the local Rabbi on a small stool, the litigants standing before him, his disciples sitting cross-legged behind him. Although she has exchanged words with the Rabbi only once or twice, she has always admired Bava ben Buta, has heard many stories of his kindness. A light explodes in her mind. His name, luckily enough, happens to be Bava. What if she broke the lamps on his head? That would be equally humiliating. But she could blame her husband and have him share in the ignominy. Bava ben Buta, she hopes, will be more understanding than her spouse and perhaps even summon him for castigation at his cruel directive.

She waits for a break in the proceedings, approaches Bava ben Buta's stool, quickly takes out the lamps, and carefully smashes them together just above his head, making it appear to onlookers that the impact to his head caused the lamps to shatter. The Rabbi, though covered with shards, is unscathed. His students quickly grab her and pull her away, instinctively protecting their master. But it immediately becomes clear that the Rabbi is neither bloodied nor the least bit hurt. He instructs his students to bring the woman forth to explain. A crazy woman, the Rabbi knows, would have wounded him, whereas this woman has skillfully avoided injury. To what end?

When she explains, apologetically, that she was following her husband's bidding, trying her best to be an obedient wife, the Rabbi immediately understands. How often have married couples approached him, having sworn the most foolhardy oaths, begging him to find a way to absolve them? At least in this case the enraged husband stopped short of an oath. No legal machinations are necessary this time. With a knowing wink he proclaims for all to hear, "You did your husband's will. May God bring forth from your belly two sons like Bava ben Buta." This marriage needs some help to continue more happily. Perhaps the blessing of children and the joint endeavor of raising them will enable the couple to put aside their minor differences.[4]

Language, Misunderstanding, Gender

Misunderstandings of language, including confusing idioms and expressions with their literal meanings, are common tropes of humor. In Gilbert and Sullivan's famous opera *The Pirates of Penzance*, a hard-of-hearing and dim-witted nursemaid mistakenly apprentices a young nobleman to a *pirate* instead of a *pilot* as the father had instructed. This opera also involves satire of the literal minded; the contract of apprenticeship states that the young man goes free on his "twenty-first birthday," but because he was born on February 29, the pirate king claims his services for eighty-four years. A contemporary children's book series *Amelia*

Bedelia, now numbering over forty volumes, features a literalistic housekeeper. Asked to make a sponge cake, she bakes a real sponge within a cake; tasked with making the bed, she makes (builds) a bed; directed to draw the curtains, she draws a picture of curtains; instructed to look for a fork in the road, she keeps an eye out for cutlery. While almost all the books have a formulaic ending whereby Amelia makes up for her errors by baking and serving a delicious pie—here, food compensating for rather than underlying the problem—the issue at hand is not child's play but a complex understanding of linguistic theory, language apprehension, and gender difference. Ms. Bedelia has featured in such erudite scholarly analyses as "Polysemy: A Neglected Concept in Wordplay."[5]

Research into differences in language use between men and women, the pivotal axis of the Bedelia series, has a long history. Already in 1912 the anthropologist Alexander Chamberlain observed in an article entitled "Women's Languages" that the men of the Caraya Amazonian indigenous tribe pronounced a certain drink *sauba* while the women pronounced it *sakuba*.[6] Literature on this topic has exploded in recent decades with a particular focus on the impact of language on relationships between the sexes. In the bestseller *You Just Don't Understand: Women and Men in Conversation*, professor of linguistics Deborah Tannen asserts that differences in the way men and women express themselves—such as women's use of indirect speech far more often than men—cannot be ascribed purely to cultural conditioning (gender expectations) but devolve from fundamental biological differences; and then, because men and women fail to appreciate the way the other sex speaks, they easily become frustrated and angry with each other. In addition, she says, men and women may have difficulty understanding each other because of their different "cultures." Culture, after all, is simply a network of habits and patterns based on past experience—and women and men have different past experiences.[7] Male-female conversation therefore can be understood as cross-cultural communication. Just as an American may have trouble understanding exactly what an Englishman or Australian means because of differences in culture, despite speaking fundamentally the same language, so men and women from the same town may not completely understand each other due to the different cultural experiences of their gender.

John's Gray's bestseller *Men Are from Mars, Women Are from Venus* also argues that men and women have different methods of communicating, actually "speaking different languages," and basically thinking very differently because of their biological and psychological differences.[8] Other scholars disagree. In *The Myth of Mars and Venus: Do Men and Women Really Speak Different Languages?*, Oxford University professor of language and communication Deborah Cameron characterizes Gray's work as "New Age psychobabble," insisting that differences in the ways men and women speak are due exclusively to social and cultural factors, to the way our society constructs gender.[9] Professor of English and linguistics Jennifer Coates takes a similar view in a series of books, *Women Talk*: Conversation Between Women Friends; *Men Talk*: Stories in the Making of Masculinities; and *Women, Men and Language: A Sociolinguistic Account of Gender Differences in Language*. John L. Locke, a professor of linguistics and author of *Duels and Duets: Why Men and Women Talk So Differently*, attributes the differences to evolutionary biology—men employ aggressive speech, in raised voices, to assert their dominance, whereas women use quieter speech to bond together. Hundreds of other studies by psychologists, linguists, and sociologists take just about every position on this topic.

Some research shows that men and women differ in their use of literal and nonliteral language, at least in some contexts. In their paper "Do Men and Women Differ in Their Use of Nonliteral Language When They Talk about Emotions?," professors of psychology Kristen Link and Roger Kreuz answer in the affirmative.[10] When husbands and wives differ both in the "gender" culture to which Tannen refers, which may involve disparate uses of literal language, and also in their home culture, as in our story, and speak a different dialectic too—misunderstandings are perhaps inevitable.

Notably, even when they disagree about causes, almost all the relationship gurus propose the same basic solution: relationships can be vastly improved if men and women remain more alert to their differences in manner of speech, communicate more openly and frequently, maintain a high level of attentiveness when conversing, and try to understand the other on his or her own terms.

Our storyteller (and the storyteller in the previous chapter) would undoubtedly agree with this sage advice. At the same time, however, the talmudic story emphasizes other, more traditional ways to strengthen one's marriage: having children and abiding by religious tradition. When the couple focuses on rearing the next generation and teaching their offspring to lead moral and spiritual lives (like Bava ben Buta), then the marriage will be directed not only to self-fulfillment but to values of ultimate worth. Misunderstandings between husbands and wives may be inevitable, but by partnering together in joint pursuit of more important goals the couple can treat those mix-ups as a source of comic relief rather than of irreconcilable discord.

Dialect and Death

The storyteller's use of different Aramaic dialects as an integral element of the plot reveals a keen understanding of an important linguistic phenomenon. Sociolinguistics, the study of language in society, includes the subfield of "dialectology," which focuses on systematic variants of a language. In centuries past, authors wrote in proper English (and other languages), the "King's English," eschewing dialects as the corrupt speech of the lower classes. By contrast, more modern authors consider rendering dialects accurately as crucial to their literary purposes. In *Adventures of Huckleberry Finn,* Mark Twain's characters speak in specific dialects, an unusual writing style that Twain felt necessary to explain with an introductory note to his readers:

> In this book a number of dialects are used, to wit: the Missouri negro dialect; the extremist form of the backwoods Southwestern dialect; the ordinary "Pike County" dialect; and four modified varieties of this last. The shadings have not been done in a haphazard fashion, or by guesswork; but painstakingly, and with the trustworthy guidance and support of personal familiarity with these several forms of speech.[11]

Twain's use of dialect creates a more realistic feeling, facilitates characterization, and allows the reader to better appreciate each character's social class, level of education, degree of sophistication, and even moral status.[12]

In other works Twain employed different dialects to create humorous interchanges. *Roughing It* includes a hilarious scene in which a rural Nevadan miner named Scotty Briggs asks a minister who has recently arrived from the East to preach at his friend's funeral. The two can hardly understand one another as the one speaks in a local dialectic with all sorts of slang and idioms and the other in sophisticated English with highfalutin vocabulary:

> [Scotty:] Well, you've ruther got the bulge on me. Or maybe we've both got the bulge, somehow. You don't smoke me and I don't smoke you. You see, one of the boys has passed in his checks and we want to give him a good send-off, and so the thing I'm on now is to roust out somebody to jerk a little chin-music for us and waltz him through handsome.

[Minister:] My friend, I seem to grow more and more bewildered. Your observations are wholly incomprehensible to me. Cannot you simplify them in some way? At first I thought perhaps I understood you, but I grope now. Would it not expedite matters if you restricted yourself to categorical statements of fact unencumbered with obstructing accumulations of metaphor and allegory?[13]

After a long back-and-forth of such confusion they eventually manage to reach an understanding and the funeral takes place.

Though Twain's primary purpose here seems to be entertainment, his portrayal of the difficulty of mutual intelligibility points to serious issues, such as the gap between the cultures of the eastern and western United States at the end of the nineteenth century. Implicit questions for Twain's contemporary American readers are where do their sympathies lie and why, and the political implications regarding the future of American culture/cohesiveness.

An extremely serious case of what is at stake in dialect differences appears much earlier than our talmudic example in the biblical book of Judges, chapters 11 and 12. The Israelites ask the warrior Jephthah to lead them in battle against the Ammonites, a neighboring people. After the Ammonites have been defeated, the northern Israelite tribe of Ephraim rebukes Jephthah for not having summoned them to the battle—prompting a civil war between the men of Jephthah's city, Gilead, and Ephraim. Losing the battle, the Ephraimites attempt to flee across the Jordan River. The Gileadites, however, intercept the retreating Ephraimite soldiers, who try in vain to conceal their identity; their Hebrew dialect gives them away:

(Judges 12:5) The Gileadites held the fords of the Jordan against the Ephraimites. And when any fugitive from Ephraim said, "Let me cross," the men of Gilead would ask him, "Are you an

Ephraimite?"; if he said, "No," (6) they would say to him, "Then say *shibboleth*"; but he would say *"sibboleth,"* not being able to pronounce it correctly. (7) Thereupon, they would seize him and slay him by the fords of the Jordan. Forty-two thousand Ephraimites fell at that time.

The Hebrew word *shibbolet* means an "ear of corn" and, more rarely, a "stream." Apparently the Ephraimite dialect rendered the "sh" sound of biblical Hebrew as an "s." Therefore the Ephraimites could not pronounce the word as *shibboleth* even if they tried, much as speakers of some languages today cannot pronounce the "th" and other sounds that do not exist in their native languages.[14] Our English word "shibboleth," meaning "a way of speaking or believing that indicates that a person belongs to a particular social group" or a "custom or usage that distinguishes one group from another," derives from this incident.

This tragic episode underscores the critical nature of the issues raised in our story. In the talmudic story the different Aramaic dialects contribute to a misunderstanding that might have led to the breakup of a marriage; in the biblical tale the different Hebrew dialects lead to the tragic death of forty-two thousand Ephraimites.

The historian and journalist Abraham Rabinovich recounts a contemporary event with echoes of the biblical story in *The Yom Kippur War: The Epic Encounter that Transformed the Middle East.* In the first confused days of fighting in the Sinai, a small garrison of forty-two Israeli soldiers tried to retreat from the fort they had been manning along the Sinai-Egypt border to join up with the main Israeli forces. Setting forth at night through the adjacent town that had been occupied by Egyptian soldiers, they proceeded into the desert, where they encountered enemy troops firing upon them:

Lieutenant Kostiga, who knew Arabic, shouted, "Are you crazy? Why are you shooting at us? We're Egyptian."

After a pause, a voice shouted, "They're not Egyptian." Kostiga had pronounced the Arabic word for crazy, *majnoon*, as it is pronounced by Palestinians, with a soft *j*; in Egypt, however, it is pronounced with a hard *g*. Fire was opened again, this time more intensely. The Israelis responded in kind.[15]

In the ensuing battle, some of the Israeli soldiers were killed and others wounded or taken captive. Life and death once again depended on dialectical pronunciation.

All of these examples illustrate the crucial importance of language to human life. The ability to speak distinguishes humans from animals. How one speaks and what one speaks determine what kind of human being one is.

5 Sufferings! Not Them and Not Their Reward!

Why do the righteous suffer and the wicked prosper? The problem of "theodicy," of God's justice, ranks among the most important religion questions. Some scholars argue that addressing this issue is in fact the primary function of religion. The goal is not necessarily to solve this difficulty—which generally cannot be resolved in a completely satisfactory way, at least in the monotheistic tradition—but to provide strategies for coping with the reality of human suffering to make it understandable, bearable, and ultimately meaningful.

After all, the problem of suffering is not merely a matter for abstract theology or philosophy, but ultimately personal; it afflicts all of us sooner or later. Like the challenges of love and marriage discussed in the previous chapters, the experience of suffering and death constitutes an inescapable part of being human.

Unjustified suffering, the Rabbis teach, is central to the Bible's account of the most direct human encounter with God: Moses ascending Mount Sinai to receive the divine Revelation. At the summit of the mountain, Moses asks God, "Now if I have truly gained Your favor, pray let me know Your ways, that I may know You" (Exod. 33:13). This request, according to Rabbinic traditions, specifically concerned the suffering of the righteous. When Moses requested to "know Your ways" he sought to understand the "ways" that God administered recompense in this world through rewards and punishments. Moses could not understand why the righteous sometimes suffered and the wicked prospered contrary to our expectations of divine justice. Therefore when Moses spoke "face-to-face" with God, as the Bible describes the meeting (Exod. 33:11), in the most intense experience of the Divine—when he could have asked any imaginable question—Moses asked specifically about the injustice of human suffering.

The standard explanation for suffering found in the Bible and Talmud devolves from covenantal theology. According to the terms of the covenant between God and the Israelites established on Mount Sinai—and in some ways going all the way back to Abraham and the biblical patriarchs—God rewards the people for obedience and punishes them for disobedience and sin. "Reward and punishment" thus serves as the divine response to human conduct, applying both to individuals and to the people as a whole. The *Shema*, for example, among the most important Jewish prayers, quotes Deuteronomy 11:13–17 in asserting: "If, then, you obey the commandments that I enjoin upon you this day . . . I will grant the rain for your land in season . . . And you shall gather in your new grain and wine and oil . . . And you will eat and be satisfied. Take care not to be lured away to serve other gods and bow to them. For the Lord's anger will flare up against you, and He will shut up the skies so there will be no rain . . . and you will soon perish from the good land." Another prayer states unambiguously: "Because of our sins we were exiled from our land, and brought far from our homeland, and our sanctuary was destroyed."[1] From this perspective, suffering, including illness and economic hardship, is evidence of sin, though the Rabbis believed timely repentance could preclude punishment.

To explain why reality sometimes contradicts this theology, why some righteous human beings suffer and some sinners prosper, the Bible employs various strategies. Occasionally an individual suffers because of his ancestors' sins, or as punishment for an unknown sinner hidden within the community, or as a goad to repentance, or to achieve a secret divine purpose. But these are ad hoc explanations; strictly speaking, according to biblical covenantal theology, such cases ought to be few and far between.

The Rabbis, on the other hand, were not satisfied with this explanation. Having experienced the destruction of the Second Temple and centuries of oppressive Roman rule, they were keenly aware of the more extensive nature of injustice in the world. The righteous, they conceded, do suffer in this world. But they added a crucial explanatory mechanism by broadening their perspective to include the "world to come." The final reckoning will take place posthumously, when God metes out true rewards and punishments. After death God will punish the wicked for their sins, either denying them a portion in heaven or subjecting them to the fires of hell, while granting the righteous a blissful existence for eternity. Indeed, according to some Rabbinic sources, the righteous are *expected* to suffer in this world: receiving punishment for their few this-worldly sins now, in effect "paying off" all their sins in this life, allows them to receive pure reward in the next. The wicked, conversely, might prosper in this world, receiving reward for their few good deeds—which would then justify their posthumous fate of unadulterated suffering.

How Difficult Are Siufferings!

A problem with this theology, apart from it sounding much like a rationalization that defies empirical verification, is that few people relish suffering. To philosophize and theologize in this way is one thing, but when most people experience pain and suffering, they lose interest in ideas. Even the Rabbis could take only so much theology, as seen in the following anecdotes from the midrash:

Rabbi Yohanan became afflicted and endured fevers for three
and a half years. Rabbi Hanina went up to visit him. He said to
him, "What has come upon you?" He said to him, "My burden

is too great to bear." He said to him, "You should not say that. Rather you should say, 'The faithful God. . . .'"

After some time Rabbi Ḥanina became sick. Rabbi Yoḥanan went up to visit him. He said to him, "What has come upon you?" He said to him, "How difficult are sufferings!" He said to him, "But how great is their reward!" He said to him, "I want neither them nor their reward."

(*Shir ha-Shirim Rabbah* 2:16)

When Rabbi Yoḥanan suffers a protracted illness, his colleague Rabbi Ḥanina pays him a call to offer consolation—but the focus shifts from comfort to theology after Rabbi Yoḥanan complains, "My burden is too great to bear." Rabbi Ḥanina admonishes his fellow Sage for protesting his condition. He offers a brief maxim, "The faithful God," that picks up on the standard rabbinic theology of suffering: God should be trusted such that the sufferings God inflicts are neither unjustified nor arbitrary. In the background rests the belief that God imposes human suffering as just punishment for sin, as motivation for repentance, or as a divine wake-up call to search one's deeds and change one's ways. Of course God would never cause suffering beyond the limits of what any given individual can handle, never inflict a punishment "too great to bear." Rather than remonstrate, Rabbi Ḥanina avers that Rabbi Yoḥanan should piously accept his sufferings as justly deserved.

Rabbi Ḥanina's perspective shifts when he himself becomes sick. In a role reversal, Rabbi Yoḥanan now pays a visit to console his former consoler. Ironically, Rabbi Ḥanina, who had directed his friend Rabbi Yoḥanan not to complain about suffering, will have none of such pious adages. His first expostulation, "How difficult are sufferings!," is not far from Rabbi Yoḥanan's original avowal that sufferings are burdens "too great to bear." Rabbi Ḥanina probably intends more than the mere observation that sickness wears one down and feels oppressive after a while. He implies, rather, that suffering is a miserable experience of which he has had quite enough. Rabbi Yoḥanan, having been chastened by Rabbi Ḥanina himself to accept suffering with equanimity, now counters with positive spin. Suffering confers great rewards, either by atoning for sin in this world so as to maximize reward in the next or simply by earning merit for the self-effacing acceptance of God's decree. A pious soul who consents to suffer with humility and submission can expect divine compensation for that faith. Look on the bright side, Rabbi Yoḥanan urges his colleague. Welcome suffering for the great opportunities it offers!

Rabbi Ḥanina's sharp retort, "I want neither them nor their reward," brilliantly undermines this "brighter side" of suffering. He will gladly forego those great rewards if only he can be relieved of his pain. In the face of the real, tangible, personal experience of sickness and hardship, Rabbi Ḥanina now abandons the very sentiments he had so confidently expressed to his friend. In other words, the storyteller seems to be telling us, you should not think you understand the phenomenon of human suffering such that you can counsel and comfort others until you have been in the same situation yourself. But then you won't be so receptive to the hollow words of your comforters, of "outsiders" whole in body and free of pain.

Sufferings of Love

This subversive perspective that essentially rejects suffering is developed in the Babylonian Talmud where a new idea, "sufferings of love," appears.

Rava, and some say Rav Ḥisda, said:

> If one sees that sufferings come upon him, let him examine his deeds, as it says, "Let us search and examine our ways, and turn back to the Lord" [Lam. 3:40].

> If he examines [his deeds] and finds no [sin], he should attribute [the sufferings] to his neglect of Torah [study], as it says, "Happy is the man whom you discipline, O Lord, the man you instruct in your Torah" [Ps. 94:12].

> If he found no neglect of Torah, he should know that these are sufferings of love, as is written, "For whom the Lord loves, he rebukes" [Prov. 3:12].

Rava, quoting Rav Seḥorah quoting Rav Huna, said:

> He whom the Holy One loves, he crushes with sufferings, as it says, "But the Lord chose to crush him by disease" [Isa. 53:10].

> Is it possible [the Holy One imposes sufferings] even when one does not accept them with love? [No!], as it says, "If he made his soul an offering of restitution" [Isa. 53:10]. Just as an offering requires consent, so sufferings [of love] require consent.

> If he accepts [sufferings with love], what is his reward? He will live a long life, see his offspring, and in addition, his

knowledge [of Torah] will endure, as it says, "Through him the Lord's purpose will prosper" [Isa. 53:10].

(*Berakhot* 5a–b)[2]

This passage combines profound theology with an artful literary structure, comprising two units of midrash (biblical interpretation) featuring tripartite divisions and a story (to follow) that also includes a tripartite structure. In the first two paragraphs Rava's explanations about the causes of suffering are accompanied by biblical prooftexts. In theory Rava explicates the biblical verses, explaining their meaning for a later audience not acquainted with the biblical idiom. In practice the interpretation may be as much "read into" the verse as "read out" of it, such that the verses serve as supports, but not the sources, of the Rabbinic ideas.

Rava opens with a thoroughly conventional understanding of the cause of suffering. He recommends that the sufferer "examine his deeds," because sufferings generally come about as punishment for sin. By stepping back and scrutinizing one's conduct the individual may become aware of ethical or religious failings that had escaped his notice and then, by changing his ways or by repenting for those sins, influence God to ameliorate his fortune. If an individual cannot identify any moral or religious failing, or find even one commandment he or she has violated or failed to perform, it stands to reason that the suffering is due to "neglect of Torah study". The Rabbis considered Torah study the highest religious vocation and greatest commandment, and they encouraged both Rabbis and laity to study as much Torah as possible. Because in theory one can study Torah every minute of the day— and even the entire night—it is very safe to say that just about everyone can be considered guilty of this offense. Who doesn't waste at least some time during the day that could have been spent more profitably studying Torah? Even the most industrious people who don't engage in idle chatter, or daydreaming, or dawdling over a coffee break can be accused of neglecting Torah study simply because they devote some extra time to their business—or to exercising, food shopping, child rearing, even sleeping. Given this impossibly high standard, one wonders whether Rava's statement worked better as a motivation to redouble one's personal commitment to Torah study than as an explanation for suffering. In any event, because neglect of Torah study is a type of sin, albeit a sin of omission, this statement continues the standard theology of suffering as divine punishment.

Rava's third statement, however, blazes an entirely new approach by introducing the idea of "sufferings of love," a concept, to the best of my knowledge, not found in earlier Rabbinic traditions and therefore an innovation of the Babylonian Talmud. It is not completely clear what Rava means. His prooftext comes from a passage found in the biblical book of Proverbs that reads in full: "Do not reject the discipline of the Lord, my son; do not abhor his rebuke. For whom the Lord loves, He rebukes, as a father the son whom he favors." In context these verses mean that God disciplines, rebukes, and punishes the humans he loves *in the same way* as a father disciplines the child whom he loves; hence presumably for the same reasons: to correct the behavior and direct the child away from sin or error. Proverbs, in other words, offers the standard theology of suffering as punishment for sin but adds emotional coloring and an insight into God's motivation. God does not cause suffering because he is harsh, mean, or callous but because God loves humans and wants to teach them proper behavior. Therefore, when God sees his human "children" misbehave, God punishes them with suffering. Rava, however, must mean something entirely different as he contrasts "sufferings of love" with the conventional theology he proposes with his first two statements.

In the next paragraph Rava develops this innovative theology by drawing on another biblical verse, Isaiah 53:10. This verse appears within a lengthy and extremely enigmatic passage that spans Isaiah 52 to 55, often referred to as "the suffering servant." It describes a righteous and faithful servant of God who, despite his innocence, is despised, oppressed, afflicted with disease, and "crushed" with sufferings because of the sins of others. Christianity interpreted this passage as a prophecy about Jesus, whereas the Rabbis generally understood it as an allegory about the Jewish people as a whole, who suffer on account of, and also for the sake of, the sins of other nations. Rava, however, takes a narrower reading of the verse, understanding it apart from the larger biblical passage. For him it concerns a righteous individual who suffers neither on account of his own sins nor because of the sins of others but due to God's special love. Rava adds that the sufferer must reciprocate by accepting the sufferings with love—that is, by willingly receiving the sufferings and not resenting or rebelling against them. People who do so can then expect to be rewarded with a long life, living children, and enduring knowledge of Torah—the family's traditions will be passed down over the generations and not forgotten. "Sufferings of love" therefore provide the righteous an opportunity for "extra" rewards. By demonstrating their faith in God, despite their seemingly unjustified suffering, they earn reward over and above what they otherwise would have received for their acts of piety.

Notably, the talmudic commentators were somewhat puzzled by the notion of "sufferings of love." The great medieval jurist and philosopher Moses Maimonides (1135–1204), author of the *Guide of the Perplexed*, insists that Jewish theology believes "all these human affairs are managed with justice; far be it from God to do wrong, to punish any one unless the punishment is necessary and merited." Nevertheless, he concedes that a minority position held by "some Sages" recognizes "sufferings of love," in which "it is possible that a person be afflicted without having previously committed any sin in order that his future reward may be increased" (3:17). By "future reward" Maimonides may be transferring the time frame from Rava's claims of reward in this world to the next. Rashi, the foremost Talmud commentator, makes a similar move: "The Holy One afflicts him in this world, without his having sinned, in order to increase his reward in the next world more than his merits deserve." This shift to the next world as the arena where rewards materialize is probably designed to address the same difficulty noted above: that some righteous who suffer do not seem to receive their rewards in this world as Rava envisions. Thus, for both "sufferings of love" and standard "sufferings for sin," the dominant Rabbinic tendency defers rewards to the next world. A later commentator, Rabbi Samuel Edels (1555–1631), however, understands "sufferings of love" more in line with the biblical passage in Isaiah—namely that the undeserved suffering of the righteous atones vicariously for the sins of other people.[3]

The difficulties these and other theologians encounter in trying to make sense of "sufferings of love" reveal how problematic the notion is, despite the advantage of separating suffering from sin. Some people indeed take great offense at the idea that God would make people suffer gratuitously. (Although, to be fair, Rava stresses that God only imposes "sufferings of love" on those who willingly accept them, and many people take equal offense at the notion that God makes people suffer as punishment for sin.)

Nevertheless, some sufferers do take great comfort in this concept. A woman I knew who was stricken by cancer at a relatively young age and eventually died from the disease could not accept the theology that her sickness was due to her failings or sins. She also rejected the idea that suffering is a "mystery," that God's reasons for causing suffering are beyond human understanding. But she took great comfort in this notion that, far from being punished by God, she was in fact the recipient of a special divine love. Her illness and death, which she had initially experienced as a completely unjustified and inexplicable fate, became bearable once she thought of it as testimony of the love of God, even if she could not fully understand why God chose that way of reaching out to her.

Other sufferers have interpreted the notion of "sufferings of love" in a different way: as expanding the human ability to love. Suffering sometimes functions as a wake-up call leading to a deeper awareness of our love of others. When we are healthy and life seems to stretch out endlessly before us, we are liable to take those we love for granted and not express how much they mean to us. When stricken by illness or staring death in the face, we may feel the urgency to communicate our love openly before it is too late. Similarly, the experience of suffering can lead to heightened sensitivity, compassion, and empathy toward fellow sufferers. When confronted with our own vulnerability we may reach out with love to care for others who share our fate.

A Talmudic Memento Mori

After a brief discussion of additional aspects of suffering, the talmudic passage continues with another story of suffering Rabbis:

Rabbi Elazar became ill. Rabbi Yoḥanan visited him. [Rabbi Yoḥanan] saw that [Rabbi Elazar] was lying in a dark room. He uncovered his arm and light shone. He saw that Rabbi Elazar was weeping. He said to him, "Why do you weep?

"[Do you weep] because of Torah, that you did not proliferate it? Have we not learned, 'All the same is a large measure and a small measure, as long as his intention is for the sake of heaven [*Mishnah Menaḥot* 13:11]?'

"[Do you weep] because of [your lack of] sustenance? Every man
does not merit two tables [i.e., riches in this world and in the next].

"[Do you weep] because of [lack of] children? This here is the
bone of my tenth child [who died, yet I do not weep]."

[Rabbi Elazar] said to him, "I weep for that beauty [of yours]
which will wither." [Rabbi Yoḥanan] said to him, "For that you
may justly weep," and the two of them wept together.

Meantime, Rabbi Yoḥanan said to him, "Do you cherish
sufferings?" [Rabbi Elazar] said to him, "Not them and not
their reward." [Rabbi Yoḥanan] said to him, "Give me your
hand." [Rabbi Elazar] gave him his hand and he healed him.

(*Berakhot* 5b)[4]

Rabbi Yoḥanan, whom we encountered in the earlier story, again
visits a sick colleague to offer solace. The patient lies in a dark
room, perhaps to facilitate his drifting off to sleep, perhaps simply due to his subdued and depressed mood, or perhaps because
in his condition light itself proves too painful. In an effort to raise
his colleague's spirits, Rabbi Yoḥanan exposes his arm, and its brilliance floods the room with light.[5] The Talmud imagines Rabbi
Yoḥanan as the most beautiful of men, whose majestic face blazes
with splendor akin to the brilliant rays of the sun. Even his limbs,
apparently, are so radiant as to shine with dazzling luminosity,
and in this way Rabbi Yoḥanan's physical presence illuminates
the dim chamber where Rabbi Elazar suffers in silent anguish.
At this point Rabbi Yoḥanan notices that his colleague weeps—
presumably due to the physical pain of his illness or the mental
anguish of approaching death.

Rabbi Yoḥanan reacts like many of us do when someone cries in our presence: we try to halt the weeping by cheering up our friend or providing consolation. Weeping signifies pain, and we naturally wish to end the hurt, even—and perhaps especially—if we stand helpless before someone else's physical sufferings. Rabbi Yoḥanan proceeds to query Rabbi Elazar about what underlies his suffering—might it be frustration at the lack of accomplishment (for a Rabbi, the failure to master a greater body of Torah), poverty, or childlessness?[6] A keen observer of human nature, the Rabbi knows well that when one is sick and depressed, no matter what the immediate cause, one cannot help but feel other travails more acutely, as if they gang up on him, so to speak. By quoting another Rabbinic tradition he assures his colleague that the quantity of Torah mastered is not important; a pious intention is what counts, namely that one studies because of a commitment to serve God and not to promote one's ego. Poverty, too, should not occasion weeping as many people do not merit "two tables"—to eat both in this world and of the bounty of the world to come. In other words, let it suffice for Rabbis like you and me to anticipate the eternal rewards we will enjoy in heaven and not concern ourselves with the deprivations of this ephemeral world. If we must choose a single "table" to merit, let the table of eternal sustenance in the hereafter take precedence over the table of earthly food in the present. Nor should one weep because of childlessness, a particularly painful condition in a culture that stresses peoplehood and the continuity of family bloodlines. Here, Rabbi Yoḥanan appeals to his personal experience; he had ten children and watched them all die. He shows the "proof" of his bitter suffering: a small bone from the tenth child he has since carried as a memento, perhaps on a chain around his neck or in his pocket. Childlessness may be miserable, he tells his colleague, but having children who die can be even worse. "I have been to that darker place and I know it," he informs Rabbi Elazar, "and I have put aside my weeping. Why then do you weep even for such miseries?"

Surprisingly, Rabbi Elazar answers with a kind of non sequitur. Personal failure, poverty, illness, childlessness do not make him weep. What does is the inevitable loss of his friend's beauty, the physical splendor of Rabbi Yoḥanan, who has illuminated the room by uncovering his radiant arm. The real tragedy is human mortality, the inexorable march of time that causes us all to age, wither, and die. In so speaking, Rabbi Elazar has effectively transcended the gap between the sufferer and comforter, the sick and the well, the insider and outsider. What remains is the shared experience of all human beings: "Yes," he tells his friend, "All those miseries are terrible. My diseased body is terrible too. But worse is the death that will overtake us all, young and old, healthy and sick, beautiful and deformed alike." That indisputable—awful— truth, Rabbi Yoḥanan concedes, provides a just reason to weep. Now, no longer the minister to the sick but a co-sufferer of the malady of human vulnerability, he begins to cry. "And the two of them wept together."

Together. They wept together. Perhaps that is the lesson the storyteller wishes to teach us. No words, however compassionate; no theology, however true; no explanation, however accurate, can really provide solace to the sufferer. So the two Sages sit together, in silence, in tears, in semidarkness, knowing that they face life's inescapable travails with friends. "It is not good that the human should be alone" (Gen. 2:19), and there is nothing more human than mortality, decline, and infirmity; no experience more lonely than suffering.

By shifting the focus to the mortality and inexorable death of his colleague, and by extension the inexorable death that awaits all humans, Rabbi Elazar transforms the dialogue into a type of memento mori or "reminder of mortality" (the term literally translates to "remember that you must die"), a genre of literature and art. Paintings in this genre typically feature a human skull or skeleton, and sometimes a faded flower or timepiece, all symbolizing the inevitability of death. In literary memento mori, authors emphasize the terrors of death, the frailties of the body, the fleetingness of life, and the vanities of wealth, in order to impress upon readers the urgency of living a meaningful life and focusing on matters of ultimate concern. In Europe during the late Middle Ages and Renaissance people often kept objects also known as memento mori, such as skulls, in their bedrooms to remind themselves of death and thereby instill a sense of humility and piety. By meditating on death, Rabbi Elazar suggests, we learn not to take life for granted but rather to live life well and meaningfully. This is a much more productive matter to contemplate than the question of why the righteous suffer, which has no satisfactory answer.

Give Me Your Hand!

Rabbi Yoḥanan gets the message. He understands from Rabbi Elazar's arresting reply that neither consolations nor explanations are helpful. Rabbi Elazar, it turns out, like Rabbi Ḥanina, does not "cherish sufferings"; he too wants "neither them nor their reward."

Thus, somewhat surprisingly, the Talmud gives us a strong protest against advocates of the standard Rabbinic theodicy, against those who understand sufferings as just punishment for sin and thereby defend divine goodness in the face of suffering and evil. And the Talmud also seems to protest against "sufferings of love," however innovative and provocative the concept, as it too seeks to rationalize the sufferings of the righteous. Do not accept sufferings, the storyteller tells us, neither them nor those who justify them, neither them nor the routine maxims that explain them.

Rabbi Yoḥanan accordingly switches from theologian to healer and cures his colleague. But how? And what are we to make of this ending? Like many talmudic Sages, Rabbi Yoḥanan possesses supernatural abilities. In this instance his arm radiates light, and with a miraculous touch alone he heals Rabbi Elazar. Alas, we humans today no longer possess such powers. Thus another gap opens—between the storyteller's world and that of the contemporary reader. Perhaps the lesson is that we too must do whatever we can to heal others, if not supernaturally then naturally. Just as Rabbi Yohanan learns that he must replace theology with empathy and action, so, too, should we by dedicating our resources to modern medicine, supporting biomedical research, and participating in clinical drug trials. And although we cannot cure with a miraculous touch, we can provide comfort and solace, visiting the sick, volunteering in hospices, serving as grief counselors, and supporting in other ways.

Yet this distance between us and the Sages of old, between our modern, scientific worldview and the miraculous and supernatural beliefs of ancient tradition, also points to another dimension of human loss. Not only are the ravages of death and suffering inexorable but also the ravages of time. We are all at a distance: at a distance from the traditions of the past, at a distance from the pious faith of our ancestors, at a distance from knowing our predecessors and forefathers and foremothers of bygone ages. And for all this, too, we may justly weep.

Job's Chat with His Friends

The biblical book of Job also rejects the conception of suffering as punishment for sin. Job, a pious and righteous man, has a large family, owns thousands of domestic animals, and prospers greatly. In fact Job is so good that God boasts of his righteousness to "the Accuser," or Satan, an angelic figure apparently granted limited autonomy by God to function as a type of oppositional force. Satan responds that Job has good reason to be righteous, as God has provided him with a wonderful life, but were God to change Job's happy fortune, then Job would blaspheme God. Immediately God delivers Job into Satan's power. Job's ten children soon die, and

Job loses all his wealth. When Job remains pious Satan causes his skin to break out in painful boils. The next thirty-five or so chapters consist of discussions between Job and four of his friends. The companions repeatedly argue that Job must have sinned, else he would not have received such punishment; he should accordingly confess and repent. Job nonetheless insists on his innocence. His "friends" condemn his protestations as blasphemous—for he is implying that God is unjust.

The authors of the Torah and most of the other biblical books never could have told this story. According to their covenantal theology, God would never have allowed an innocent individual like Job to suffer misfortune and disease.

The author of the book of Job has a different worldview. Indeed, his very purpose is to challenge the dominant theology of the Bible, subsequently embraced by the Rabbis: that God rewards righteousness and punishes sin. The righteous can and do suffer, he insists. Premature, unnatural death (such as that of Job's ten children), disease, poverty, and other misfortunes afflict the righteous through no fault of their own. From this perspective to accuse the righteous of sin adds insult to injury—and, what is more, is tantamount to blasphemy, as it presumes to know the ways of God. In short, the standard biblical and Jewish theology is now standing on its head.

What, then, is the author's explanation for why the righteous suffer? In the book's last five chapters (38–42) God provides Job an answer of sorts. Speaking to Job "out of the whirlwind"—that is, manifesting as a tremendous natural force like a tornado or cyclone—God confronts Job with a relentless series of rhetorical questions emphasizing God's colossal power and the unbridgeable gap between the divine and the human:

Where were you when I laid the foundations of the earth? Declare, if you have the understanding. . . .

Have you commanded the morning since thy days began, and caused the dayspring to know its place? . . .

Have you surveyed unto the breadths of the earth? Declare, if you know it all . . . (Job 38:1–14)

The questions carry on. In other words, Job cannot and should not expect to understand the ways of God, whose power far exceeds human comprehension.

In the face of this divine onslaught Job concedes as much, admitting his infinitesimal stature vis-à-vis God and abandoning the search for an explanation of his sufferings. God also castigates Job's friends for their false claims about God's methods—namely the notion that God justly punishes the sinful and rewards the righteous. God is unknowable. How dare they have the audacity to assert why God does what God does?!

Ultimately, though, the author of Job fails to provide a coherent explanation for the suffering of the righteous, and for this reason scholars largely consider the book of Job to be a failed theodicy. The author appears to be much more adept at polemicizing against others' theodicy (e.g., suffering does not result from sin) than articulating his own (e.g., its causes are impenetrable mysteries).

The author nonetheless strongly believes in God and in particular God's ruling the universe with a firm hand. One could almost say the author's problem is that he has too powerful a God conception. There *are* explanations for the suffering of the righteous; we just cannot hope to comprehend them because God's massive, awesome powers transcend understanding in human terms. It is like trying to explain multivariate calculus to a toddler.

This theological perspective contrasts with more extreme skeptical views, such as the idea that God has totally abandoned the world to its own devices or, worse, abandoned the world to an evil power, or the deist view that God created the world but does not intervene in history, to say nothing of atheist and materialist views that deny the existence of God completely. All these beliefs in one way or another deny that God is directly responsible for human suffering, whereas the author of Job, like the Torah, believes that God is accountable.

A well-functioning religion or theology does not necessarily explain the problem of suffering but helps make that suffering meaningful. The author of Job would likely hold that suffering has meaning—even if that meaning is incomprehensible to us humans.

Even if this theology of the book of Job may strike us as unsatisfying, paradoxically it has a certain appeal in its negation of explanations that attempt to make sense of suffering, especially those that associate suffering with sin. For example, contemporary theologians have almost unanimously resisted explaining the sufferings of the Holocaust along the lines of the standard covenant theology. A theology that rejects the possibility of comprehending such colossal suffering may be somewhat more appropriate even if not completely adequate. On a personal level, too, some people may prefer to leave the causes of their own suffering as mysterious and inscrutable while holding on to the belief in a God who governs the cosmos. The great Hasidic master Rabbi Levi Yitzhak of Berdichev prayed: "Master of the Universe! I do not ask you to reveal to me the mysteries of your ways. I could not understand them. I do not even want to know why I suffer. But I do want to know that I suffer for Your sake."

Part 2 Virtue, Character, and the Life of Piety

6 The Ugly Vessel

"Grace is deceitful, and beauty is vain; but a woman that fears the Lord, she shall be praised" (Prov. 31:32). So states the hymn known as "A Woman of Valor," which men have traditionally sung at the Sabbath table to their wives. The verse expresses the conventional wisdom found in many religious and philosophical writings: physical beauty is superficial and meaningless; true goodness lies within.

Most of us would probably agree that this idea is sound in theory, while recognizing that real life proves far more complicated. In fact a talmudic tradition addresses the natural human inclination to make judgments based upon physical appearance. In ancient times, the Talmud tells us, the "daughters of Jerusalem" used to dance in the vineyards on two occasions each year at a betrothal festival:

The beautiful [maidens] among them—what would they say?
  "Young men! Set your eyes on beauty, since women are most prized for beauty!"

The [maidens] of noble lineage among them—what would they say? "[Young men!] Set your eyes on family!"

The ugly [maidens] among them—what would they say?
  "[Young men!] Make your acquisition [of a wife] for the sake of heaven . . . !"

(*Ta'anit* 26b)

The Talmud recounts that nubile damsels put their best foot forward, as it were, appealing to their greatest strength as they tried to attract the attention of prospective husbands. Women lacking both good looks and noble birth evidently had no choice but to entreat the young men to think of higher, more spiritual motives for marriage. Rather than insisting "beauty is vain" or pointing to inner beauty as paramount, this text offers a remarkably candid and sober understanding of the inevitability of aesthetic judgments.

If the experience of weighing physical beauty cannot be avoided, it nonetheless does not grant license for insensitive treatment of others as the Rabbinic protagonist of the following story learns.

Our Rabbis taught: "A person should always be soft like a reed and not hard like a cedar."

Once Rabbi Shimon ben Elazar[1] was coming from his master's house of study in Migdal Gedor. He was riding on a donkey, traveling slowly along the bank of the seashore. He felt great happiness because he had studied a great deal of Torah.

He chanced upon a very ugly [mekho'ar] man, who said to him, "Peace be upon you, Rabbi!"

Rabbi Shimon did not answer his greeting but said to him, "Scoundrel [reiqa]! How ugly you are! Perhaps all the people of your village [irkha] are as ugly as you are?"

He said to him, "Go and say to the craftsman who made me: 'How ugly is this vessel that you made.'"

Realizing that he had sinned, Rabbi Shimon got down from his donkey, and prostrated himself before the man, and said to him, "I humble myself before you. Forgive me." He said to him, "I will not forgive you until you go to the craftsman who made me and say to him: 'How ugly is this vessel that you made.'"

Rabbi Shimon traveled slowly, following after [the man] until he reached his village.

The people of the village came out to greet him, and they were saying to him: "Peace be upon you, our Rabbi!"

The man said to them, "Whom are you calling 'Rabbi'?" They said to him, "That one following after you." He said to them, "If he is a Rabbi, may there not be many like him in Israel!" They said to him, "For what reason?" He said to them, "He did such-and-such to me." They said to him, "Nevertheless, forgive him, for he is a man of great knowledge of Torah." He said to them, "I forgive him for your sake, providing that he does not make a habit of acting in this way."

Immediately Rabbi Shimon ben Elazar entered [the study house] and taught, "A person should always be soft like a reed and not hard like a cedar."

(*Ta'anit* 20a–b)

Why does Rabbi Shimon insult a man he considers physically ugly? At first glance, we might think that his remark had just slipped out inadvertently, the result of an unthinking, spontaneous reaction. Most of us cannot help reacting in certain ways upon beholding various sights: we feel awe at beauty, revulsion at ugliness, desire at delicious food, and other emotional responses beyond our control. We typically "screen" such sensibilities and keep them inside our heads while behaving and speaking politely.

Sometimes they spurt forth because our filters fail, because our emotions overwhelm us before our rational faculties can regain control, or in moments of weakness, as when people clap their hands to their mouths immediately after making an utterance as if to say, "I can't believe I actually said that."

Alternatively, is it possible that the Rabbi feels annoyed that this man has interrupted a blissful reverie? Perhaps his solitary and silent contemplation of the lovely sea—probably the Sea of Galilee—and lush vegetation on its banks, his appreciation of the magnificence of nature as he "travels slowly" and leisurely along, has been disturbed by this human interloper whose seeming "ugliness" contrasts sharply with the splendor around him.

However, neither of these possibilities appears to be the case here. The man first greets the Rabbi with politeness and respect. Given this opening, it is hard to imagine that the Rabbi reacted negatively to him because the Rabbi had unexpectedly and suddenly beheld the man. Nor is there any intimation that the surroundings were particularly attractive or the seascape anything out of the ordinary.

Rather, the Rabbi's pride at having "studied a great deal of Torah" seems to have motivated his nasty comment. Returning home from "his master's house of study," Rabbi Shimon has probably spent some weeks or even months toiling over his studies for ten, twelve, or more hours per day. Understandably he feels proud of his dedication, self-sacrifice, efforts, and accomplishments in the realm of the highest spiritual pursuit. Not so understandably this healthy sense of self-respect and "great happiness" turn into arrogance and a supercilious attitude. Indeed, to make this point abundantly clear, some versions of the story add that the Rabbi was feeling "full of himself." His haughtiness is also communicated by the difference in postures: the Rabbi rides on a donkey, elevated and comfortable, while the man walks on the ground and presumably has to raise his head to view the seated and almost literally "stuck up" Sage.

Rabbi Shimon's insult is particularly gratuitous. He not only belittles the man ("How ugly you are!") but extends the abuse to all the residents of his hometown, perhaps assuming that the man dwells close to members of his extended family. If the ugly man deserves opprobrium, the Rabbi thinks, why not his relatives too?

That he calls the man "scoundrel" is also excessive—and somewhat puzzling. What makes Rabbi Shimon so sure that this man, who has saluted him so appropriately, is a rogue? Here the Hebrew contains a wordplay deriving from the words for "ugly" (*mekho'ar*), "scoundrel" (*reiqa*), and "village" (*irkha*), pointing to the Rabbi's (illogical) assumption that the three are connected, that the man lives in a village of ugly scoundrels.[2]

More important, Rabbi Shimon mistakenly infers that the ugly countenance signals ugly deeds. Conflating superficial appearance with inner reality, he ignores the talmudic saying, "Do not look at the vessel but at what it contains" (*Mishnah Avot* 4:20)—in our idiom, "Do not judge a book by its cover." In such a case we might have expected him to reprimand the man as a sinner and call him to repent rather than belittle his physical appearance.

The real issue for Rabbi Shimon, then, is the man's lack of knowledge of Torah. Overweening pride at his own worthy vocation has led him to disparage those who do not devote themselves to full-time study, as if their mundane work renders them shirkers of Torah, ipso facto malefactors and "scoundrels." His own impressive accomplishments induce him to deprecate an individual whom he perceives as "lower," inferior and undeserving of honor. An ugly exterior, for Rabbi Shimon, results from an interior made ugly by its unembraced beauty of Torah.

Rabbi Shimon has learned "a great deal of Torah"—but what kind of Torah is this if it leads him to degrade others? Or has he forgotten his Torah upon leaving his master's house? Has he overlooked that Torah must be applied in all of life's circumstances and not confined to the rarefied space of the Rabbinic academy? Has he also misjudged the man? That the man responds to the insult by invoking a profound theological insight suggests he may not be as ignorant of Torah as the Rabbi assumes.

In this respect the story is a cautionary tale for Rabbis and other spiritual elites, warning them not to think so highly of themselves and so contemptuously of the laity lest their arrogance lead them to sin. By extension it can function as a cautionary tale for anyone today who has achieved significant accomplishments through hard work and sacrifice, and especially for those who supervise or employ others. Self-satisfaction and pride can lead to experiencing a sense of superiority and then to blaming others for their seeming lack of ability or achievement. This in turn can become an assault on their character: "How lazy/stupid/incompetent/unmotivated/inept/derelict you are!"

After making this didactic point at the expense of the Rabbi, the storyteller returns to a respectful, even saintly, portrayal of his protagonist. Rabbi Shimon immediately recognizes his sin, humbles himself by descending from the donkey, and, prostrating himself before the man, apologizes, asks for forgiveness, continues to seek forgiveness by following all the way to the man's home, and silently endures public humiliation before the villagers. He never attempts to cover up his error; rather, he even publicizes it, by teaching the lesson he learned to his contemporaries in the study house, presumably recounting his experience in the course of his homily. That he has acted appropriately is also suggested by the repetition of the description of the Rabbi "traveling slowly" (*metayyel*) as he follows the man, which points to measure-for-measure atonement for his sin. Just as he was traveling slowly, at leisure, when he insulted the fellow man, so he travels slowly, in distress, pleading for forgiveness. Typically an important man leads while his attendants, admirers, or students follow, but here the other man leads and the respected Rabbi trails behind, signs of contrition and acknowledgment that the Rabbi has been transformed into the student. More evidence of the storyteller's fundamentally high opinion of Rabbis is apparent in the villagers' reactions. They greet the Rabbi with great respect, direct the man to forgive him, and—despite hearing of the Rabbi's offense—praise him as a man of "great knowledge of Torah." In the storyteller's view the study of Torah does not guarantee immunity from sin but nonetheless deserves tremendous honor and respect, as it still counts as the highest spiritual activity.

An interpretive question worth pondering is whether the man behaves appropriately or whether he too exhibits a moral failing. Should he have forgiven the Rabbi immediately, or at least somewhat sooner, without having to be persuaded by his fellow villagers? His first response to the Rabbi, "Go and say to the craftsman who made me: 'How ugly is this vessel that you made,'" effectively teaches the lesson: humans are created by God and in God's image, hence an insult to the appearance of any human insults God Himself. The man then repeats this response with even greater intensity after the Rabbi has humbled himself and apologized: "I will not forgive you until you go." What is the purpose of the repetition? It no longer serves to provide the Rabbi insight into the implications of his offense, as his actions and words of apology demonstrate that he understands that his slur was sinful. Nor does the man really want the Rabbi to carry out this directive as to do so would undermine the very lesson he wishes to teach.

The man's repetition of his demand therefore could be interpreted as a gratuitous and mean-spirited rejoinder to achieve a type of revenge. By refusing to accept the offender's humbling apology perhaps he wishes to rub the sinner's face in his sin.

Meanwhile, by narrating that in his quest for forgiveness Rabbi Shimon follows the man until he arrives at his village, the storyteller implies that the Rabbi continues to atone along the way with further entreaties and pleas. And, upon arriving at the man's home, the Rabbi does not desist or slip away, despite his awareness that a private offense will now become public, the embarrassment of apologizing before an individual soon turning into a community spectacle. Furthermore, even after publicly humiliating the Rabbi Shimon by making known the insult, the man does not forgive him. How much must any individual, and certainly a learned Rabbi, have to debase himself before he or she deserves forgiveness?

It takes the pleas of his friends to persuade the man to forgive, and when he finally does so his intention appears to be to gratify them and not to sincerely pardon the Sage. It is not even clear that he has recounted to his friends that the Rabbi apologized and followed him for miles seeking forgiveness; possibly he has shared only the insult, "he did such-and-such to me."

In his refusal to be pacified has the man become "hard as a cedar" just as quickly as the Rabbi? On the other hand sometimes an apology feels "cheap," as if by just saying "sorry" and expressing contrition one can make up for a heinous act that causes real damage. Is the man's repetition of the lesson and refusal to forgive the Rabbi's fitting and measured response intended not to punish the Rabbi excessively but to ensure that, given the severity of the sin, the lesson is fully internalized so that it never happens again?

In our own lives when do we accept apologies and graciously forgive the offender, and when do we refuse the gesture and bear a grudge?[3] What does it take for us to truly forgive? When respected public figures lapse, under what terms should they be forgiven?

Image of God

At the heart of the story lies one of the most profound theological beliefs of both biblical and Rabbinic Judaism: *imago dei*, all human beings are created in the image of God. The man's reference to the "Craftsman who made me" alludes to Genesis 1:26:

"And God said, 'Let us make humanity in our image, after our likeness.'" His retort therefore unmasks a double offense in the Rabbi's insult. To impugn a creation impugns the skill of its creator. To judge a human ugly essentially charges the divine Creator with poor skill and a flawed creation. More important, because God created humanity in God's own divine image, any ugliness found in a human necessarily reflects negatively on the essence of God. Rabbi Shimon has therefore not only disparaged God's skill in creating but God's very form and being (however we understand such concepts). In other words, through his utterance he has essentially committed blasphemy. This realization quickly moves Rabbi Shimon to contrition.

For the Rabbis, God's Creation of humans in the divine image was a central theological idea. They developed it in numerous ways. The Mishnah teaches: "Therefore humanity was created as one individual, to teach the greatness of the Holy Blessed One. For a man strikes many coins from the same die, and all the coins are alike. But the King of Kings, the Holy Blessed One, strikes every human being from the die of the first human being, and not one is identical to his fellow" (*Mishnah Sanhedrin* 4:5) The incredible diversity of human appearances, yet basic similarity of human form, testifies to God's grandeur and simultaneously affirms the fundamental holiness of each and every human being.

Based on this theology Rabbi Akiva even considers bathing to be a mitzvah. When his surprised disciples ask him why this is the case, he replies that just as those workers who clean the statues of the emperor are paid for their work and esteemed among their peers, "We, who are created in the image, in the likeness, as is written 'In His image did God make humanity' (Gen. 9:6), all the more so [should we clean ourselves]" (*Va-yiqra Rabbah* 34:3). Because the human body contains the divine image, caring for the body performs a service for God and therefore should be understood not merely as an act of hygiene but as an act of piety. John Wesley's axiom "Cleanliness is next to Godliness" is thereby apropos, even though the eighteenth-century theologian did not derive it from the Scripture of any tradition. For the Rabbis the body was godly and so cleanliness of the body was indeed part of godliness.

The Rabbinic understanding of the commandment to procreate also devolves from the theology of Creation in God's image: "Rabbi Elazar ben Azaryah says: [One who does not engage in procreation] diminishes the divine image" (*Yevamot* 63b; cf. Tosefta *Yevamot* 8:17). Procreation increases the presence of God in the world by creating additional likenesses of God, whereas failure to procreate ultimately causes a decrease in divine images when individuals die. For this reason, the Rabbis teach, immediately after creating human beings God instructed them: "Be fertile and increase, fill the earth and master it" (Gen. 1:28). In each generation human beings continue to complete the work of Creation by filling the cosmos with God's presence and holiness.

Yet even when these theological ideas appeal to our rational faculties—even if we understand that a physically unattractive human being is also created in the image of God, or that ugliness and beauty are not "objective" categories but subjective and culturally determined, or that true beauty and ugliness lie within—we sometimes react involuntarily when beholding what we perceive as ugliness. The Rabbis accordingly formulated a blessing for these circumstances:

One who sees an Ethiopian, a person with red spots, one with white spots, a hunchback, or a dwarf, or a person with dropsy should say, "Blessed is He who varies the forms of the creatures."

One who sees a person with missing limbs, or a blind person, or one with a flattened head, or a lame person, or one who suffers from boils, or pock-marked should say, "Blessed is the true Judge."

(*Berakhot* 58b)

The first category, according to the Talmud, includes what we could call "natural" characteristics, conditions a person bears from birth, while the second pertains to those whose deformed states derive from accidents or diseases or the like. The larger goal is to turn one's emotional reaction into a more sober and meaningful one. However strange or ugly or disgusting certain people may appear to us, the "varied forms" should move us to think of the great diversity of life that God has created, both animal and human, and how this variety enriches the world. By articulating a blessing we acknowledge the source of life and thus focus on God's role in Creation, much as the man in the story induces the Rabbi to do. The second blessing recognizes God as "the true Judge," thus acknowledging the divine role in the suffering and fates of humans while again directing us to think about our shared mortality and vulnerability.

These blessings, like many other rituals and commandments, function in part to move us away from our animal natures to a higher and holier plane of existence. The dietary (kosher) laws, for example, address the natural need for food, which people share with all animals, and the instinct to put any tasty food item in one's mouth when hungry and thirsty. Spontaneous aesthetic reactions to ugliness likewise are to be elevated to a high spiritual level that forms part of the Rabbinic vision of the life of piety.

The Divine Craftsman and the Human Vessels

The metaphor of God as a craftsman or artisan and the human being as a vessel features in many Rabbinic prayers, homilies, and ethical teachings. The imagery ultimately derives from the book of Jeremiah, in which God directs the prophet to visit a potter sitting at his wheel and then speaks to him: "O House of Israel, can I not deal with you like this potter? Just like clay in the hands of the potter, so are you in my hands" (Jer. 18:6). With this vision and the interpretive analogy God teaches the Israelites that God controls their destiny and can "shape" it for good or for evil. The Hebrew in fact contains a double entendre; the word for "potter," *yotzer*, also means "Creator." Also, the word for "clay," *ḥomer*, evokes the Creation of human beings: God forming Adam out of the dust of the earth (Gen. 2:7). Similarly, in one of his bitter complaints about his fate, Job cries out: "Your hand shaped and fashioned me, then you destroyed every part of me. Remember that you fashioned me like clay; will you turn me back into dust?" (Job 10:8–9). God is both the metaphoric *yotzer*-potter and the literal *yotzer*-Creator, who crafts people according to the divine will.

Whereas God employs the metaphor to instruct Jeremiah, the Prophet Isaiah adopts it to beg God for forgiveness: "But now, O Lord, You are our Father; We are the clay, and You are the Potter. We are all the work of Your hand. Be not implacably angry" (Isa. 64:7–8). Isaiah quotes God's words back to him as grounds for compassion. Just as artisans treasure their creations and do not destroy them, so God should show mercy to the Israelites by refraining from punishing them gravely.

One of the most beautiful liturgical prayers (*piyyutim*) recited on Yom Kippur develops the imagery in vivid fashion.

As the clay in the hand of the potter
He expands it and contracts it at will
So are we in Your hand, O Preserver of kindness,
Look to the covenant and ignore the Accuser.

As the stone in the hand of the cutter
He grasps it and smashes it at will
So are we in Your hand, O Source of life and death,
Look to the Covenant and ignore the Accuser.
As metal in the hand of the smith . . .

Four more verses continue with additional similes, comparing God to a sailor, a glassblower, an embroiderer, and a silversmith working with their materials, respectively an anchor, glass, cloth, and silver.

This prayer has been understood in two primary ways. According to the first interpretation God must forgive the people (by focusing on the covenant and ignoring the accusations of sin): having formed human beings God is therefore accountable for their natures. Just as artisans bear responsibility for any weaknesses or defects in their creations, just as a potter cannot blame the pot for its cracks and flaws, if God's human worshippers have moral and religious failings, God cannot cast the blame upon them.

Some interpreters, however, focus more on the materials, arguing that all substances place limitations on what craftsmen can create. The size, consistency, and quality of the clay restrict the types of pots and other products a potter can form. Similarly, the other materials mentioned in the prayer differ in their potential; a sculptor cannot do with stone what she can do with metal. The prayer accordingly asks God to do the best God can with the human materials, the souls and selves that each human offers the Divine, but it does not absolve us humans from responsibility for that which we present to God.

The following Rabbinic midrash employs the craftsman imagery for yet another didactic teaching:

"A broken and contrite heart, O God, You will not reject" [Ps. 51:19]. . . . Rabbi Alexandri said: if an ordinary person makes use of a broken vessel, it is a shameful thing. But the Blessed Holy One only makes use of broken vessels, as it is written, "God is close to the brokenhearted" [Ps. 34:19]. (*Va-yiqra Rabbah* 7:2)

Rabbi Alexandri combines the figure of the "broken heart" from the book of Psalms with the idea of human beings as "vessels" or creations of God to describe all people as "broken vessels." This is an apt characterization of the human condition, as what person is perfect and intact? Even those who have not suffered disabilities, handicaps, and/or illnesses bear the scars of life on their bodies and hearts. How then does God "make use" of broken people? They do God's work in the world: help others, perform deeds of loving-kindness and charity, fight for good and justice. Human beings discard dishes and tools and other vessels when they break but the divine craftsman continues to value God's flawed human creations.

These considerations led Rabbi Eliezer Judah Waldenberg (1915–2006), one of the leading modern authorities on Jewish law, and many other contemporary rabbis to rule that it is forbidden to undergo plastic surgery and for doctors to perform plastic surgery solely for the sake of beauty. Waldenberg emphasizes that one may not gratuitously endanger one's life, as surgery always entails some risk, and also condemns the notion of "chang[ing] oneself according to his own tastes and to outsmart the form with which his Creator engraved him." Disagreeing with Waldenberg, some rabbis sanction some cosmetic procedures that entail minimal risk and might improve the individual's mental health and self-image. Waldenberg, on the other hand, doubts whether one is even permitted to pray to God for beauty, let alone undergo surgery. He contends: "How much more should one not be overly wise with himself to change nature with these [surgical] interventions. And this is tantamount to saying to the craftsman who made him, 'How ugly is this vessel that you made.'"[4] To Waldenberg, people who consider themselves insufficiently attractive, or believe that a certain body part warrants cosmetic surgery, are guilty of directly insulting God. Like Rabbi Shimon in the story they are saying of themselves, "How ugly is this vessel that You made."

In other words, not only are we to appreciate the diversity of human shapes, forms, and appearances as manifestations of the divine presence in all its complexity, we must also accept ourselves—bodily flaws and all. For many of us, this can be the greatest challenge.

The Cedar and the Reed

The story of Rabbi Shimon ben Elazar opens with a hortatory saying, "A person should always be soft like a reed and not hard like a cedar," and closes with Rabbi Shimon repeating the same lesson in the Rabbinic house of study. The conclusion thus cycles back to the beginning, both in the repetition of this teaching and in the reversal of the Rabbi's "coming from" the house of study at the outset to his returning there with newfound wisdom at the end. The contrast between the inside and outside of the study house complements the contrast between the external appearance and the inner qualities of the man. Here the storyteller intimates that the Rabbis must not distinguish the inside from the outside of the study house: the teachings and practice of Torah should not be limited to the private domain of the Sages but applied outside too. Musicians sometimes say, "What happens on tour, stays on tour," and others say, "What happens in Vegas, stays in Vegas"— but what happens in the Rabbinic house of study should be modeled outside as an example to all. Likewise, lessons learned outside, including from the laity, should be shared inside the house with an audience of Rabbis and disciples.

In the context of the story the hard or harsh cedar represents an inflexible and arrogant person who disparages those who are different and cannot abide alternative perspectives. When such individuals rigidly judge other people according to stereotypes and fixed notions, they become incapable of learning from others. The soft reed that bends pliantly when powerful winds blow signifies an individual open to other people and their different ideas. Rabbi Shimon realizes he has judged the man harshly, reacted with excessive pride at his own accomplishments, and, like the tall and magnificent cedar, taken a high and mighty attitude toward the stranger. It is far better to act humbly and unassumingly—to be like the smaller, thinner, and suppler reed in being ready to change and "bend" one's beliefs. The Rabbi acknowledges that he has learned a valuable principle from the very man he once stereotyped harshly.

The Talmud follows Rabbi Shimon's praise of the reed as the model for pious behavior with a brief coda: "Therefore the reed merited that quills be fashioned from it to write Torah scrolls, tefillin, and *mezuzot*." Scribes who write out scrolls of Torah and the small parchments with biblical verses for tefillin (phylacteries) and *mezuzot* use finely cut slivers of reed as quills. The personification of the reed receiving this reward for its "softness" aptly matches the story's lesson about the importance of being open to learning. Just as the individual who emulates the yielding nature of the reed will be able to learn from others, so the reed itself serves as the instrument for writing out the Torah scrolls learned by the pious.

Contrasts of reeds or soft, pliant foliage with strong and firm trees appear throughout world literature and especially in classical fables and moralizing tales. In fact the Hebrew word for "quill," *qolmos*, derives from the Greek word for "reed," *kalamos*. In Sophocles's tragedy *Antigone,* the heroine Antigone buries the body of her brother Polyneices, in violation of King Creon's prohibition against burial as punishment for his traitorous act of attacking their city of Thebes in a civil war. Creon sentences Antigone to death, prompting his son Haemon, who is betrothed to Antigone, to try to persuade Creon to relent. Haemon argues that he, together with many Theban citizens, believes that Antigone carried out a noble deed. She had an ethical obligation to her brother and therefore should not undeservedly die:

> Do not bear this single habit of mind, to think
> that what you say and nothing else is true. . . .
> For a man, though he be wise,
> it is no shame to learn—learn many things,
> and not maintain his views too rigidly.
> You notice how by streams in wintertime
> the trees that yield preserve their branches safely,
> but those that fight the tempest perish utterly. . . .
> Yield something of your anger, give way a little. . . .
> It is good also to learn from those who advise well.[5]

The soft foliage on the banks of a river that bends when strong currents or stormy waters flow through it does not break despite the powerful forces. Harder, more rigid trees, on the other hand, those that do not yield to the rushing waters, are quickly destroyed. And so, Haemon counsels, Creon too should learn from and yield to this different advice, although he is father and king and his son and other Thebans are his inferiors. There is danger in sticking to one's views "too rigidly," thinking that "nothing else is true," and refusing to entertain alternative perspectives. The willingness to rethink matters, to be open to others' views, and to change one's policies accordingly is not a weakness, Haemon insists, but a strength. Sophocles would have us understand that yielding is learning—admitting that one has made a mistake or an error in judgment and will now adopt a different path.[6]

Creon rejects this sound advice and remains as hard as the unbending trees. Later the blind prophet Tiresias cautions him: "All men can make mistakes; but, once mistaken, a man is no longer stupid nor accursed who, having fallen on ill, tries to cure that ill, not taking a fine undeviating stand. It is obstinacy that convicts of folly. Yield to the dead man."[7] Yet Creon is unmoved until Tiresias unleashes a terrifying prophecy of doom as punishment for Creon's stubbornness. At this point Creon has a crisis of confidence: "My mind is all bewildered. To yield is terrible. But by opposition to destroy my very being with a self-destructive curse must also be reckoned in what is terrible."[8] Finally he agrees to forgive Antigone and rushes to save her—but it is too late. His son Haemon has also killed himself upon finding Antigone's lifeless body, and Creon's wife, too, commits suicide out of grief.

Antigone, a tragedy, ends with heartrending misery. We, the audience, appreciate the lesson even if Creon takes too long to learn it. The talmudic story, on the other hand, is not a tragedy but a didactic tale. Rabbi Shimon quickly appreciates the importance of yielding to other perspectives. He endures some humiliation along the way but otherwise emerges a wiser and better person: a role model for the talmudic audience and for us.

Beauty and Brains

A different approach to beauty and ugliness appears in a talmudic story about Rabbi Yehoshu'a ben Ḥananya:

The daughter of the Roman emperor said to Rabbi Yehoshu'a ben Ḥananya: "Woe to glorious wisdom [such as yours, which is contained] in an ugly vessel."

Rabbi Yehoshu'a ben Ḥananya said to her: "Does your father put his wine in clay vessels?"

The Emperor's daughter said to him: "Rather, in what should he put it?"

He said: "You, who are so important, should put it in vessels of gold and silver."

She went and told her Father, "Put the wine in vessels of gold and silver."

[He did so and] it turned sour.

They told the Emperor. He said to his daughter: "Who told you to do this?"

She said, "Rabbi Yehoshu'a ben Ḥananya."

The Emperor summoned him and said to him: "Why did you tell her this?"

He said: "Just as she said to me, so I said to her."

The Emperor said to him: "But there are beautiful people who are learned."

Rabbi Yehoshu'a ben Ḥananya replied: "Had they been ugly, they would have been even more learned."

(*Ta'anit* 7a)

This story is almost a mirror image of the story of Rabbi Shimon ben Elazar. Instead of a Rabbi disparaging a Jewish man as ugly, a gentile woman slights a Rabbi as unattractive. In place of the victim undermining the insult with the notion of humans as vessels, the offender bases the insult on this very premise: how unfortunate and inappropriate, the emperor's daughter thinks, that the beautiful wisdom of the Rabbi resides in his ugly physical body. Intellectual beauty should go hand in hand with physical beauty; you cannot have one without the other.

To expose the fallacy of this line of thought, Rabbi Yehoshu'a ben Ḥananya appeals not to metaphoric vessels and their theological implications, as in the man's response to Rabbi Shimon, but to real, tangible containers. The daughter's superficial ideas must be countered by concrete experience: "Just as she said to me, so I said to her." Beautiful objects (the wine), she learns, are ruined by beautiful containers but preserved in ordinary, ugly clay jars. Were it not for his ugly appearance, Rabbi Yehoshu'a would not have become such a brilliant Sage. Indeed, we witness Rabbi Yehoshu'a's brilliance immediately in his quick retort to the emperor's empirical counterexample to his claim. That some Sages are handsome proves—however we make sense of the sour wine—that human wisdom is compatible with beauty. Yet Rabbi Yehoshu'a offers the last word in the cross-cultural discussion: had those same Sages been ugly, they would have been even more knowledgeable!

Why is that the case? The great talmudic commentator Rashi explains that beautiful people cannot be humble and are more likely to forget what they have learned, apparently due to divine punishment for their arrogance. The talmudic commentators known as the Tosafists suggest that those who "despise beauty become superior scholars." Because they devote no time and effort to their appearance they make more progress in their studies. The Tosafists understand the beauty at issue in the story not as natural good looks but rather attractiveness achieved through primping and preening oneself. Their view is eminently plausible today given the monetary and personal resources that are expended on the cult of beauty—including the cosmetics industry, cosmetic surgery, fashionable clothing, hairstyling, personal makeovers, and so forth. Alternatively, perhaps Rabbi Yehoshu'a means that God in God's infinite wisdom compensates people for deficiencies by blessing them with other gifts and talents. If God chooses not to favor certain individuals with beauty presumably God balances this lack by adding to their intelligence. Or maybe those disadvantaged in some respects are naturally motivated to work harder, persevere, redouble their efforts, and thereby end up accomplishing more than they otherwise would have achieved.[9]

Perhaps the larger lesson here is to accept the fact that we humans are all "broken vessels," uniquely imperfect in one respect or another. Rather than lamenting our fate with resignation we might best employ our unique qualities and talents to maximize our potential as partners with God in Creation. Our actions may then fill the cosmos with God's presence and holiness.

7 An Arrow in Satan's Eye

Yom Kippur, the Day of Atonement, is well known as the most solemn and holy day on the Jewish calendar. Another of its titles, the Day of Judgment, nicely sums up the theology of the day. All humans stand in judgment as God—the divine judge, jury, and witness all in one—decides who will live and who will die, who will flourish and who will suffer, who will be at rest and who will wander. God's judgment is based on one's deeds of the previous year, a calculus of sins against righteous actions. Yet no matter how evil or sinful the individual's acts, the Rabbis believed that sincere repentance, *teshuvah*, could atone for sin, cleanse the slate, and ensure a favorable verdict.

The lengthy prayers that developed for the day, along with the biblical commandment to "practice self-denial" (Lev. 16:29), which the Rabbis understood to prohibit eating, drinking, and other material comforts, encouraged repentance. Yet in and of themselves, without sincere remorse and a commitment to change one's ways, these rituals were deemed to be empty gestures that would not change one's fate. When the Prophet Isaiah's contemporaries complained to God, "Why, when we fasted, did you not see? When we starved our bodies, did you pay no attention?," Isaiah explained: "Because you fast in strife and contention, and you strike with a wicked fist! Your fasting today is not such as to make your voice heard on high" (Isa. 58:3–4).

Jewish tradition recognized the challenges inherent in transitioning from mundane life to experiencing the solemnity of Yom

Kippur in a frame of mind conducive to repentance. Additions to the daily prayers for the preceding weeks and other rituals are designed to help facilitate this process. For example, prayers during the period between the celebration of Rosh Hashanah (the New Year) and Yom Kippur, known as the "ten days of repentance," include supplications and liturgical formulae that remind the worshipper of the urgency to act. Rabbis exhort their congregants to give charity and to perform good deeds during this time as signs of their commitment to a righteous way of life.

But of course an absolute prerequisite to repentance is the awareness of one's faults and shortcomings. One who denies having sinned cannot engage in true introspection or change for the better. In the following story a Rabbi with an overconfident sense of his own piety learns a harsh lesson about his own moral failings.

Pelimo was in the habit of saying each day, "An arrow in Satan's eye!"

One day, on the eve of the Day of Atonement, Satan appeared to him [disguised] as a poor person.

He came and knocked on the door.

They brought him a loaf of bread.

He said to them, "On such a day as this—everyone should be inside and I remain outside?!"

They brought him inside, and they brought him a loaf of bread.

He said to them, "On such a day as this—everyone [has a seat] at the table and I remain alone?!"

They brought him [in] and sat him at the table.

Satan was sitting, and his body became filled with boils and sores, and they were discharging pus upon him, and he was doing disgusting things with them [e.g., picking at the sores].

Pelimo said to him, "Sit nicely!"

Satan said to him, "Give me a drink."

They gave him a drink.

He coughed and threw up phlegm into the cup.

They rebuked him.

Satan fell down dead.

They heard it being said, "Pelimo killed a man! Pelimo killed a man!"

Pelimo ran away and hid himself in a latrine.

Satan went after him.

[Pelimo] fell down before him.

When Satan saw how much Pelimo was suffering, he revealed himself to him.

Satan said to him, "Why do you speak thus?"

Pelimo said to him, "How then should I speak?"

Satan said to him, "My master should say, 'May the Merciful One rebuke Satan'" [cf. Zech. 3:2].

(*Qiddushin* 81a–b).

Pelimo, a learned Sage (though not designated by the honorific "Rabbi"), regularly boasted of his immunity to sin by exclaiming, "An arrow in Satan's eye". This phrase exudes the self-confidence that he has triumphed over his "evil inclination," personified here as Satan, the demonic power associated with sin and wickedness. Pelimo thereby taunts "the evil tempter," as Satan is sometimes called: because Pelimo is completely pious (or so he believes), were he and Satan to battle, his (metaphoric) weapons would wound Satan and he would prevail.

Insulted by these provocative barbs, Satan resolves to test Pelimo. Satan comes to his house in the guise of a beggar on the eve of the Day of Atonement while Pelimo and his family enjoy the meal before the fast. Members of Pelimo's family first bring the beggar some bread outside, as perhaps is their routine when vagrants come to the door. When Satan persists and asks to enter the warmth of the house, Pelimo and his family acquiesce but seat him alone in a separate room, not at the family table. Only when he remonstrates again do they admit him to full fellowship with them, offering him a seat at the table. We understand that Pelimo reluctantly and begrudgingly extends hospitality to the needy; he is hardly the paragon of piety he believes himself to be.

Endowed with a deep bag of tricks, Satan has not finished bringing Pelimo's failings to light. Not only does he afflict himself with suppurating sores all over his body, he acts in a disgusting manner. Unable to stomach such behavior, Pelimo and his family instruct the visitor to knock it off and sit appropriately for the important meal. Satan then ratchets up his antics, requesting a cup to drink—having only been given bread to this point—and coughing up mucus, phlegm, and spittle into the cup. This proves too much for Pelimo's respectable family, who rebuke Satan for such revolting conduct.

Satan now pretends to die. The news spreads quickly throughout the neighborhood, as bad news tends to do and not always accurately. The neighbors need not mean that Pelimo committed murder but that he was somehow responsible for a man's death. How many righteous people have men drop dead at their dining room tables? It is also possible, as the commentator Rashi explains, that Pelimo imagined that he heard such words, conflating his anxieties as reality. Or perhaps Satan was speaking, projecting his voice like a ventriloquist. Whether the words are real or imagined Pelimo becomes distraught and flees to an outhouse, a public latrine. In antiquity, aristocrats may have had a private outhouse or even a lavatory of sorts, but most people had to use public latrines, generally located on the fringes of the village.

Not yet through with Pelimo, Satan pursues him to the filthy latrine. We do not know what goes through Pelimo's mind when he beholds the beggar now looking very much alive. He may think this is the beggar's spirit or ghost harassing him for causing the death. Or he may believe a demonic vision has been inflicted upon him as punishment. At last Pelimo falls down before the poor man, a sign of contrition and atonement.

At this point Satan takes mercy on Pelimo, reveals himself to the Sage, and brings home the lesson: Pelimo should not have "spoken thus," should not have boasted "An arrow in the eye of Satan." Pelimo is hardly a consummately righteous figure as Satan easily defeated the Sage by inducing him to sin. Now Pelimo takes his lumps and accepts Satan's admonition, humbly asking about the appropriate language. Satan (and Satan should know!) teaches the Sage to ask God for help in resisting temptation: "Let the Merciful One rebuke Satan." Even holy Sages are susceptible to moral failings and in need of divine assistance to maintain their piety. If they do in fact prevail against sin they should not take too much pride in their accomplishment, for failure is as close as a poor person at the door.[1]

The Beggar at the Door, or How Not to Give Charity

"Pelimo" was probably chosen as protagonist for this tale because this uncommon name may be related to the Greek word *polemos*, meaning "war" or "strife" (as in "polemical"). His daily affirmation, "An arrow in Satan's eye," points to the nature of the battle he has waged for many years. This is not a military campaign on the battleground, but Rabbinic combat: a struggle against sin, temptation, and the forces of evil. Having resisted sin for as long as he can remember, Pelimo not only brags of his conquest but asserts his prowess by assault laden with belligerent imagery. The precise meaning of his expression emerges clearly in a talmudic saying attributed in another passage to Rav Ḥisda: "The fact that I am superior to my colleagues is because I married at the age of sixteen, and had I married at fourteen I would have said to Satan, 'An arrow in your eye'" (*Qiddushin* 29b–30a). Rav Ḥisda's comparatively early marriage spared him from sexual temptation and sin, and had he wedded at an even younger age, he would have been so impervious to depravity that he could have provoked Satan to battle, secure that his "arrows" and (figurative) armaments would defeat the weapons of his adversary. The phallic imagery of the arrow and the penetration of an orifice here fit the context of sexual temptation, but in Pelimo's case the sense is broader: he considers himself completely righteous and therefore not susceptible to any type of transgression.

In the Bible and Talmud, Satan is a shadowy figure. The Hebrew verb *satan* means "to lie in wait," "to oppose," "to be an adversary." Certain human enemies and opponents are described as *satan* in various biblical passages; for example, "the Lord raised up an adversary [*satan*] against Solomon, the Edomite Hadad" (1 Kings 11:14). A celestial figure called "the Satan," usually translated as the "Adversary" or the "Accuser," appears among God's angelic retinue in several late biblical books. Almost devoid of personality this "Adversary" functions mostly as a prosecutor of sorts, bringing accusations before God against human beings. Best known from the prologue to the book of Job (see chapter 5), "the Satan" disputes God's claim of Job's righteousness, asserting that Job's piety results exclusively from his good fortune; God then grants "the Satan" license to test Job in the cruelest ways. Even here, however, "the Satan" does not have independent power but can act only when God gives him dispensation. Some writings from the Second Temple period, including Christian Scripture, portray Satan (now a proper name) as a malevolent, demonic figure, an autonomous and evil being who tempts, corrupts, and punishes humans. In these texts Satan has almost grown into his medieval character—"the Devil," ruler of hell and nefarious power, only slightly inferior to God.

Classical Rabbinic literature, however, depicts Satan in a much weaker manner, typically as a minor demon and troublemaker. In many sources Satan seems to be an embodiment of sin or of the "evil inclination" that the Rabbis believed to be an inherent part of the human psyche: free will entails that we choose to follow our good inclination (*yetzer ha-tov*) and suppress our evil inclination (*yetzer ha-ra*). Thus Rabbinic texts may speak interchangeably of individuals struggling against (or succumbing to) the evil inclination, sin, or Satan. Where Satan appears as a character, especially in a few colorful talmudic stories, he has a complex and multifaceted personality, sometimes serving to admonish rather than to punish and experiencing a range of emotions including sorrow—hardly the consummately evil being of later ages.

Still, for humans to challenge Satan is not the wisest of moves. A common folk proverb quoted in the Talmud states, "Do not open your mouth to the Satan" (*Berakhot* 19a)—that is, do not provoke Satan with overconfident or hubristic utterances. Bragging about piety invites Satan to investigate, test, and expose false assertions, sometimes at a very high cost. Much better to "lie low" religiously and not call attention to oneself.

Pelimo, however, made it a *habit*, a ritual in and of itself to recount his outstanding track record. Even if he muttered the saying under his breath as a type of personal encouragement rather than in public as a proclamation of his greatness, he must have intended his adversary—*the* adversary—to hear. And Satan cannot resist the challenge.

The temporal setting, the eve of the Day of Atonement, is what anthropologists call a "liminal" time, from the Latin *limen*, meaning "threshold". Similarly, the doorway where Satan stands, the threshold between the world outside and Pelimo's private house, is liminal space. Liminal times and places lie on the border, the unclear and indistinct boundary between and betwixt two well-defined areas or periods. Often they play a role in transitions from one state or status to another and typically have an uncertain, ambiguous, or even dangerous quality. The *mezuzah* placed on the doorpost at the liminal area marking the entrance to a house, in many anthropologists' view, originated as a device to protect against the dangers of this threshold space.

Thus our story takes place at the threshold of the Day of Atonement, the boundary between mundane and holy time, between feasting and fasting, between everyday activities and spiritual devotion. Inside the house Pelimo and his family prepare for the holy day by joining together in a communal meal, separated from external society. Satan's approach at the door threatens that separation, and soon Pelimo will experience a transition fraught with unexpected danger.

Probably Pelimo believes he will have a short list of sins designated for confession on the Day of Atonement. Presumably he takes equal pride every year as he looks back upon twelve months of seemingly exemplary conduct as he does daily with his ritual recitation declaring the triumph over his evil inclination. Perhaps he has even invited some honored guests, Rabbis and scholars whom he considers worthy to share his table fellowship. Known as the "final" or "separation feast" (*se'udah mafseqet*), this meal immediately prior to the fast was considered a commandment in and of itself. Part of the preparation for a smooth fast involved consuming a festival meal with plenty of food the previous night.

No doubt Pelimo took this precept very seriously as he surveyed the sumptuous banquet laid out before him. We can picture the scene as he instructs his family at the dinner table of the importance and solemnity of the approaching holy day, speaking of how he has dedicated himself to the pious life and expects no less from his flesh and blood. He may have placed his hands lovingly on the heads of his sons and daughters and declaimed the special "Children's Blessing"; this prayer, recited specifically on the eve of the Day of Atonement, petitions God to help children become pious and studious and to grant them health, life, and sustenance in the coming year. Pelimo may have donned a *kitel*, a white garment, as was the custom in later centuries, to symbolize innocence and purity.

This banquet scene exuding warmth, family, connection, harmony, plenty, and piety contrasts with the situation outside the happy home: a beggar, hungry, lonely, empty, perhaps feeling a cold autumn chill. The storyteller is directing us to broaden our vision and evaluate Pelimo's treatment of those beyond his circle of intimates. Is this "separation feast" also indicative of his separation from the needy? The family's initial response to the beggar-Satan, bringing him some bread but dismissing him to the emptiness beyond while they return to their warm table, seems particularly coldhearted. The poor man seeks human fellowship, companionship, inclusion. Pelimo's type of charity serves to emphasize, rather than erase, the distance between the haves and the have-nots. So, too, the family highlights that distance by initially seating the beggar apart from the table. Only until he repeats his woeful cry, "On such a day as *this* . . ," do they seat him with the guests. The thrice-repeated narration, "They brought him . . . They brought him . . . They brought him . . ." indicates both their obliviousness to the beggar's plight and hesitancy to treat him appropriately.

Even after having seated the beggar at the table the family seems not to have provided the beggar with wine or drink, as he must subsequently request a cup. When prodded they will do the minimum, not very pleased about being imposed upon in this way. On the eve of Yom Kippur, when thoughts of religious conduct should be foremost in one's consciousness—when Pelimo supposedly prepares for the holiest day of the year in the most sober of ways—his attitude to the poor reveals the superficiality of his piety and the falseness of his religious pretentions. He fails to uphold even the elementary precepts of hospitality and charity. Such a man has no business challenging Satan to combat.

From the Festival Table to the Latrine

If Pelimo fails the first test, he fares no better at the second, which, as is often the case in such didactic dramas, becomes much more difficult. The storyteller leaves to our imagination Satan's nauseating behavior—perhaps he picks at the boils, or wipes the pus on his clothes, or flicks away the scabs from his skin. This affliction, astute readers will recognize, offers an ironic reversal of Satan's torments of Job: Satan "smote Job with sore boils from the sole of his foot even unto his crown" (Job 2:7). Lamenting "My flesh is covered with maggots and clods of earth. My skin is broken and festering," Job observes that people now "abhor me and keep their distance from me" (Job 7:5, 30:10). Of course in this case Satan's self-affliction is an artifice designed to test and ultimately afflict Pelimo. Will he keep his distance from the pitiful beggar the way Job's "comforters" kept their distance, or will he extend a sympathetic response to another human being suffering from a terrible dermatological condition?

Pelimo fails miserably. He cannot overcome his sense of disgust and cannot appreciate the suffering of his fellow human being. He offers neither medicine nor kindness, making no effort either to ameliorate the illness or to express compassion at the discomfort. Presumably he has the resources to summon a physician to attend to the suffering soul in front of him. Or has he no salve or ointment in his home? Focused instead upon the ugliness of the world outside invading his private domain, upon the disturbance to his comforting meal and personal serenity, Pelimo attempts to suppress—not mitigate—the wretchedness. And, in fact, his response exacerbates the poor man's plight by humiliating the poor man in the family's presence. "Sit nicely," Pelimo reprimands him. Pelimo's subsequent rebuke, noted but not detailed by the story-teller, calls further attention to his guest's embarrassing condition.

Sores suppurating pus and expectorations of phlegm and mucus place this tale in the category of the "grotesque." As a literary genre, the grotesque involves body parts, often depicted in distorted or exaggerated form, bodily orifices, and substances exuding from and entering the human body, sometimes "transgressing" their appropriate boundaries—creating either a humorous or disgusting effect, or both. In our story we have to laugh as Satan, step by little step, disrupts the solemn and holy meal, advancing ever closer to Pelimo's table and then "grossing out" his host in the most offensive ways. Picture the look on the Sage's face as his unwanted visitor methodically peels off the scabs from his boils and then coughs up his phlegm for all to view.

The grotesque, often associated with "the common folk" and with "low" culture, may function to erase or reverse accepted social hierarchies, bringing down the high and mighty to the level of their shared humanity. Here indeed the educated and affluent Pelimo, who considers himself among those elite and holy figures immune to sin, is brought ignominiously low. First, Satan's revolting antics swiftly remove the veneer of his piety to expose a rather average individual, mighty far from a "holier-than-thou" Sage. Second, his flight to the latrine, a place of filth, reduces him to the most debased of states. The storyteller achieves a stunning reversal by shifting from a holy meal abundant in fine food, in preparation for the holiest time of abstention from eating, to a foul place of dirt and excrement where that food is eliminated from the body.

No matter how elite and pure and holy we consider ourselves to be, our core humanity and equality with all others is marked by inescapable excretory functions.

On Yom Kippur our fasting and the white garments we may don symbolize angelic aspirations: our attempts to distance ourselves from bodily needs and even our human status, as angels have no need for sustenance. But only for a day. The latrine gives Pelimo a painful reminder of his very human nature, including the propensity to sin. At the same time the latrine concludes a reversal of the vivid imagery of Pelimo's boast: the "arrow in the eye." In contrast to Pelimo's penetrating Satan's bodily orifice with his weapon, Satan first brings forth phlegm from his orifice at Pelimo's table, almost rubbing it in Pelimo's face. Then he causes Pelimo to end up in the latrine, the place where filth comes forth from the orifices of the body. No doubt Pelimo realizes that human orifices are far more vulnerable than Satan's eye, which he boasted of penetrating.

Pelimo's flight to the latrine results from the beggar's apparent death. Whether Pelimo really judges himself responsible, or whether he panics and bolts, is not completely clear. He may think his lack of immediate attention to the beggar's need for food and healing resulted in the death, hence that he caused it if only through inaction. Pelimo may even imagine that the beggar's feelings of humiliation at being rebuked caused him to die: the nexus between death and embarrassment, "whitening the face in public," as the talmudic expression translates, is a trope in other talmudic stories. Or Pelimo may simply feel shocked at the presence of death in his own home and horror at the (inaccurate) charges of his complicity.

In any case this death in the context of the eve of Yom Kippur creates a powerful effect. Within an hour or two, on the Day of Judgment, Pelimo and his colleagues are to begin their prayers for life in the year to come. Ironically Pelimo cannot even make it into the synagogue to offer those prayers as the beggar's death confines him to the latrine at this crucial time. And what would people think were he to recite the confessional of sins now that word has circulated that he has killed, among the worst sins imaginable?

While we can understand why Pelimo absconds to the latrine, his flight results in the transgression of one of the most important precepts in Jewish tradition: care of a *meit mitzvah*, literally "a dead [person whose care is] commanded," namely a corpse with no family or other responsible party to attend to the purification and burial. So important is this duty that the Rabbis ruled it takes precedence over Torah study, circumcision, and various other commandments. Even the High Priest is to render himself impure so as to participate in the burial—an act ranking among the purest mitzvot and considered an example of "true righteousness" because it can never be paid back. Burial devolves from our obligation to all human beings, not because they are our kin, not because of their wealth, but simply because they, too, are created in the image of God. To recognize this is to understand our responsibilities to all others regardless of status.

Yet Pelimo flees from this obligation too. Having failed the beggar during his life, Pelimo now fails him in death as well.

The latrine, partially as a result of its grotesque associations, is a place of danger. A talmudic passage mentions a "demon of the toilet" who resides in the latrine, intent on causing harm, and who may even follow a person for a distance of half a mile after he uses the facilities (*Gittin* 70a). Elsewhere the Talmud instructs that before entering a latrine a liturgy is to be recited addressed to the angels that constantly escort each individual but will not enter into that unholy domain: "Be honored you honored and holy ones that minister to the Most High. Give honor to the God of Israel. Wait for me until I enter and do my needs and return to you" (*Berakhot* 60b). Pelimo, then having fled into the latrine, has perforce lost his angelic retinue and entered the realm of the demonic, leaving him particularly vulnerable. Fittingly he encounters Satan, the demon chief, the otherworldly opponent of the good angels whose protective presence Pelimo has forfeited. This second encounter with Satan has shifted from Pelimo's home turf to that of his adversary, and with it comes the loss of any security Pelimo might have possessed.

Satan pursues the panicking Sage in order to be certain of Pelimo's remorse. Again we can only imagine Pelimo's reaction at seeing the dead beggar show up so quickly in his hideaway: a mixture of astonishment, dismay, confusion, bewilderment, distress, and misery. "What foul demon of the night hounds me relentlessly?" he may be thinking. What irony: his colleagues and fellow worshippers will soon bow low before God in emulation of the ritual of Temple times; Pelimo himself is bowing low, imbibing the filth of the latrine in abject surrender before an unidentified man with a nefarious power.

Enhancing this irony is the awareness that, according to the Talmud, Yom Kippur stands out as the one day of the year when Satan has no power over human beings: "Rami bar Ḥama said, The Satan . . . on 364 days he has permission to act as accuser, but on the Day of Atonement he has no permission to act as accuser" (*Yoma* 20a). Another talmudic tradition explains that the shofar is sounded on Rosh Hashanah "so as to confound the Satan" and prevent him from bringing accusations before God. For Pelimo, unfortunately, Satan has seized the window of opportunity just before his one-day suspension of activity. The confounded has become the confounder, turning the tables on his prey with machinations of his own.

When his opponent's boasts become bows, demonstrating that Satan has triumphed completely, Satan quite unexpectedly takes pity on poor Pelimo. This reversal offers the deepest irony of our text as Satan notices the suffering of the Other and acts with the compassion that Pelimo failed to exhibit. Indeed Satan is the true hero of our story as he succeeds in bringing Pelimo to sincere repentance—and then immediately ceases the charade. Pelimo now understands the didactic point. Humbly he asks his tormentor-turned-mentor what he should say to remind himself of the constant battle again sin. With remarkable self-understanding of his own modest stature (the precise character trait Pelimo lacked) Satan offers not a grandiose taunt of triumph ("There is nothing you can say to combat my incredible powers, you inveterate sinner. . . .") but rather judicious advice politely proffered with a courteous salutation, "My master should say. . . ." This respectful mode of third-person speech, which can be paraphrased as "You, my good sir, should say . . ," puts Pelimo back on something of an equal footing with Satan and restores a measure of his dignity.

The locution "May the Merciful One rebuke Satan" rephrases an enigmatic biblical passage from Zechariah 3, in which the prophet receives a vision of Joshua the High Priest standing "in filthy garments" before an angel with "the Satan/Accuser" nearby "to accuse him." At this point either God or the angel states, "The Lord rebuke you, Satan!"[2] The biblical precedent provides the crucial lesson that humans cannot defeat "Satan"; for example, they cannot resist, without divine help, their evil inclinations and propensity to sin. Not grandiose braggadocio but humble appeals to God constitute our best strategy against Satan's wiles. Even the High Priest Joshua of halcyon biblical age wears "filthy garments," like Pelimo's latrine-stained clothes, which can only be replaced with pure robes by intercession from above.

Earlier the overconfident Pelimo had rebuked the beggar-Satan, and here Satan essentially—yet much more kindly—rebukes him with instruction as to whose place it is to offer Satan rebuke: God's. Fortunately for Pelimo (and for the rest of us too) it is not incumbent upon each human being to achieve the degree of perfection at which Pelimo initially imagined himself. As Rabbi Akiva expounds in a teaching about Yom Kippur: "Happy are you, Israel! Before whom are you purified, and who purifies you [of sin]? Your Father in heaven." Before and with the assistance of the "Merciful One," Pelimo—and all other human beings—can hope to prevail over Satan and the evil inclination he represents (*Mishnah Yoma* 8:9).

Disgust and Its Discontents

Recent ethical, political, and psychological works have explored the role of disgust in human culture. We tend to feel disgust at both physical and social phenomena, such as human waste, rotting corpses, vomit, and crawling masses of insects on the one hand, and cannibalism and bestiality on the other. Some of us may also be disgusted by racist speech or the divisive nature of contemporary politics. How do we account for the diverse phenomena that elicit this response? What function does disgust serve from an evolutionary and sociobiological perspective? Is it natural or learned? Is it common to all societies or culturally specific? Should feelings of revulsion play a role in our personal morality or public policy? Because a central axis of our story turns on Pelimo's disgust at Satan's boils and sores, and then locates the climactic conclusion in a disgusting place, we may gain some insights regarding the motif from this body of theoretical literature.

Some philosophers argue that the emotion of disgust can be a moral compass of sorts, a natural intuition that certain acts are unethical. They claim, for example, that our natural feelings of repugnance at necrophilia or obscenity or even human cloning indicate that these acts are inherently depraved.[3] Other thinkers point out that some practices considered disgusting in one society are accepted by another, or even by different groups and members within a given society.[4] Moreover, some practices others consider disgusting have been held up as grounds for discrimination and persecution against those who partake in them.

In many societies disgust serves a social function: to reinforce the social hierarchy. Those higher on the hierarchy can keep the "low" in their proper place by assessing them as contemptible and repugnant and therefore as deserving of their inferior status. Throughout history the noble and upper classes considered the poorer classes to be dirty, loathsome, barbaric, and repulsive, and portrayed them accordingly in art and literature. In "caste" systems like that of India, this is taken to an extreme with a prohibition against any touching or contact between the higher castes and "untouchables." Some scholars also believe that rituals and laws surrounding menstruation in both Jewish and non-Jewish societies, such as those that call for the separation of women, are motivated by men's feelings of disgust and therefore ultimately by misogynistic tendencies.

Because certain responses of disgust are automatic and involuntary, and some physical substances—such as human feces, rotting corpses, and diseased flesh—are considered disgusting across most cultures, many theorists believe that at least a part of our disgust "system" evolved to provide humans with an evolutionary advantage for survival. A leading theory, though by no means the only one, points to "poisons and parasites" as the original force behind the disgust response: we first evolved the system of disgust to protect ourselves from poisons and parasites as the involuntary reaction makes us shrink back from and avoid these threats.[5] However, because identifying contaminants and dangers is difficult and imprecise, we involuntarily react to many substances that are not themselves dangerous but that resemble noxious poisons and parasites, such as a large pile of worms or a creeping mass of flies. Human excretions and other bodily emissions, including festering wounds, suppurating sores, and similar indications of disease, likewise elicit disgust because they can be harmful if ingested or even touched. Over the course of time we "adapted" or "co-opted" our own disgust system for other purposes by consciously or unconsciously directing feelings of disgust against various natural and social phenomena. For this reason many of us might feel disgust from time to time: vegetarians when presented with a juicy steak, those who keep kosher when seeing a big ham, pacifists when exposed to explicit images of violence.

Pelimo's involuntary feelings of disgust at Satan's boils, sores, phlegm, and other expectorations are therefore natural and instinctual. As a self-professed paragon of piety, however, he must subdue this understandable response just as he subdues his evil inclination every day. Indeed, throughout history those pious caregivers who ministered to lepers, cared for social outcastes such as those who were deformed, and prepared dead bodies for burial have had to transcend feelings of revulsion. In the Middle Ages, for example, Catherine of Siena (1347–1380), a famous Christian mystic, drank the pus exuding from the sores of those she attended, rubbed her nose in it, and ate scabs and lice in order to overcome her nausea at such ailments. In fact, there is a startling parallel between an account of Catherine's response to her feelings of disgust and our story. Once, when she was dressing the cancerous sore on the breast of an old woman that exuded a foul stench, Catherine vomited. She judged this to be the work of the devil, causing her own flesh to revolt, and addressed her body as follows:

I shall make thee not only to endure the savor of it, but also to receive it within thee. With that she took all the washing of the sore, together with the corrupt matter and filth; and going aside put it all into a cup, and drank it up lustily. And in so doing, she overcame at one time, both the squeamishness of her own stomach and the malice of the devil.[6]

As Catherine faced the old, sick woman, she understood that she was being tested by the devil and resolved to approach, not reject, the source of repugnance so as to transcend it. Another medieval Christian holy woman, Angela of Foligno (1248–1309), drank the water in which she washed the sores of lepers.[7] Perhaps we cannot demand this exaggerated level of piety (admittedly bordering on madness) from our friend Pelimo, but we can expect a little more kindness.

Indeed, some would even claim that love itself is the "suspension of disgust," as it requires "a willingness to pardon normal failings of the other's body, such as bad breath or ugliness that attend puberty and growing old."[8] Likewise, overcoming disgust is almost a prerequisite for loving parenthood, as William Ian Miller observes in his *The Anatomy of Disgust*: "Changing diapers, overcoming the disgust inherent in contaminating substances, is emblematic of the unconditional quality of nurturing parental love."[9] Doctors, nurses, and family members who care for the sick also have to confront such feelings: "[O]vercoming revulsion of body products is one of the issues faced by carers. When the carer is a partner, this can put an extreme stress on the relationship."[10] If not acts akin to those of Catherine of Siena, certainly this much love of the poor man could be expected of Pelimo; after all, the Bible commands, "Love your fellow as yourself" (Lev. 19:18).

The oft ubiquitous role of disgust in human experience invites us to reinterpret the beginning scene in sharper relief—to understand disgust as the deeper reason Pelimo neither admits the beggar to his house nor seats him at his table. In particular, hygiene has always presented a challenge for the poor. The rich often judge them to smell foully, to insist, as George Orwell succinctly put it, that "The lower classes smell."[11] Beggars in Pelimo's day and age probably did not bathe regularly and would have exuded foul body odors, bad breath, and other such catalysts of the disgust reflex— and we can be sure Satan adopted many such pungent aromas for his test. Pelimo naturally wished to keep the putrid-smelling panhandler away from the table so as not to be confronted by his revolting presence.

For precisely these reasons a virtuous man or woman must overpower the instinctive physical reaction and treat the poor with dignity. Pelimo's unimpressive response to this trial reveals his average, if not below-average, level of holiness.

The denouement appropriately takes place in the outhouse, where Pelimo faces his antagonist amidst the foul odors and disgusting discharges from human bodies—and probably the repulsive flies, maggots, and other denizens of such locales. Latrines in antiquity were more exposed than our modern public restrooms, lacking the partitions and stalls we construct for a modicum of privacy, though we, too, cannot escape the smells and sounds. Unlike Pelimo's rarefied home, from which Pelimo had initially attempted to exclude the "baser" social stratum, this shared social domain is open to everyone. If Pelimo could hardly suppress the contamination from the beggar's sores and spittle in his own home, here he can do even less to prevent contagion from the excreta of many others.

Clothing, another signifier of class differences, is stripped away in the latrine as bodies are exposed to perform their animal functions. Perhaps the storyteller is conveying that this setting, too, forces Pelimo to appreciate the common denominator of all human bodies, of all human beings, aristocratic or lower class. While death is often considered the great human equalizer, during life the toilet has a similar function. In this way Pelimo is knocked off his pedestal of self-righteousness and brought low: both in the awareness of the deficiencies of his conduct toward his fellow human beings and in his ultimate bow of capitulation.

Law, Ethics, and Disgust

Disgust has gained recognition as a factor in contemporary law and engendered a copious amount of legal literature debating the parameters of its legitimate function. Some state jurisdictions, for example, accept claims based on disgust as considerations either for stringency or leniency in murder cases. A killer who professes that he was moved to act out of disgust at the victim may receive a lesser penalty. For example, in 1988 a Texas judge accepted a murderer's plea that he had killed two men due to his revulsion at their homosexuality and sentenced him not to life imprisonment but according to the guidelines for voluntary manslaughter.[12] On the other hand, some state laws impose harsher penalties on the perpetrator of a murder that is "outrageously or wantonly vile, horrible, or inhuman," that is, that we find particularly disgusting. Thus a murderer who kills by dismembering the body with an electric saw and not with a "conventional" shotgun may receive the death penalty rather than life imprisonment.[13]

Jewish law recognizes disgust as a factor in a number of legal realms. The Mishnah rules that women are entitled to receive a divorce from husbands afflicted with boils or with an oral lesion causing bad breath, and also from those who work as tanners, gatherers of excrement, and copper refiners (*Mishnah Ketubot* 7:10). Tanners used excrement and other such substances in the process of treating leather and, like copper miners, exuded foul odors. If these conditions and professions are sufficiently disgusting to the women that they cannot tolerate their husbands' presence (or perhaps cannot tolerate engaging in sexual relations with them), they therefore have a right to a divorce.

Sabbath law, too, includes a category of things "set aside on account of disgustingness [*muqtzeh maḥamat mi'us*]," which generally may not be touched or moved, including vomit and animal and human excrement. This touching does not violate any prohibition, as no work is done, but it is said to detract from the holiness of the day. The precept recognizes the general incompatibility of sanctity—in this case the holiness of Sabbath time—with items that elicit disgust. Similarly, Jewish law prohibits prayer and Torah study if feces and urine are nearby and can be seen or smelled.

Disgust in the story of Pelimo presents a challenge to overcome. And yet the emotion can also function constructively in helping us to lead lives of piety. This positive use of disgust results from our ability to feel revulsion not only through direct sensory experience but by imagining disgusting substances, recalling revolting smells, and other cognitive processes. Thus the Mishnah advises, "Be very, very humble, for the end of humans is worms," that is, the worms that will infest our bodies after our death (*Mishnah Avot* 4:4). By picturing a rotting human corpse infested by worms, an image typically eliciting disgust, and then understanding that no human can avoid this fate, that even the most beautiful, powerful, and rich ultimately wind up as a disgusting mass of decaying flesh, we appreciate the lowly stature of all human beings, especially ourselves. This realization of our repulsive future state should in principle counter any pride or hubris we may feel about our own beauty, importance, or greatness.

In a variation of this idea, a Rabbi advises:

Contemplate three things and you will not come to sin: Know

Whence you came, and

To where you go, and

Before whom you will ultimately give an account and reckoning.

"Whence you came"—from a putrid drop.

"To where you go"—to a place of dust, worms, and maggots.

"Before whom you will ultimately give an account and reckoning"—before the King of Kings, the Holy One, Blessed be He.

(*Mishnah Avot* 3:1)

Jewish tradition thus recommends that we not only focus on the disgusting state that awaits us all but be mindful of our ignominious origins in a "putrid drop," that is, a driblet of semen. To imagine ourselves not as glorious and dignified people, but as devolving from fetid glops of sperm, should remind us of our baseness and lowliness. This perspective should counter sins of pride, haughtiness, and self-importance, and also their negative ramifications: self-serving acts of greed, self-aggrandizement, and insensitivity to others. A medieval commentator, Rabbi Obadiah ben Abraham Yare of Bertinoro, adds: "Anyone who contemplates where he is destined to go, to 'a place of dust, worms, and maggots,' will be saved from desire and from lust for money" (commentary to *Mishnah Avot* 3:1). Why struggle to amass a fortune and envy the wealth of others when we all wind up rotting in the grave in due course?

Two stories about resisting sexual sin illustrate how this process is supposed to work. A talmudic tradition relates that the wife of a certain Roman wished to disgrace Rabbi Akiva as revenge for the Rabbi's besting her husband in arguments. An exceedingly beautiful woman, the wife adorned herself, approached Rabbi Akiva, and "uncovered her thigh" so as to seduce him. Rabbi Akiva, however, spat and, when she asked why he did so, explained: "You came from a putrid drop." The disgusting spittle, signifying the sexual fluids in which her life had begun, helped Rabbi Akiva resist temptation; looking beyond her superficial beauty and sexual appeal, he saw a deeper truth about a repulsive aspect of all humans.[14] Yet another story about Rabbi Akiva relates:

When Rabbi Akiva travelled to Rome, he was slandered to the governor. The governor sent him two beautiful women. He had them bathe and anoint themselves, and he adorned them like brides for their grooms. They fell upon the Rabbi the entire night: This one said, "Come be with me." That one said, "Come be with me." But he sat between them and spat, and did not look at them.

The next morning they went and complained to the governor. They said, "Our master! Death is preferable to us than to be given to a man like that." The governor summoned Rabbi Akiva and said to him: "Why do you not do with these women as is customary for men to do with women? Are they not beautiful? Are they not human beings like you? Did He who created you not also create them?"

Rabbi Akiva said to him: "What can I do, for their stench came upon me like that of carrion and swine?"

(*Avot d'Rabbi Natan* 16:2[15])

The Roman governor's motivation to implicate the Rabbi in an extramarital ménage à trois is unclear, but the mention of "slander" suggests he seeks a pretext to disgrace and perhaps imprison Rabbi Akiva. The Rabbi, however, resists the beautiful women that night by spitting so as to mobilize his disgust reflex. The lascivious women, in the storyteller's imagination, cannot stomach this rejection and inform their master that they would rather die! When the Roman prods Rabbi Akiva, emphasizing the women's shared humanity and observing that they, too, are created in the image of God, the Rabbi points to disgust as the source of his aversion. Because the women had bathed and anointed themselves, beautifying techniques in antiquity, they did not give off a bad smell in reality. Rather, through the power of his imagination Rabbi

Akiva associated them with the dead flesh of animal corpses and the offensive meat of pigs, and in that way maintained his virtue.

Thus the emotion of disgust is a tricky force in the struggle to lead a moral life. Like many emotions (jealousy, rage, lust), it must be transcended and overcome when it pulls us away from virtue. But it can also be summoned as a strategic ally to counter other emotions that may seduce us to vice.

8 The Land of Truth

Sefer ha-Ḥinukh (*The Book of Education*), one of the most influential medieval digests of the 613 biblical commandments, emphasizes the importance of truth:

> Falsehood is abominable and despicable in the eyes of all. Nothing is more disgusting than it, and desolation and curses are found in the houses of those who love it, because God is a God of truth, and everything about Him is true. Blessings come exclusively to those who emulate God's attributes in their deeds, to be truthful just as He is a God of truth. . . . Therefore the Torah admonished us to distance ourselves from falsehood greatly, as it says, "Keep distant from a false matter" [Exod. 23:7]. The Torah uses the word "distant," which is not mentioned in other admonishments, because falsehood is extremely disgusting. (Commandment 74)

The unknown author's passionate and vivid language would seem to allow for no compromises whatsoever. God stands for the truth, and humans, who are charged to imitate God in all their ways, must exhibit complete devotion to truth too. In hopes of persuading us as readers to abhor anything false, the author attempts to marshal our emotion of disgust (a sometimes-effective technique, as discussed in the previous chapter).

Rabbi Elijah Eliezer Dessler (1891–1953), however, provides an opposing perspective on when to tell the truth with the following guidance:

> What is truth and what is falsehood? In our early education we were taught that truth is telling things just as they happened, and falsehood is when one deviates from this. However, this applies only to simple situations, but in practice there are many situations in which this is not the case. Sometimes it is forbidden to tell things the way they are, for example to say something that would negatively impact another person when there is no benefit or necessity. Sometimes it is in fact necessary to deviate from the truth, such as cases when the truth will not help but will cause injury. In such cases that which appears to be truth is in fact falsehood, as it causes evil consequences, while that which appears to be falsehood brings about the truth.[1]

Underscoring the complexity of the ethical calculus underpinning lies and truths, Dessler dismisses as childish the notion that the truth corresponds to things as they are. Only the naïve and immature conduct their lives in this way, oversimplifying ethical decisions that require a more sophisticated sensibility. Focusing less on the facts as such and more on the consequences of the words uttered, namely whether they are kind or harmful, Dessler arrives at the paradoxical notion that in certain circumstances lying should, in fact, be considered "truth," namely the right action, while telling the truth—if it is a hurtful, mean-spirited truth— should be considered "falsehood," that is, an immoral deed.

What is more, often there are numerous choices between the two stark alternatives. We have developed a nuanced terminology to capture the many points along the spectrum: fib, half-truth, untruth, shade the truth, deception, dishonesty, dissemble, misspeak, perjury, equivocate, mislead. A "lie" may be further modified to distinguish its precise character: white and black lies, polite and serious lies, lies of omission and lies of commission, interpersonal lies and intrapersonal lies (a lie to oneself), self-centered lies (that benefit the liar) and other-oriented lies (that benefit someone else).

When to tell the truth, when to lie, or when to embark on something in between is no easy decision. "The Ethicist" column in the *New York Times Magazine* reveals some of the moral questions we wrestle with today: Should I tell my child that his father is not his biological father? Must a mental illness be disclosed on a first date? Must I pretend to like my artist friend's work? My parents told me not to tell my sister that she is adopted—should I preserve the lie? Do I have to tell my aged mother-in-law that she is dying of cancer, or can I just tell her she is sick? Can I identify my non-biological children as black because my husband is, although they are of Hispanic Caucasian parentage? My friend, who is the long-time girlfriend of another friend of mine who is ill, swore me to secrecy that she found another love—should I break my promise to her? When I'm showing a property to sell, I sometimes arrange for friends to make bogus telephone calls to me, which I answer with a monologue of sales talk designed to be overheard; is this deception ethical as long as everything I say is true?

Research shows that almost every day most of us utter falsehoods, albeit telling ourselves that we indulge not in full-blown lies but rather in half-truths, deceptions, and "white" lies. (If one has, or works with, young children, the number may be astronomical.) One 1977 study found that people are lied to as many as two hundred times per day.[2] A 2009 British study found that men lied six times per day on average, twice as much as women.[3] A 2002 study published in the *Journal of Basic and Applied Social Psychology* found that 60 percent of the subjects lied at least once in a ten-minute conversation.[4] ("Nice haircut!" "I didn't mean it." "Sorry, I'm busy on Wednesday." "I love your gift—it's exactly what I wanted.") Noting that many of these daily lies are told to those closest to us, a *Wall Street Journal* column, "A Guide to Little White Lies," provided advice on when such lies are appropriate and when to avoid them.[5] A 2017 *National Geographic* cover story explored "Why We Lie: The Science Behind our Complicated Relationship with the Truth."[6]

What is the cumulative effect of compromising the truth on this scale? How many of these lies are for the noble purposes Dessler delineates? Is there an alternative? Consider this thought-provoking talmudic story:

Rava said: Once I used to think that there is no truth in the world.

Until a certain Sage—his name was Rav Tavut (and some say his name was Rav Tavyomi)—who would not lie even if given all the possessions in the world—told me [this story]:

"One time I came to a certain place, and its name was Qushta [Truth]. The residents did not 'modify their words' [lie], and no one living there died prematurely.

I married a woman from among them and had two sons from her.

One day my wife was sitting and washing her hair. A neighbor came and knocked on the door. I thought, 'It is not proper [to tell the neighbor that my wife is washing].' I said to the neighbor, 'She is not here.' Her [my wife's] two sons died.

The residents of the place came to me. They said, 'What is this?' I told them what had happened. They said to me, 'We

beg of you: leave our place and do not stir up death against
the rest of us.'"

(*Sanhedrin* 97a)

Rava understandably believed that this world is devoid of truth,
given the typical daily experience of being lied to, cheated, and
deceived. Notably, among the terms the Rabbis use for the "world
to come," that posthumous world of heavenly bliss, is "the world of
truth"—thus distinguishing it from our current existence in the
"world of lies" (perhaps better translated as "the world of illusion").

Then Rava hears from a colleague named Rabbi Tavut (or Tavyomi) about a town named Qushta, the Aramaic word for "truth,"
an elusive place where all the residents conduct all their dealings
with perfect honesty. No one there ever "modifies his words," a
talmudic euphemism for lying. Apparently truth can be found in
this world after all.

Because of their virtue, God has blessed the residents of Qushta
with only natural deaths. In traditional Jewish theology premature deaths, whether by illness or accident, indicate divine punishment, as otherwise one would enjoy a normal life-span. The
reward for the townspeople's exemplary commitment to truth renders Qushta a utopia, and we should probably infer that, together
with the absence of early death, the town is free from discord and
other social ills. Who would not wish to dwell among such par-
agons of virtue? Rabbi Tavut/Tavyomi naturally settles there,
marries a local woman, and starts a family. But he does not live
happily ever after . . . .

His blissful existence comes to an abrupt end when confronted
with an awkward situation. A neighbor comes to visit his wife
while she washes her hair, perhaps sitting naked as she leans over
the tub or washing trough. Even were she not undressed, mar-

ried Jewish women in talmudic times covered their hair in public, as exposed hair was considered erotic. The Mishnah rules that a married woman who appears in public with uncovered hair violates "the laws of [modest] Jewish women" and can be divorced with forfeiture of her marriage payment. Elsewhere the Talmud tells the story of Kimḥit, whose seven sons all served as the High Priest in the Jerusalem Temple because "the ceiling-beams of her house never saw the plaits of her hair"—that is, she never uncovered her hair even within the privacy of her house, far exceeding the normal expectations of modesty (*Yoma* 47a).

From this perspective, the Rabbi judges it "not proper," or immodest, to state that his wife is washing her hair, even to another woman. This might be analogous to saying something like "she is on the toilet" today. So the Rabbi tells a "white lie," a seemingly innocuous, well-intentioned mistruth never meant to cause harm to anyone and solely uttered to protect his wife's privacy. Alas, this is the town of Truth.

The couple's two children immediately die. The storyteller calculatingly refers to them as "her sons" to emphasize that the Rabbi, the outsider, has brought premature death to the offspring of a longtime resident of the town, children who otherwise should have lived to ripe old age. The feminine possessive also underscores the irony that in attempting to protect his wife, the Rabbi ends up causing her great injury.

Within the Qushta ethic of absolute commitment to truth there lies no gray between the black and white of truth and falsehood, no sliding scale of truth (white lie, deception, fib)—a lie is a lie is a lie. The town therefore loses its immunity from the consequences of sin. It, too, becomes subject to the evils that plague human existence in this world, "the world of lies." And the pious residents dismiss Rabbi Tavut/Tavyomi, the liar, from their town before he can afflict them with further disasters.

At first glance, the story seems to offer the straightforward message that any and all lying is wrong and cannot be justified, no matter what the motivation. Were we all committed to telling the truth, our society would be much better off.

Yet this story clearly should not be taken as a "true" (!) report of what actually happened to an itinerant Rabbi. The symbolic names signal that the story is a parable, a didactic fiction, despite the autobiographical pretenses. The town's name, "Truth," is patently fictional. So too is the protagonist's name, Rav Tavut, which might be rendered in English as "Rabbi Goodness" or "the Good Rabbi," based on the Aramaic word for "good," *tav*, or, per the alternative tradition, "Rabbi Good Day," from the Aramaic words for "good" and "day," *yom*. Moreover, the story belies its own claims to reality with an internal contradiction: Rava asserts that the audience should believe the story because of the protagonist's impeccable honesty; he "would not lie even if given all the possessions in the world." Yet that same Rabbi lies about his wife's whereabouts when, as far as he knows, much less is at stake. The source of the tale, Rava wants us to understand, cannot be trusted.

The town of "Truth" therefore does not exist—and furthermore we should not believe that such a society would be a utopia or ideal. In fact, Rava's very point would seem to be that a town such as Qushta not only does not but cannot exist.

He provides us with a type of thought experiment. Here, Socrates or another Hellenistic philosopher might have offered a philosophical discourse, setting forth arguments about the advantages and problems of such an ideal and to what extent an absolute insistence on truth constitutes the apex of ethical life. But a talmudic Rabbi does not speak in philosophic idiom; he tells a story. In this case he offers a complex counterfactual narrative for us to ponder and decode. In theory, Rava suggests, were all people to always tell the truth, they would have a perfect society, presumably free of the ravages of disease and death that generally devolve from sin. However, in practice such a society would not work, because all sorts of innocent departures from truth are necessary to uphold other values.

The particulars of our story are not intended to distract us from this general principle. The reader is not meant to argue, for example, that the root problem is the value of modesty—that were we, say, to live in a society where people washed their hair and went to the bathroom and had sex in public, then we could always tell the truth without worrying about privacy and thus enjoy a truly blissful life. Rava would claim that such a society is immoral in its lack of commitment to those other values. And even were we to compromise on modesty and privacy, truth will inevitably conflict with other ethical commitments, such as avoiding harm when telling the truth. The problem is, given the complexity of human experience, values inevitably conflict, and any total allegiance to one overriding principle proves too crude a moral compass to live by. It would be wonderful to make a total commitment to truth. So, too, it would be wonderful to make a total commitment to justice, peace, kindness, generosity, hospitality, modesty, humility, and other values. But one cannot simultaneously live in the Land of Truth and also in the Land of Justice, the Land of Peace, the Land of Humility, and the other worthy Lands.

The Sages "Modified Their Words"

Several talmudic passages embrace the notion that lying is sometimes necessary. We see this, for example, in the Talmud's treatment of one of several lies within the biblical story of Joseph and his brothers. In an exceptionally dramatic scene toward the end of the saga, Joseph's brothers become exceedingly worried after the death of their father Jacob: "What if Joseph still bears a grudge against us and pays us back for all the wrongs we did him?" (Gen. 50:15). Perhaps, they conjecture, Joseph didn't want to cause his father additional grief by punishing his brothers for selling him into slavery, and therefore he has patiently waited until his father's death to avenge his brothers' wrong. The anxious brothers accordingly send Joseph the message: "Before his death your father left this instruction: So shall you say to Joseph, 'Forgive, I urge you, the offense and guilt of your brothers who treated you so harshly'" (Gen. 50:16–17). The Bible relates no such instruction among Jacob's dying words, nor among any of his other words for that matter, suggesting that the message has been fabricated. The Talmud, however, takes the brothers' clever ploy as a precedent that one may "modify one's words"—the same euphemism for "lie" that appears in the Qushta story—for the sake of "peace," either referring to the preservation of the brothers' lives or the general peace among members of a family (*Yevamot* 65b).

A stronger precedent, this talmudic passage continues, can be found in the biblical account of the Prophet Samuel's struggle to anoint David as king. After deciding to replace King Saul with David, God directs Samuel to journey to the abode of David's father, Jesse, in Bethlehem for the anointing. Samuel, however, protests: "How can I go? If Saul hears about it, he will kill me" (1 Sam. 16:2). God seems to have overlooked the fact that kings hate to be replaced, especially by poor shepherds of a lower-class family, and generally employ their armies to murder all involved in such attempts. Point well taken, Samuel! After this very reasonable objection God refines the plan, instructing Samuel: "Take a heifer with you and say, 'I have come to sacrifice to the Lord.' Invite Jesse to the sacrifice, and I will show you what to do. You are to anoint for me the one I indicate" (1 Sam. 16:2–3). Surprisingly, God does not reassure Samuel, "Don't worry about Saul's puny army, as I will direct the divine minions to take care of them," or "I'll cloak you with my invisibility force field until you arrive." Rather, God tells Samuel to lie, to pretend that he is visiting Bethlehem for the purpose of performing a sacrifice rather than in order to perform an anointment. Here before us is the divine authority to prevaricate! The Talmud accordingly concludes that lying is not only an option but a commandment—a mitzvah—when done to preserve peace, in this case meaning to save Samuel's life or to prevent the pogrom Saul would have perpetrated had he learned the truth.

In another passage the Talmud reports: "The Sages are accustomed to modifying their words in these three areas: tractate, bed, and hospitality" (*Eruvin* 53b). The commentaries understand "tractate" to refer to a Sage's mastery of a tractate of Talmud. He may lie, saying that he does not know a certain tractate well even when he has studied it fully, so as not to come across as bragging or showing off. "Bed" refers to details of a Sage's sex life or intimate relationship with his wife. Should someone inappropriately inquire into such matters, a Sage need not answer truthfully so as to protect his and his wife's privacy. "Hospitality" refers to the generosity of a host. A Sage is not to praise the fine meals or comfortable accommodations he received as a guest at another's home, lest that individual be overcome by others seeking hospitality and alms. Thus the talmudic Rabbis recommended compromising truth when it conflicted with the values of humility, modesty, and privacy.

A famous talmudic discussion of honesty and dissembling relates to the practice of praising the bride on her wedding day, as part of the general precept of bringing joy to the bride and groom:

How does one dance before the bride? The House [school] of Shammai say: "The bride as she really is." And the House of Hillel say: "A beautiful and graceful bride!"

The House of Shammai said to the House of Hillel: If she were lame or blind, would one say of her: "Beautiful and graceful bride"? Does the Torah not say, 'Keep distant from a false matter' [Exod. 23:7]?

The House of Hillel said to the House of Shammai: "According to your reasoning, if someone makes a bad purchase in the market, should one praise it in his eyes or deprecate it in his eyes? [As opposed to your reasoning,] clearly one should praise it in his eyes."

Based on this, the Sages say: "One's disposition should always be pleasant toward others."

(*Ketubot* 16b–17a)

Imagine the bride decked out in her wedding dress, her hair and makeup beautifully prepared for the occasion, radiantly beaming at the guests who approach to offer their best wishes just before the ceremony. You approach to "dance before" her, that is, to entertain her, to praise her beauty, to make her happy on her wedding day. As you are about to say, "You look so beautiful," you suddenly realize that in fact she is not beautiful at all. In fact, she is exceedingly ugly, with a deformed foot sticking awkwardly out from the hem of the dress, and apparently almost blind, with thick glasses in a gaudy frame perched on a crooked nose. What are you to say?

The House of Shammai refuses to condone a patent lie such as to call an unsightly bride "graceful." After all, an explicit divine command in an unambiguous biblical verse warns to keep away from false matters, and praising such a bride is manifestly false. Yet it seems hard to believe that the House of Shammai means for us to tell the bride the truth as we experience it: "I have never seen a bride as ugly as you. It's amazing you found a husband. With all my best wishes on your special day."

The talmudic commentators explain that the House of Shammai mean that one is to praise a beautiful aspect of the bride, such as her hands or her hair, or something graceful she has done, to avoid an outright lie. The House of Hillel, by contrast, advocate lying: no matter how disagreeable the bride's appearance, one tells her how graceful and beautiful she looks. Surprisingly, they offer no biblical support to counter the House of Shammai, no apparent authority for their position other than to invoke the common practice in this analogous situation: when a friend proudly displays something he has already bought, obviously (according to the Hillelites) one should praise the object, even if he has overpaid or otherwise made a poor transaction, as the deal is done and the purchase final. To deprecate his purchase will accomplish nothing other than to make him miserable. Later Sages conclude that the House of Hillel believes "pleasantness" to trump the truth in such cases. A still later talmudic discussion of this source, on the other hand, suggests that the House of Hillel bases its position on the duty to "preserve life," as shaming the bride by speaking honestly is tantamount to causing her to experience a metaphoric death from public embarrassment.

This debate between the schools is most likely a fiction, with the standard Rabbinic position attributed to the Hillelites and a hypothetical counter position put into the mouths of the Shammaites. The talmudic Rabbis were known to employ fictitious debates to explore many issues, creating imaginary dialogue, advancing different arguments and counterarguments, offering refutations and objections. What would life look like if we always told the truth? What would we say to a hideous bride on her wedding day when required to offer words of praise? What would they say in the Town of Truth? If we should lie in this case, what justifies it, given the biblical injunction to keep away from falsehoods?[7]

The Neighbor and the Murderer at the Door

The neighbor who comes to the door looking for the Rabbi's wife in Qushta is reminiscent of a similar scenario related to the theory of ethics proposed by the philosopher Immanuel Kant (1724–

1804). Kant believed that ethical actions must be grounded in universal principles or "maxims"—unconditional demands or "imperatives" that ultimately devolve from moral duties and apply in all circumstances. Kant formulated what he called the "categorical imperative," the criterion by which rational agents should determine ethical duties, as: "Act only according to that maxim whereby you can at the same time will that it should become a universal law." For example, if I am faced with the question of whether it is permitted for me to steal money to pay for my college education, I would ask whether such theft could be a universal law such that everyone would be permitted to do the same. This would clearly lead to an impossible situation as people would then steal back from me, and steal from colleges, and I would not achieve my goal. The self-contradiction in the universalization of the maxim means that it cannot be an absolute law; hence it cannot be an ethical course of action. Kant argued that "Do not lie" is an absolute principle, as universalizing the dispensation to lie would entail that no one could ever believe anyone else, and my lie too would not be effective.

Challenging Kant's ethics, the philosopher Benjamin Constant (1767–1830) rejected the possibility of absolute moral duties. Constant presented the following example: suppose my friend arrives at my door and hides in my house, having fled from a murderer trying to kill him. A short time later the murderer arrives at my door and demands to know if my friend is inside. Should I tell the truth to the murderer? (Some contemporary philosophers modernize this case as Nazis at the door searching for Jews during the Holocaust.) Constant argued that I should lie so as to save a life because the murderer "has no right to the truth." When Kant learned of this challenge, he penned the essay "On a Supposed Right to Lie from Benevolent Motives" (1797), which held that the duty to tell the truth was categorical and applied even in this situation. Kant's several arguments included the proposition that had my friend fled the house through a back door unbeknownst to me, and the murderer, who otherwise would have searched my house, departed because of my lie only to encounter and kill my friend, then I and my lie are responsible. For more than two hundred years philosophers have debated the merits of these arguments, providing alternative defenses for Kant's views and different objections against them (including the rather commonsensical notion that one could avoid lying by simply slamming and locking the door in the murderer's face). This question has even become a staple of college courses in moral philosophy and a frequent topic for final exams.

The contrasts between the dynamics of the neighbor at the door in the talmudic story and the murderer at the door in Constant's assessment should not mask the fundamental similarity in outlook. The Rabbi lies to protect his wife in Qushta, and death results. Constant argues that if one does not lie to the murderer to protect one's friend, then death results. The lack of a true answer undermines the utopian life in Qushta, whereas the lack of a false answer destroys the life of the friend in Constant's example. Yet both converge with a similar message. Constant concludes that, "The moral principle, 'it is a duty to tell the truth,' would, if taken unconditionally and singly, make any society impossible."[8] Likewise, the parable of Qushta illustrates the inconceivability of that society. The underlying affinity between these two views thus reveals a shared critique of an absolute prohibition on lying and probably should also be understood as paradigmatic for all ethical absolutes. Who knew the Talmud anticipated eighteenth-century moral philosophy so pointedly!

From The Twilight Zone to Liar, Liar

Film and television have also employed the conceit of a character constrained to tell the truth. An episode of the television series *The Twilight Zone* entitled "The Whole Truth" featured an unethical, smooth-talking, used-car salesman named Honeycutt, who shamelessly lies to potential buyers about the junky cars on his lot. One day he buys a "haunted" car from a mysterious old man that compels him to be honest. All of a sudden Honeycutt is advising customers not to buy the car they settled upon, confessing, "If the car were one year older, Moses could have driven it across the Red Sea," and adding that he has nothing worthwhile to show them because "every car on this lot should have been condemned years ago." He tries to tell his wife he won't be home until much later that night because he has to take inventory but can't help admitting that he will be playing poker with his buddies. When an employee inquires about a raise Honeycutt had promised, he discloses not only that he had lied about the raise but that "the day you get more money out of me will be below zero in the Fijis."

Because Honeycutt operates by dishonestly deceiving everyone else—customers, employees, and his wife alike—the negative repercussions of his compulsion to tell the truth satisfy us as "justice served!" Yet the episode provokes some deeper questions. After having new signs commissioned for the cars on his lot that say "Not Dependable," "Not Ready To Go," and "Not Guaranteed: In Poor Condition," his assistant cries out, "There is a limit to honesty, boss!" Is this the case? What are those limits? A politician becomes suspicious after having offered Honeycutt $60 for the "haunted" car, only to receive a counteroffer of $25 from Honeycutt. Subsequently learning that the car compels its owner to be honest, the politician refuses the deal on the grounds that, "I am in politics; if I had to tell the truth, I couldn't make a single political speech." Of course this is not news to any of us, but the frank admission of chronic political dishonesty is telling. The episode concludes with Honeycutt somehow managing to sell the car to Nikita Khrushchev and telephoning the White House to report this happy development. The lesson? Perhaps: absolute truth could be useful if imposed on our enemies, but we would never want to be in that situation ourselves! Or maybe: whatever the salutary implications of absolute honesty in business and domestic affairs, it could never work in politics or international diplomacy.

The 1997 film *Liar, Liar* employed the same premise of the compelled truth-teller for comedic purposes. Fletcher Reede (Jim Carrey), an unscrupulous lawyer, irresponsible ex-husband, and deceitful father, constantly neglects his paternal obligations. His son Max is so disappointed in his dad that he makes a birthday wish for one day on which his father cannot tell a lie. When the wish comes true, Fletcher's life quickly disintegrates, in amusing ways. When his boss seduces him, he tells her honestly that he has experienced better sex; when stopped by a police officer for speeding, he confesses to dozens of other traffic violations; when asked about the raise he denied his assistant, he admits that he gave her false reasons for rejecting her request and adds that the gifts he gave her were fake and cheap. Nor can he lie in court; he ends up objecting to himself and goading his own clients to admit to actions that undermine their cases. Desperate, he beats himself to a pulp in the court bathroom, hoping the trial will be adjourned—but truthfully must admit to the judge that he was not assaulted by an intruder, that he inflicted the damage himself, and that, despite his condition, he is capable of continuing the trial. Ultimately he winds up in jail, miserable and alone; no one is willing to bail him out. Lesson learned. Then his assistant takes pity on him and posts bail, Fletcher realizes his erring ways and reforms, and the film ends on a happy note.

Fletcher, like Honeycutt, is a scoundrel (though a very likeable one), and consequently, as in the episode of *The Twilight Zone*, most of the occasions on which he is compelled to tell the truth strike us as appropriate. He should not be lying constantly to his son and ex-wife for selfish, opportunistic reasons. Nevertheless, in certain scenes, problematic and troubling aspects of a mandate for total truth lurk just below the veneer of the cinematic humor.

When asked, for example, what he thinks of his colleagues and senior executives at his firm, a bunch of conniving and manipulative lawyers much like him, he insults them in offensive (though hilarious) ways. But how many of us would wish to candidly and publicly reveal our true opinions of our coworkers and bosses— and our friends and relatives too? In most cases the aftermath would be anything but humorous.

What if the truth "victim" were a regular, decent person, not a swindler like Honeycutt or Fletcher? The journalist A. J. Jacobs conducted just such an experiment by adopting a philosophy of "radical honesty" for one month. Describing his experiences in the *Esquire* essay "I Think You're Fat,"[9] Jacobs recounts how he told the truth in all sorts of situations in which he normally would have lied: he informs a five-year old that her bug is not napping but dead; discloses to a friend that he's forgotten the friend's fiancée's name, although they have been together for years; answers his stepmother that he did not like the gift certificate she sent him for his birthday because it essentially gives him an errand to run; interrupts a barber making conversation with him to say that he is tired and wants to read; and tells his wife's college friends he does not want to get together with them since he doesn't even have enough time to see his own friends. When his wife asks if he wants to hear the end of a story she was recounting about an annoying event of her day, he honestly responds, "Well . . . is there a payoff?"—and receives an expletive in response.

The aftermath of his truth-telling efforts is often negative or mixed, although Jacobs reports some salutary results. He learns that relationships can tolerate more truth than he had thought. They don't fall apart, for example, just because he tells a friend that he just does not feel like having lunch that day as opposed to making up an excuse about a doctor's appointment. His commitment to the truth generally opens the door to truthful responses from his friends and colleagues, which makes for more honest and meaningful relationships. Even his boss reacts well when Jacobs truthfully writes that he resents the delay in getting back to him about a memo in a timely fashion. More honesty among colleagues at work can be productive.

Yet Jacobs cannot bring himself to be truthful in certain occasions. When an old, retired man whose wife recently died sends Jacobs some poems for his opinion, he cannot answer that he did not care for the poems; he lies, saying they are very good. Jacobs wonders whether it might have been more compassionate to offer the man the "authentic caring" of an honest assessment and whether his lie "is simply avoiding of responsibility." In the end, however, he admits that despite his commitment to the truth, "I can't trash the old man," proving himself to be a sort of kindred soul of Rabbi Tavut.

At the end of the month, Jacobs feels tremendous relief to be able to return to the white-lies, half-truths, and other deceptions that most of us practice on a daily basis. The experiment apparently failed. But from another point of view it succeeded, in that it demonstrates how problematic sticking to "the whole truth and nothing but the truth" can be. Ironically, in some cases Jacobs's uncompromising truth telling renders him almost as offensive as Fletcher's and Honeycutt's relentless lying. For example, Jacobs tells an attractive magazine editor at a breakfast meeting that he would try to sleep with her if he were single and telephones a friend to say that he fantasizes about his friend's wife. He concludes that had he been honest 100 percent of the time, rather than the 90 percent he achieved, he "would have gotten beaten up, fired, and divorced."[10]

"We all value truth and yet we are *all* ordinary human deceivers; we neither want to know all the truth nor tell it all," the philosopher David Nyberg writes in *The Varnished Truth: Truth-Telling and Deceiving in Ordinary Life,* within the chapter appropriately titled "Truth Telling Is Morally Overrated." Deception, he says, "is not so much a plague as it is part of the atmosphere that sustains life."[11] He concludes: "A healthy, livable human lifetime of relationships with others is to me inconceivable without deception . . . . We deceive, among other reasons, so that we might not perish of the truth."[12]

Nyberg brings us full circle from Qushta, where lying produces death, to the claim that not lies, but too great a commitment to truth, will cause us to perish.

The Heavenly Truth

A fascinating Rabbinic tradition found in midrash *Bereshit Rabbah* 8:5 recounts a debate among the angels about the advisability of creating human beings.

Rabbi Simon said:

At the time when the Holy Blessed One prepared to create the first human being, the ministering angels formed themselves into factions and divisions. Some of them said, "Let him not be created!" Others said "Let him be created!" Thus it is written, "Kindness and Truth fought, Righteousness and Peace clashed" [Ps. 85:11].

[The Angel of] Kindness said, "Let him be created, for he will do kind deeds."

[The Angel of] Truth said, "Let him not be created, for he is full of lies."

[The Angel of] Righteousness said, "Let him be created, for he will do righteous deeds."

[The Angel of] Peace said, "Let him not be created, for he is full of strife."

What did the Holy Blessed One do? He took [the Angel of] Truth and threw him to the ground. This is what is written, "And you threw Truth to the ground" [Dan. 8:12].

The ministering angels said before the Holy Blessed One: "Master of the Universe! Why do you despise your own seal? Let [the Angel of] Truth rise from the earth!" Hence it is what is written, "The Truth will rise from the earth" [Ps. 85:12].

This imaginative story, almost a myth, is based on an obscure biblical passage, Psalms 85:11–12, that describes encounters between "kindness," "truth," "righteousness," and "peace." Whatever this verse means in context, the Rabbinic tradition interprets it to refer to a meeting of angels at the time God set about creating humankind. The angels, who often form a divine council of sorts, debate whether God should continue with the divine plan to create humans. The Angels of Truth and Peace advise against it on account of the human propensity toward lies and violence. Why bring falsehood and strife into God's perfect world? The Angels of Righteousness and Kindness, on the other hand, recommend that humans be created, given the good deeds that humans, and no other species, can perform. Facing a deadlock between his counselors, God expels the Angel of Truth from his heavenly retinue and throws him down to earth. Problem solved: the votes for the creation of humans now exceed those opposed, while the relegation of the Angel of Truth to earth should counter the human propensity toward lying.

The angels, however, protest the expulsion of their fellow, pointing out that God's very seal contains the truth within its emblem.

Their claim picks up on an oft-quoted Rabbinic maxim: "The seal of the Holy One, Blessed be He, is truth." In antiquity a seal or cylinder seal, typically pressed into wax to leave an impression, functioned as a mark of identity, like a signature today. God's primary identifying characteristic, in other words, is truth. As a divine and heavenly entity, like holiness, truth rightfully belongs with God, in God's celestial domain. In the end, either the angels or God beckon the Angel of Truth to rise up from the ground and return to heaven.

The story ends abruptly, with the Angel of Truth presumably on his journey home, precariously poised between earth and heaven. Perhaps that image captures the story's message. Truth functions as a link between the world of humans and the realm of the divine. Without a sufficient commitment to truth, when lies and deceit proliferate on earth, the connection to heaven weakens and society implodes. But neither can absolute truth comfortably dwell on earth among humankind, as humans cannot live up to its angelic and divine standard. Beyond the human propensity to sin, too much truth can prove corrosive to human relationships. Only among God and his angels can truth reign supreme.

9 Torah for Richer or Poorer

Study of Torah for the Rabbis was far and away the greatest religious value. As much as they valued charity, deeds of loving-kindness, prayer, and observing all the divine commandments (mitzvot), the Rabbis considered Torah study to be the essence of Judaism. Not only was Torah study the foundation of all other aspects of religious life, but the Rabbis viewed it as an activity that literally kept the universe going. Without Torah study to maintain it, all of existence would dissolve back into nothingness. Thus Torah study was very much a "universe-maintaining activity," to use the term scholars employ for the ritual acts that are believed by the faithful to sustain the cosmos. For this reason the Rabbis profess that "Torah study is equal to all of them"—to all the other commandments taken together.

However, in ancient times, just as now, excuses for avoiding Torah study were readily available. "I need to earn a living" or "I must work to support my family" were probably among the most popular and plausible justifications for neglecting the regular study of Torah. In pre-modern times the vast majority of the population eked out a living through subsistence farming and other such backbreaking work; it would seem harsh to fault poor laborers for failing to find the opportunity—or energy—to study. Yet the pressures today are no less intense. Depending upon one's profession, work weeks routinely may extend beyond forty hours to fifty, sixty, or even more. To earn enough to afford the necessities (or perceived necessities) of modern life—a suburban house, family vacations, private school and college tuitions, bar and bat mitzvah celebrations, music and sports lessons—and still to demand one find time and energy for Torah study seems equally unfair. Who has enough time for his or her spouse and children, or for his or her parents, let alone for him- or herself these days?

A common psychological strategy in these types of situations is "deferral"—to defer involvement in a worthy occupation until we have the time and opportunity: "I will cut back my hours at work when I have put away some savings," "I will read more when my workload lightens up," "I'll go on a diet when the holidays conclude," "I'll attend synagogue when my children are older." Here, too, a typical response begins: "I will study Torah when . . . ." But as we all know too well, this type of deferral, or procrastination, often stretches beyond the anticipated endpoint until . . . well . . . until we set another endpoint, which in turn is replaced by another and another. How many times do we find ourselves making the same New Year's resolution as last New Year? Thus the quip: "My New Year's resolution this year is, first, to carry out last year's resolution."

To gain perspective on difficult choices and trade-offs we make in our lives, contemporary preachers and spiritual leaders sometimes ask us to imagine the eulogies that will be delivered at our funeral. The point of view of death can provide perspective on life. Imagine: if you died today, would you be pleased with the eulogy that would likely be recited as your coffin stands before all those who gather to mourn you? Or would you wish for other words—words about what you had accomplished, those aspirations that up until now had lived in the realm of your hopes and intentions? Would you look back, your soul hovering about your coffin, satisfied at a life well lived or regretful that you had not found the time and opportunity for those enterprises?

In this talmudic passage, the Rabbinic storytellers adopt a similar strategy, depicting the soul standing before the heavenly court for judgment in the world to come. The court calls each individual to account for his or her commitment to that primary Rabbinic value—Torah study—asking very directly: "Why did you not busy yourself with Torah?" When various excuses are proffered, the court does not respond with rebuke, accusations of lies, or by adducing incriminating evidence, but with stories! Here we have an outstanding example of the didactic function of Rabbinic stories: even the heavenly court, presumably staffed by God's angelic retinue and perhaps presided over by the Holy One, endeavors to instruct a wayward soul by telling a story.

Our Rabbis taught: the poor man and the rich man will come for judgment in the next world.[1]

To the poor man they [the heavenly court] will say, "Why did you not busy yourself with Torah?" If he should say, "I was poor and was preoccupied with my sustenance," they will say to him, "Were you poorer than Hillel?"

It was said of Hillel the Elder that every single day he would work and earn one *tarpiq*. He would give half to the guard of the academy, and he would use half to support himself and the members of his household.

Once he was not able to earn [the money], and the guard of the academy would not allow him to enter. He climbed up and sat upon the aperture [in the roof] so that he could hear the words of the living God from the mouths of Shemayah and Avtalyon.

It was said that that day was the eve of the Sabbath, and it was the winter season, and snow fell upon him. When dawn broke

Shemayah said to Avtalyon, "Avtalyon, my brother. Each day this building is light, and today it is dark!" They looked about and saw the figure of a man in the aperture. They went up and found him covered with three cubits of snow. They extracted him and washed him and rubbed him with oil and sat him next to the fire. They said, "This one is worthy of having the Sabbath desecrated on his behalf."

(*Yoma* 35b)

Hillel eked out the barest of incomes. We do not know the manner of work, but presumably he was a day laborer or someone who did odd jobs, hiring himself out to whomever needed a hand that day, earning what we would call "minimum wage." From other sources we know that a *tarpiq* was a very modest sum of money, hardly enough to buy food for one day.

The story reveals the extent of Hillel's poverty. He splits his daily wages between the bare necessities for his family and the entrance fee for the academy, with nothing left over. As a result, when once he fails to earn that meager daily income, he has no savings to draw on, nothing set aside for this "rainy day," nothing even to tide him over until the morrow.

Living almost literally "day to day," hand to mouth, we might expect Hillel to forgo Torah study entirely, setting aside the "surplus" half of his daily wage to build a modest savings for emergencies, either those sporadic occasions when he could not earn a daily wage or even more serious crises. Who could blame him for deferring Torah study until such a time when he had stockpiled some funds to ensure that his family did not suffer from periodic interruptions to his earnings? Had financial planners been around in Hillel's time, I have no doubt they would have advised: "You need to start saving for difficult times, for a crisis, for your retirement. You must economize for the time being, cut out your Torah study expenses until you have some financial assets in the bank."

Apart from the concern for saving, Hillel would certainly have had other uses for the half-*tarpiq* at his daily disposal. He could have improved his family's circumstances by buying new clothes or shoes or even toys for his children. He could have amassed funding for a new piece of furniture or a home repair. If he aspired to use his money exclusively for religious purposes, he could have bought some delicacies for the Sabbath meal, or—after a period of time—candlesticks for his wife or a beautiful menorah to enhance their Hanukkah celebration.

Hillel does none of these things. Instead, every evening, following his hard day of work, he uses all his remaining money to pay the entrance fee to the academy so as to learn Torah from the great sages of his generation, Shemayah and Avtalyon. I picture Hillel watching as the overseer carefully counts out his pay and then, just as carefully, dividing the money, wrapping up half for his household and hustling to the academy and plunking down the other half as fast as he can for the guard . . . . Inside, finding his spot and joyously listening to the words of Torah uttered by the great Rabbinic masters . . . . A few hours later, departing, now walking somewhat slower, repeating with each step the Torah he has heard so as to commit it to his memory . . . .

He arrives home late in the evening, exhausted, famished, spent, but his face is beaming as if illuminated by an inner flame. Before sitting down to eat, he dutifully hands to his wife the half of his wages set aside for the next day's necessities. As he hungrily devours the meal she has prepared, Hillel relates to her the wonderful jewels of Torah he has absorbed that day, law and lore, biblical interpretation and story, logical inference and dialectical argument.

A Figure in the Aperture

Like many talmudic stories, this story of Hillel and the subsequent tale of Rabbi Elazar ben Ḥarsom (quoted below) are gapped, requiring us as readers to use our imaginations to fill in descriptive details that will make the stories more intelligible—and more entertaining. We should probably assume that when Rabbis taught the stories to their students in the academy or integrated them into sermons preached in the synagogue, they added a great deal of coloring, perhaps adapting the story to their time, place, or the situation at hand. Using this model, in this chapter I offer extensive creative retellings (rather than the literary analysis used in other chapters) of both stories as a means of fleshing out the stories' dynamics and didactic messages:

> One Friday Hillel cannot find employment. What to do? If, during optimal circumstances, when he earned his daily wage he could not be faulted for deferring Torah study until better times, how much more so now when he has no way to pay? Or is this an opportunity? A blessing in disguise? Unable to work despite his best efforts, he has the whole day free to study! With this one full day of learning he can equal the amount studied during the evenings of the whole of the previous week. Hillel will join the ranks of those pious sages who spend the entirety of each and every day engaged in the ultimate mitzvah of Torah study! With a mix of trepidation and hopefulness Hillel treks to the academy and entreats the guard to let him in: he is a regular patron, well-known to the sages inside; he typically pays the requisite fee, but today is an exception. Surely the guard knows that work has been scarce lately, that Hillel is no freeloader, no slacker; that he would gladly labor in any job were one available. Alas, the guard at the door is unmoved.

So close to the living words of Torah, Hillel can even hear through the door the distant buzz and hum of the Sages as they repeat their traditions, debate the law, argue a ruling, parse a biblical verse. He cannot bear the thought of retracing his steps with nothing to show for the day. As unfortunate as it was to have failed to find work, to have failed to find Torah is infinitely worse. And so, if he can practically hear the Sages from outside the front door, maybe there is a way . . . .

Hillel remembers a skylight of sorts near the far side of the academy. A hole in the roof had been covered by a crude, almost opaque slab of old Roman glass. When the sun shines brightly, it provides much-needed illumination for the aging eyes of the senior Sages; from time to time they have even competed for those precious seats on the benches beneath the glass.

Shuffling away from the guard, Hillel circles around to the back. He spies the aperture, not far from the roof's edge. How to climb up? He sees a large pile of firewood stacked along the back wall. By moving some of the log bundles around to form a makeshift series of steps, he just manages to reach the roof edge and haul himself up. Success! Now with his ear to the aperture, Hillel is able to listen to the words of Torah from the shadowy figures below.

The hours pass. Day becomes twilight. As the sun sets, the cold night of the winter season takes hold. Hillel hardly feels the temperature dropping, warmed as he is by a numinous, inner flame. Typically after work he can stay at the academy for at most an hour or two, but here he has been listening the entire day! Never before has he experienced such a sustained, continuous flow of words of Torah!

He knows that soon it will be the Sabbath, that his family expects him, that the learning must soon end as the Sages depart for their Sabbath meals. More than once he gathers himself to leave, but each time he tarries just a little longer, first drawn in by a brilliant insight, then by a riveting argument, again by a new tradition. At last he dozes off.

The next day, the Sages and students of the academy awake to a brisk and chilly Sabbath morning. It has snowed throughout the night, a rare event, though the sun shines now, slowly melting the slight accumulation on the ground. The Rabbis and their disciples take their usual seats in the academy. Stamping their feet to shake off the slush, rubbing their hands together for warmth, they begin the Sabbath prayers. But something is different, something slightly amiss. "Avtalyon, my brother," says Shemayah, one of the two leaders, "Each day this building is light, and today it is dark!" They gaze toward the aperture in the roof. Could it be? Even through the crude glass they discern the figure of a man, his dark clothes contrasting with the snow that covers him. Alive? Dead? Somewhere in between?

Shemayah and Avtalyon raise the alarm. Their students rush out to the back, find the improvised stairs, ascend to the roof, frantically dig through the snow, haul out the man, pass him back down again, and carry him into the academy. Someone detects a faint pulse—the man is still alive. Quickly they wash off the caked ice and snow, rub him with oil to restore his circulation, and seat him next to the fire. At this point many recognize Hillel—he is the fellow who faithfully shows up day after day in the early evening, who sits quietly at the back of the academy, who always appears to be enraptured by the discussions of Torah even if he seldom participates. Slowly the story is pieced together: the guard turned him away as he had no money for the fee; he clambered to the roof to listen, stayed the entire day, fell asleep, and almost froze to death. All this out of dedication to the mitzvah of Torah study!

Shemayah and Avtalyon turn to their students and say, "The preservation of human life takes precedence over the Sabbath and over almost all of the commandments, as you know. But it is specifically one such as this, a man who surmounts every obstacle to study the life-giving words of Torah, a man who risks his life for the sake of Torah, who is truly worthy of having the Sabbath desecrated for his sake."

An Embarrassment of Riches

The rich man's excuse for neglecting Torah study would seem to be much less compelling than that of the poor man. Not having to worry about providing for his family, perhaps not even having to work at all—what could possibly stand in the way of study? Indeed, it would seem that the richer the individual, the weaker the excuse.

Yet in practice, the richest tycoons routinely plead that their immense wealth entails the burden of unceasing responsibilities that leave them no time for study. So the heavenly court recounts to them the story of Rabbi Elazar ben Ḥarsom.

To the rich man they [the heavenly court] will say, "Why did you not busy yourself with Torah?" If he should say, "I was rich and was preoccupied with my possessions," they will say to him, "Were you richer than Rabbi Elazar ben Ḥarsom?"

It was said of Rabbi Elazar ben Ḥarsom that his father left him one thousand cities on land and one thousand ships in the sea. But he never went to see them. Rather, the whole day and the whole night he would sit and busy himself with Torah. Each day he would put his daily bread upon his shoulder, and he would go from city to city and from region to region to learn Torah.

Once his servants happened upon him and imposed forced
service upon him. He said to them, "Please leave me be." They
said to him, "By the life of Elazar ben Ḥarsom we will not leave
you be." And he did not wish to reveal to them that he was
their master.

(*Yoma* 35b)

Continuing my retelling:

Few could match the riches of Rabbi Elazar ben Ḥarsom, scion
of one of Judea's wealthiest families, heir to a real estate fortune—a massive international conglomerate of properties span-
ning the length and breadth of the Roman Empire—and a ship-
ping empire to match. No one was sure just how vast Ḥarsom
Industries was, though it often was said that the corporation
encompassed one thousand cities and one thousand ships. The
elder Ḥarsom had built the business from nothing through
hard work and good luck, and he gave thanks to God daily for
his good fortune. More than once he had seen the divine hand
at work behind his deals, as risky ventures upon which he had
gambled paid off handsomely time and again.

His one disappointment was his son, Rabbi Elazar, who dis-
played little interest in the corporation and, truth be told, even
less of an instinct for business. However much Ḥarsom tried to
teach his son the trade, to groom him to assume leadership of
the empire he had built, Rabbi Elazar never seemed to learn.
When it came to buying and selling, "hondeling" and haggling,
posturing and bluffing, he was clueless. He spent more of his
time hanging around the house of study, listening to the Rabbis'
lectures that his father supported with his hard-earned profits
and babbling about the new interpretations he had heard. In

fact Ḥarsom wasn't sure that his son was any better a student of Torah than a student of business. His persistent dedication to that spiritual life nonetheless could not be denied, and Elazar eventually earned the honorific title "Rabbi"—though Ḥarsom always suspected there had been more charity and politics than merit behind this accolade.

When Ḥarsom died suddenly at a relatively young age, Rabbi Elazar prematurely inherited his father's business operation. Surprisingly, he rose to the occasion. Even his detractors and skeptics conceded that he coped far beyond their expectations. If the business did not grow, it did not fall apart, despite the fact that Rabbi Elazar managed the holdings from his office in the village and never came on site. Profits steadily rolled in. The employees were satisfied. New challenges were successfully navigated. Crises were avoided. Those not intimately involved in core company operations hardly noticed any transition in upper management.

As the years passed, Rabbi Elazar ben Ḥarsom found that his corporate success brought him little satisfaction or happiness. His responsibilities were endless. Each day dozens if not hundreds of reports flooded in as his managers submitted records, requisitions, sales figures, and other data. Countless decisions had to be made. Hundreds of problems confronted him. A waiting list of business owners, suppliers, and entrepreneurs sought a piece of the action. Between meetings, letters, and interviews, Rabbi Elazar ben Ḥarsom rarely had time to sleep and eat, much less to spend time with his wife and kids. Torah study hardly figured on his "to do" list. At least twenty times a day he would wistfully look out the window toward the local study house, recalling the texts he had studied, the Sages' discussions, the beautiful interpretations. More than once he had attempted to block out a few hours to attend a study session . . . but something urgent always came up.

In the face of such pressures Rabbi Elazar ben Ḥarsom found a radical solution—he fled! Eschewing the costly clothes of his position—his secretary bought him only the finest and priciest fashions—he donned the ordinary tunic of one of his household servants and, late one night, slipped out into the darkness. The black of night made the going slow, but before dawn he had covered enough miles to arrive at a nearby town. Rabbi Elazar ben Ḥarsom knew he should continue on so as to increase the distance from home—news traveled slowly in antiquity, but not all that slowly, and news of the disappearance of one of the richest men in the country would move quickly. But he could not help himself. Free at last, after a quick breakfast he slipped into the local study house, took the most unobtrusive seat in the shadows in the back, and blissfully listened to the words of Torah flowing forth from the Sages. He was transported to another world. The hours raced by, and before he knew it, night had descended.

It had taken just one day, but Rabbi Elazar ben Ḥarsom knew then and there what he must do. He could not go back to his former life. Nor could he remain close to his hometown, as he would inevitably be discovered, exposed, and dragged back to his duties. So he acquired the garments and accoutrements of an itinerant grain peddler: old trousers, a waterskin, a hard loaf of bread, a worn sack for his shoulder. He let his beard and hair grow long and thick. He wandered from town to town and village to village, studying Torah wherever he went. He stayed for a few days in one place, a week in another: always long enough to learn the novel interpretations and creative traditions of that study house, but never so long that the locals would ask too many questions or someone become suspicious. After a few months he could barely remember the details of his business—the cities and ships, the shops and supply lines, the debtors and creditors. Or had he consciously made an effort to forget all this? Perhaps the Torah he learned each day had crowded out his former memories?

One spring day Rabbi Elazar ben Ḥarsom was walking spirit-
edly toward his next destination, a town a few miles distant,
reputed to have a small but eminent school. As he approached
the outskirts he smiled at the familiar hubbub of activity ever
present at the entrance to the main thoroughfare: drivers with
their mules laden with wares, fruit and vegetable dealers hawk-
ing their produce, day-laborers seeking work, fortune-tellers
advertising their trade, amulet writers, beggars of all sorts and
sizes. About to pass into the town proper, he heard a gruff voice
calling from the side: "Hey, you there. Come over here." Star-
tled, Rabbi Elazar ben Ḥarsom stopped in his tracks and turned
in the direction of the voice. A stocky, muscular man with a
wax writing board in his hand, standing under a palm tree a
few yards away from the road, was staring straight at him.
"Yeah, you. Get over here," the man commanded. When Rabbi
Elazar ben Ḥarsom approached, the man continued: "What is
your business here?" "I am a wandering student of Torah," said
Rabbi Elazar ben Ḥarsom. "I have come to spend a few days in
the study house in this place. I will be no trouble." The man
smirked. "Wonderful. But you'll have to delay your studies for
a week. I am conscripting you for the *angarya* [forced service]
to repair the road over yonder. It has needed work for years,
and the winter rains did a lot of damage. You'll be on my crew
for a week or so."

Rabbi Elazar ben Ḥarsom could not believe his bad luck. The
angarya was part of the oppressive array of Roman taxes. The
"wicked kingdom" afflicted its subject peoples in every way
imaginable: billeting soldiers and officials in their homes; tram-
pling fields; confiscating crops; taxing produce, herds, flocks, and
all commercial activity. Roman officials routinely conscripted
locals for "forced service," commandeering their mules and pack
animals to move Roman supplies; coercing blacksmiths, carpen-

ters, and other artisans for their building projects; and forming corvées of unskilled laborers to work on roads, bridges, walls, and ditches. This "temporary slavery" could strike almost anyone at almost any time. And the Rabbi had unwittingly walked straight into this ambush.

"Please let me be," pleaded Rabbi Elazar ben Ḥarsom. "I am a student of Torah, come to study in the town's study hall." The overseer laughed derisively. "By the life of Elazar ben Ḥarsom we will not leave you be! Torah students are just about last on the list of exempted professions. Can't say we are taking you away from your fields or vineyards or other productive activity now, can we? You'll probably be last off the detail at week's end. Next time make up some other line of work, not that I wouldn't have figured out the truth. Men like me . . . ."

Shocked at the mention of his name, Rabbi Elazar ben Ḥarsom hardly heard the rest of this speech. What was going on? The man didn't seem to recognize him, and he hadn't told the man his name. How on earth could this overseer invoke his name—and apparently to justify his conscription? "Elazar . . . son of . . . Ḥarsom . . . ?" he stuttered, uncomprehendingly. "Yes, you dolt," interrupted the other, "Ḥarsom Industries contracted with the Romans to fix this road. They manage most of the building projects around here. So they have imperial authority for the job—conscriptions, requisitions, corvées—you name it. The rich bloke who owns the whole thing is Elazar ben Ḥarsom. He's the only son of the founder, I believe. Got a finger in every pie. By his life I swear you will work until we're done."

Aha! Rabbi Elazar ben Ḥarsom came to his senses. Arrangements of this type had crossed his desk. Apparently his father had engineered this innovative idea—a "project farming" he'd called it. Like the tax farmer who purchased from the Romans the right to collect taxes from a given region in exchange for a large lump sum up front, Ḥarsom had subcontracted with the Roman masters to construct and repair their infrastructure. Armed with the authority to conscript and requisition at will, the work went quickly and the profits rolled in. Ironically, Rabbi Elazar ben Ḥarsom's employees had inadvertently conscripted their employer; he was "hoist by his own petard."

What could he do? There was no chance this functionary would believe he was a Rabbi. In any case revealing his identity would blow his cover. He'd be dragged back into the business, and that would be the end of his study of Torah for good.

So reluctantly Rabbi Elazar ben Ḥarsom accepted his fate. He sat down quietly alongside the other miserable wretches snatched in the same way. And once a few others had been seized to make up the full complement, all day long he toiled as part of the group. Pick and shovel in hand, he cleared the debris and damaged stones of the old road and hauled the new gravel into place.

Rabbi Elazar ben Ḥarsom found that he did not mind the physical labor all that much—there was something refreshing about exercising his body. But with each passing minute he grew increasingly frustrated about the time he was wasting that could have been spent studying Torah. "Wasted time," *bittul zeman*, the Sages called it—time spent in almost any occupation other than Torah study. After three days the Rabbi was almost frantic with anxiety.

Six days later Rabbi Elazar ben Ḥarsom was released. He made straight for the house of study, pulled up a bench, closed his eyes, and blissfully listened to the words of Torah circulating all about him. He was home.

And for the rest of his days Rabbi Elazar ben Ḥarsom went from village to village, from study house to study house, never again seeing his one thousand cities and one thousand ships.[2]

When the Rich Do Not See

Hillel and Rabbi Elazar ben Ḥarsom constitute two ends of the spectrum: extreme poverty and extreme wealth. Neither the one nor the other—and, by extension, any point in between—provides a valid reason for neglecting Torah study. Therefore, the stories teach us, the time to dedicate ourselves to Torah study is right now, hopefully many years before we stand before the judge of the heavenly court.

Yet there is more to these stories. Why, for example is there a guard at the house of study who won't admit poor students without payment? On whose authority does he turn them away? Only one other Rabbinic source mentions such a guard, and that source says nothing about the guard collecting an entrance fee. This probably reflects an elitist and aristocratic perspective, namely that Torah study should be limited to a wealthy and scholarly elite, and not extended to the common people. The guard functions as a gatekeeper who denies those who do not meet these standards the opportunity to study Torah. And functionally, without the guard, there is no story, as nothing would have prevented Hillel from entering the academy. The guard's rebuff propels Hillel up to the roof, and that poignant image stays with us as we absorb the lesson that poverty does not provide sufficient excuse for those truly dedicated to Torah study.

What then does the rest of the story add? Why not end with the image of Hillel lying prone, straining to hear the discussions of Torah below?

To a certain extent the snow and the cold weather magnify Hillel's heroism. Harsh conditions fail to deter him, and we picture him not only with his ear pressed to the skylight but with teeth chattering and frozen extremities too. Yet even without this additional dramatic coloring, the audience can appreciate the moral.

The second half of the story can be seen as criticism of the Rabbis in the academy (and perhaps was added to the original story at a later time by another storyteller).[3] Shemayah and Avtalyon, the leading Sages, notice the darkened room and the figure blocking their light, but they have not noticed the poor students struggling to pay the admission fee each day. They evidently did not realize that the guard—their guard?—turned away those who lacked funds. Either they put the guard in place themselves or did not object to whatever authority instituted this arrangement. In any event the Rabbis have not made Torah fully accessible to the regular folk, which should be their responsibility as communal leaders and spiritual exemplars. Another metaphor: inside the academy the (wealthier?) Sages warm themselves around a blazing fire, oblivious to their poorer brethren (shivering?) without.

The story of Rabbi Elazar ben Ḥarsom also harbors an internal tension. The first half of the story elegantly illustrates how the richest of men refuses to be trapped by his own wealth; he runs away from all his possessions to be free to study Torah. In the second half, though, this solution does not work, due to the ironic seizure by Rabbi Elazar ben Ḥarsom's own agents.

Through this elaborate construct, the storyteller thus further illuminates the theme of the dangers of affluence. Not only does great wealth inevitably entail demands and responsibilities that encroach on time available for Torah study, but such demands contain unforeseen traps and snares that will afflict even those with the best intentions. (Think today of charity dinners; expectations to serve on boards of synagogues, federations, and other communal institutions; fundraisers pleading to be given a hearing; solicitation by politicians, etc.)

In this way, the second half of the story also levels criticism against the wealthy, even against those aristocrats committed to Torah study. For how many years did Rabbi Elazar ben Ḥarsom (along with his father, their managers, overseers, and partners) conscript poorer folk for his business enterprises, probably preventing many of them from studying Torah themselves? Until Rabbi Elazar ben Ḥarsom fell into that very snare—a snare of his own making—he was oblivious to how his commercial empire affected those with less affluence, power, or privilege.

The Costs of Piety

These texts, then, are deceptively complex, combining profound lessons concerning the nonnegotiable importance of Torah study with subtle criticism of both Rabbinic and aristocratic social elites.

The lack of excuse for neglecting study is an eternally relevant message, though particularly apposite these days with our increasingly demanding professions. Email and texting on mobile phones means the office is always present. Organizing our children's lives with their myriad afterschool activities, clubs, and sports sometimes feels like a second work week in and of itself.[4] The typical predicament today is probably more akin to that of Rabbi Elazar ben Ḥarsom than Hillel, as the demands and pressures of material success squeeze out the time available for study.

In some respects the social criticism in the Hillel story—the Sages consciously or inadvertently standing in the way of the people's Torah study—is not as pressing for us today. Contemporary rabbis and Jewish institutions have become so alarmed about the dearth of knowledge of Torah and Judaism, especially in the Diaspora, that they provide opportunities for Torah study at little or no cost. Many resources also are available on the internet, such that one could hardly claim that the doors to the study house have been shut in one's face. At the same time, though, some Jewish institutions are prohibitively expensive for many people today. Synagogue memberships, sometimes required for High Holiday seats, can cost several thousand dollars per year. Membership at Jewish community centers likewise typically runs into the thousands. Kosher chicken and beef typically cost 50 percent to 200 percent more than their nonkosher equivalents, and a portion of the sales is disbursed to the organizations providing kosher certification.[5] Jewish day schools have become so expensive that some financial aid forms ask about the financial resources of grandparents. Thus there is truth in the hackneyed joke that the cost of Jewish education is the most effective form of birth control.[6] Many an article has argued that leading an observant Jewish life is beyond the means of the middle class.[7]

Who should be called to account for this situation? Unfortunately we find many guards at the doors of Jewish establishments preventing modern-day Hillels and their children from entering. The Rabbi Elazar ben Ḥarsom storyteller would cast blame on the wealthy members of the Jewish community—whether or not they study Torah—for not sufficiently subsidizing Jewish institutions so that Torah study is available to all who wish to enter them. After all, even an indigent laborer like Hillel could eventually become a great Rabbi whose teachings would bring inspiration to many generations.

The two stories challenge us as readers to surmount whatever personal difficulties we confront so as to lead lives more committed to tradition. When the heavenly court asks each of us whether we have done so, what will our answer be?

10 Heroism and Humor

Rabbinic Judaism has often been called a "this-worldly" religion on account of its focus on piety, devotion, and righteous action in the here and now. The Rabbinic values of marriage, raising a family, and building a community indicate an interest in the structures of the present time that differ from the single-mindedness with which some religions direct energies to earning rewards and avoiding punishments in the next world. Rabbinic sources have relatively little to say about the specific nature of the world to come, offering us few visions of the heavenly delights the righteous can expect or the cruel tortures in store for the wicked. Even the existence of hell is not completely clear: some talmudic sources refer to *Gehinnom*, a type of hell or purgatory in which sinners receive posthumous punishment before being admitted to the world to come, while other passages give the impression that sinners are simply consigned to oblivion after their deaths and thus miss out on heavenly bliss.

At the same time Rabbis of the talmudic period absolutely believed that the world to come existed and served as the arena in which true rewards and punishments materialized. In fact, expectation of a "share in the world to come" never receded too deeply below the surface of Rabbinic religious consciousness. As expressed by one Rabbinic adage: "There is no reward for fulfilling the commandments in this world"— only in the next (*Qiddushin* 39b). The suffering of the righteous and prospering of the wicked in this life would thus be reversed in the eternal world to come (as discussed briefly in chapter 5).

This tenet of faith naturally raises questions: how righteous must one be to earn heavenly rewards? How difficult is it to earn a share in the world to come? Who qualifies as a truly righteous individual? The following story provides one Rabbinic perspective on this important issue:

Rabbi Baroqa of Ḥuzestan was standing in the market of Beit Lapat. Elijah the Prophet came and appeared to him. Rabbi Baroqa said to him, "Is there anyone in this market who will enter the world to come?" Elijah said to him, "No one."

Meanwhile he saw a certain man come by wearing black shoes and not wearing a blue thread [in the fringes] of his cloak. Elijah said, "This one will enter the world to come."

Rabbi Baroqa ran after him. He said, "What is your occupation?" The man said, "Go away today, and come back tomorrow."

On the morrow, Rabbi Baroqa said to him, "What is your occupation?" He said to him, "I am a jailer, and I confine men by themselves and women by themselves, and I place my bed between the men and the women so that they do not sin.

"When I see a Jewish girl whom the gentiles have set their eyes upon, I risk my life to save her.

"Once there was a betrothed maiden with us whom the gentiles set their eyes upon to assault. I took dregs of wine and scattered them on the bottom of her skirt, and I said to them, 'See, she is menstruating.'"

Rabbi Baroqa said to him, "Why do you not have a [blue] thread [in your fringes] and wear black shoes?" He said to him, "I go in and out among the gentiles such that they do not know that I am a Jew. When they decree a persecution, I inform the Sages, and they pray and annul the decree."

"What is the reason when I said to you, 'What are your deeds?' you said 'Go away today and come back tomorrow?'"

He said to him, "Just then they decreed a persecution. So I thought, 'First let me go and inform the Sages in order that they pray and annul the edict.'"

Meanwhile, two brothers passed by. Elijah said, "They too will enter the next world."

Rabbi Baroqa went to them and said, "What are your deeds?" They said, "We are jesters. We make jokes for those who are unhappy. Also, when we see two who have a quarrel between them, we exert ourselves and make peace."

(*Ta'anit* 22a)

Rabbi Baroqa, like several other talmudic Rabbis, enjoys special intimacy with Elijah the Prophet. He wishes to know if righteous individuals can be found in the marketplace of Beit Lapat, evidently an area known for vice and depravity. Elijah points him to a certain character dressed in gentile garb and without the blue thread on the fringes of his shawl that both marks him as a Jew and attests to his piety. Rabbi Baroqa tries to interview the man but is deferred until the next day. On the morrow he learns that the man, contrary to appearances, is not only a Jew, but a heroic one at that. Employed by the government as a jailer, he prevents male and female prisoners from engaging in immoral sexuality by separating the sexes on each side of the cell and setting his bed between the two. In this way he will bar any man or woman who tries to cross the median to commit adultery, harlotry, rape, or other nonmarital sex.

Moreover, this anonymous jailer goes out of his way to save Jewish women from sexual assault. The separation of sexes and intervening bed cannot guarantee that an attractive Jewish woman will not be victimized when the gentiles "set their eyes upon" her, a talmudic idiom for illicit desire. A physical confrontation, however, may require our pious warden to blow his cover as a Jew, or he, too, will be overwhelmed by the dissolute inmates, and so he resorts to yet another ruse: sprinkling the bottom hem of her skirt with red wine dregs and pointing out to the male prisoners that she is in a state of menstrual impurity. Zoroastrianism, the dominant religion in Persia, like Judaism, has a complex system of ritual impurity that includes menstruation, so this tactic will work on Jews and Persian gentiles alike (and perhaps upon other men who are simply "turned off" by such bloodstains).

The gentile disguise, the jailer explains to the Rabbi, enables him to save not only an occasional Jewish maiden but the entire Jewish community. His clothing allows him to go about the gentiles undetected. Perhaps he drinks with them in taverns or strikes up chats in the marketplace. In one way or another, by masquerading as a gentile, he learns about plans to institute persecutions against Jews and quickly informs the Rabbis, who in turn pray for divine assistance. Indeed, the jailer means no disrespect by brusquely deferring Rabbi Baroqa's initial question until the following day—he is just rushing to apprise the Sages of a new threat.

Elijah now interrupts the conversation to identify two other men destined for the world to come, and Rabbi Baroqa turns his attention to them. They are jesters—entertainers or comedians—who cheer people up and make peace when friends or acquaintances quarrel. These ordinary, unexceptional gestures would seem to pale in comparison to the heroic and risky deeds of the jailer. Yet such acts, Elijah's testimony assures us, are so holy that they, too, secure entry to the next world.

A Rabbi Went to Market

With brief strokes the storyteller takes us far from the center of Rabbinic society to the domain of the "Other." Rabbi Baroqa is not mentioned elsewhere in the Talmud, so despite being identified as a Rabbi, he stands out as somewhat of an alien figure. He is not from the main area of Rabbinic settlement, but far south of it, as he hails from Ḥuzestan, one of the more important provinces of the Persian Empire in talmudic times. Beit Lapat, the capital of Ḥuzestan, served as the summer capital of the Persian emperor and his court, and therefore signifies the power of the authorities and the domain of the gentiles.

Markets in antiquity were the quintessential public spaces, the areas where peoples of all sorts mixed and interacted with minimal supervision. As such, the marketplace represents both danger and licentiousness. The Mishnah rules that a wife who spins thread in the market, thereby participating in this precarious cosmopolitan culture, violates "the custom of Jewish women" and can be divorced without payment of her marriage settlement (*Mishnah Ketubot* 7:6). In the Mishnah's view, to "expose" oneself in such an open and public space violates the norms of modesty expected of pious Jewish women. Similarly, the Talmud has some reservations about whether Torah study should ever be conducted in the market, noting that "Once, Rabbi Yehudah ha-Nasi decreed that they should not teach disciples in the marketplace" (*Mo'ed Qatan* 16a–b). The "market of Beit Lapat" thus constitutes the polar opposite of both the pious Rabbinic house of study and the private home.

Against this background, Rabbi Baroqa asks a particularly apposite question: is there anyone in this market sufficiently righteous to receive posthumous reward in heaven? In other words, do those who spend time in the market, or those whose occupations require them to work in such places, thereby lose any hope for a share in the world to come? How exclusive are Rabbinic expectations of otherworldly salvation?

Normally this type of question would be a matter of speculation, as those who have access to the world to come typically cannot return to our land of the living to report back. Even the greatest religious authority's pronouncement on this matter may be treated with a degree of skepticism ("I'll believe it when I see it myself . . . ."). Our Rabbinic storytellers, however, have a technique to overcome this obstacle.

Enter Elijah the Prophet. The Elijah of the Talmud differs a great deal from Elijah of the Bible, who appears to be a typical prophet, though perhaps with a penchant for colorful miracles. The talmudic Elijah is more of an angelic figure, passing time with God and the angels in their heavenly abode but also returning periodically to earth on various divine errands. Unlike the angels, however, whom God also dispatches to earth on occasion, Elijah functions more as a mediator between the Rabbis and God, often conveying to the Rabbis God's reaction to their dealings and to other terrestrial events. In this respect Elijah retains his prophetic function, as biblical prophets function primarily to disclose the divine will and often divine reactions—especially disapproval—of human behavior. Yet the talmudic Elijah, by shuttling back and forth to heaven, brings eyewitness testimony of God's heavenly activities. This peripatetic Elijah will later play an important role in Jewish liturgy, attending Passover sedarim, where a special cup is set aside for him, and circumcisions, where the special chair is designated the "Seat of Elijah the Prophet." The Talmud also reports that Elijah frequently accompanies particularly holy Sages in their day-to-day lives, thus providing them with immediate access to privileged divine information.

Here Elijah appears to Rabbi Baroqa, whose lack of surprise suggests that such visits are not rare or unexpected. The Rabbi seizes the opportunity to inquire as to the posthumous prospects of the market folks, obviating the difficulty noted above of the veracity of such information. Presumably the market of Beit Lapat, the summer capital of the Persian emperor, must be a vast and bustling area, crowded with hundreds or thousands of people. Nevertheless Elijah—and Elijah would know!—at first confirms the audience's suspicions that anyone who spends his or her day in the market must be involved in some desultory occupation and cannot, almost by definition, rank among the righteous. This answer gives the impression that gaining entry to heaven is extremely difficult, as not one of the multitude of folks in the market makes the cut. However, while still conversing Elijah identifies someone who has suddenly entered the public thoroughfare as a future denizen of the world to come. Surprisingly to the Rabbi, the man's dress marks him as a gentile. The black shoes characterize gentile dress, while the lack of blue thread in his fringes likewise suggests that he cannot be a Jew, or at least not a pious one. Numbers 15:38, part of the *Shema* prayer, requires Jews to wear a blue thread in the corners of their garments, and both the storyteller and the Rabbi appear to assume that no good Jew would fail to observe this precept. Notably, the fact that the man is a gentile would not in and of itself disqualify him from entry to heaven. Rabbinic theology has a mixed view of gentiles, but many Rabbis believed that righteous gentiles would receive a share in the next world.

This man, however, seems to brush off the Rabbi's question and hustle away, indicating a lack of respect for Rabbis and an uncouth demeanor—and certainly not furnishing evidence as to why he counts among those particularly righteous individuals. Thus the storyteller begins with an enigma: a clash between superficial appearance and the inner truth as revealed by Elijah, which Rabbi Baroqa, together with the audience, must puzzle out.

The next day we learn that little in the story is as it first seemed. Appearances were deceiving; the man is indeed both Jewish and righteous. The man's non-Jewish dress does not indicate that he has adopted the ways of the gentiles and abandoned his people, but rather that he can discover the ways of the gentiles so as to save his people. Far from initially avoiding or rebuffing this Rabbi or Rabbis in general, the man was in fact rushing to the Rabbis to convey crucial information.

Then, as now, the profession of jailer was typically associated with cruelty and complicity with the rulers, and prison guards were notorious for abusing prisoners, especially females, under their authority. When the man begins, "I am a jailer," the Rabbi (and audience) may well think of him along these lines. Yet this jailer acts in the complete opposite way, scrupulously preventing abuses of those in his charge while subversively thwarting the intentions of the gentile magistrates.

This contrast between appearance and reality also features in the deception whereby he saves the betrothed maiden, as the assailants, prompted by our hero, incorrectly interpret the red wine stains on her skirt as menstrual blood. Thus the storyteller fashions a parallel between the man's two saving acts. In both cases the perpetrators fail to carry out their plans because they cannot see through the appearance of things: the gentile authorities mistake this man for a gentile and disclose the planned persecution of Jews, while the potential assailants of a Jewish maiden cease their actions because they mistake red wine blotches for blood.

This story is unusual in its vivid mention of colors—the black shoes, the (lack of) blue fringes, the red on the dress. Yet not one of these colors correctly signifies what it should: the black shoes and lack of blue thread do not reliably identify the man as a gentile, and the red stains are not trustworthy signs of blood. So, too, the audience should understand: we will inevitably make mistakes in assessing human beings' true character unless we penetrate beyond externals to deeper truths.

Vision accordingly looms large in the story. At the outset, Rabbi Baroqa "saw" a certain man in gentile dress. Later the jailer relates that he risks his life when he "sees" a maiden whom the gentiles have "set their eyes upon" for sexual assault. The two jesters also act when they "see" a quarrel break out. An even more subtle allusion to the importance of sight may appear in the symbolism of the absent blue thread. The Bible explains the function of the thread and the fringes: "*Look* at it and recall all the commandments of the Lord and observe them, so that you do not follow your heart and eyes in your lustful urge" (Num. 15:39). While the blue thread and fringes clearly serve as reminders of the commandments in general and as restraint against all sins, the verse specifies the danger of "eyes" that lead to "lustful urges," suggesting sexual transgressions in particular. The King James Bible captures this nuance nicely by translating: "that ye seek not after your own heart and your own eyes, after which ye use to go a-whoring." Picking up on this cue, another talmudic story relates that the fringes of a potential sinner's garment miraculously prevented him from consorting with a whore (*Menaḥot* 44a). This biblical idiom has parallels in the story's expression of lust, that the men "set their eyes" upon the woman. Despite the lack of a blue thread, the jailer "sees" the lustful urges of others and foils the intended sexual sins. That he accomplishes the blue thread's purpose without in fact seeing it rehearses the story's lesson that we not value sight too highly.

The man's vocation as jailer points to a second theme of the story: boundaries. As prison warden, he enforces the boundary between criminals and the rest of society. In addition, he enacts new boundaries: segregating the sexes by placing his bed and body between them and separating the betrothed Jewish maiden from would-be oppressors. Conversely, by religiously cross-dressing he violates the boundary between Jews and gentiles that distinctive clothing otherwise establishes—a necessary transgression to uphold the survival of his people. The story's fundamental question also concerns crossing a boundary, probably the most important boundary of all: who will cross over from this world into the next? By identifying the cross-dressing, boundary-violating Jewish jailer among those privileged to "enter" that world, the answer to the question becomes exceedingly complex. Even someone who looks like an ordinary gentile may be a disguised holy man.

For this reason the storyteller reverses the direction of the normal back-and-forth between Rabbis and laity. Typically the layman asks questions and the Rabbi, the master of Torah, provides the answers. In our story, however, Rabbi Baroqa asks four questions of the jailer and one question of the brother-jesters, and these non-Rabbis respond. Add the initial question to Elijah and the Rabbi ends up asking a total of six questions while offering not one reply. On this difficult issue of posthumous reward, the storyteller informs us, Rabbis do not have all the answers. They, too, cannot always rely on what they see to assess the righteousness of others.

The concluding interchange with the jesters offers a variation of this didactic point. These two brothers cannot point to any heroic acts to their credit like the jailer's. Their merits seem to fall short even of those we might expect of exemplary lay Jews—such as taking care of orphans, visiting the sick, or other charitable activities. In their case, too, the challenge to the reader is to see beyond the surface. One might think that such clowns devote themselves to frivolous activities, or at least trivial pursuits of little worth: providing "light" entertainment for those with time on their hands to enjoy distractions. Rabbis, on the other hand, dedicate their lives to the serious business of Torah study, while other virtuous individuals, like the jailer, scurry about saving lives and preventing sin. How high on the scale of merit does comedy rank when the gentile authorities can decree a persecution at any moment?

As the storyteller relays to us, this superficial view of matters fails to appreciate the true worth of the brothers' deeds. To relieve another person of sadness or depression, if only for a short time, counts for a great deal. So, too, the importance of making peace between those who quarrel, of restoring bonds of friendship, cannot be underestimated.

The two examples of righteous human beings thus describe two different types of peacemaking. While the jailer works at keeping the peace between Jews and gentiles by foiling the persecution of Jews and protecting a betrothed Jewish maiden, the jesters seek to restore the peace among quarreling Jews.[1] Whereas the jailer endeavors to prevent physical or sexual persecution, the brothers strive to assuage emotional harm or melancholy. The storyteller invites us to equate the merit of the two parties, as Elijah identifies both for heavenly reward.

To gain entry to the world to come, it turns out, requires neither great acts of religious devotion nor heroic deeds of self-sacrifice. Certain sensitivity to the emotional states of others or "exertion" to help heal rifts between one's fellow human beings suffices.

Lacking Elijah's supernatural knowledge of the heavenly prospects of all human beings, the storyteller implies that we would do well to give others the benefit of the doubt in this regard. Who knows whether the people before us, despite some indications to the contrary (the wrong clothes, or shoes, or etiquette), have carried out courageous exploits to save other people's lives or dignity, resolved long-standing quarrels, or brightened the lives of the downtrodden? From this vantage point, who among us is not a potential inhabitant of the world to come?

Talmudic Humor

The Talmud's high esteem for jesters (*badḥanim*) and their humor is noteworthy. Many religions frown on humor, or at least see comedy or laughter as incompatible with the weighty matters of service to God and religious devotion. Early Christian thinkers often expressed such sentiments. As one literary scholar put it: "Early Christianity had already condemned laughter. . . . John Chrysostom declared that jests and laughter are not from God but from the devil."[2]

Chrysostom, known for his brilliant preaching (the sobriquet *chrysostom* means "golden-mouthed" in Greek), lived in the fourth century CE, and was therefore a contemporary of many talmudic Rabbis. Gregory of Nyssa, an important theologian who also lived in the fourth century CE, claimed, "Laughter is our enemy because it is neither a word nor an action ordered to any possible goal."[3] The early rule books for monks forbade laughter, and Basil of Caesarea (330–379) required that "anyone in the monastery who inclines to jocularity should be banished for a week."[4] Although humor was commonplace in Greco-Roman culture, and the comedies of Aristophanes still count among the classics of Western tradition, some leading philosophers frowned upon excessive laughter. Epictetus, an important Stoic philosopher, cautioned: "Your laughter should not be loud, frequent, or unrestrained."[5] Islam, too, has tended toward a negative view of humor. A tradition (*hadith*) ascribed to Mohammed's wife Aisha reports: "The Prophet was never seen laughing until his uvula was revealed."[6] That jokes often include untruths is particularly problematic, as another Islamic tradition cautions: "A man may say something to make his companions laugh, and he will fall into Hell as far as the Pleiades because of it."[7]

Theologians and philosophers particularly objected to humor that targeted individuals, and thus served to embarrass, mock, scorn, or ridicule someone else. Humor of this sort was understood as a cause of humiliation and inducement to retaliation, leading to strife. Plato accordingly writes of his utopian Republic: "A comic poet, or maker of iambic or satirical lyric verse, shall not be permitted to ridicule any of the citizens, either by word or likeness, either in anger or without anger."[8] Augustine of Hippo (354–430) observed that mockery and humorous insults were particularly pernicious, as the offenders take pleasure in "watching other people's pain, like spectators of gladiators, or those who mock and ridicule others."[9]

The Talmud's overall view on humor is mixed. Some talmudic traditions echo the sentiments of these Church theologians. Rabbi Shimon bar Yoḥai reportedly stated: "It is forbidden for one to fill his mouth with laughter in this world, as it says, 'Then will our mouths be filled with laughter and our tongues with joyous singing [Ps. 126:2]'" (*Berakhot* 31a). He interprets the biblical verse as describing the Messianic Age and reads it hyperliterally: "Then," in messianic times, and only then, should our mouths be filled with laughter but never now, never in this world. The Talmud proceeds to note that: "It was said of Rabbi Shimon ben Laqish that never was his mouth full of laughter in this world after he heard this tradition." Similarly, a brief anecdote relates: "Mar, son of Ravina, made a wedding celebration for his son. He saw that the Rabbis were joking a lot. He brought a valuable cup worth four hundred *zuzim* and broke it in their presence, and they became sad" (*Berakhot* 30b–31a).

Four hundred *zuzim* was a great sum in talmudic times—the cup, according to the commentaries, made from white glass, constituted a rare and valuable work of art. (Some talmudic commentators cite this passage as the source of the common Jewish custom of breaking a glass at a wedding, though even the most pious Jews do not smash valuable glasses any longer.)

The Rabbi might have been objecting to his colleagues' jocular comments on this occasion, or, more generally, he might have disapproved of any and all joking, especially if he felt it was derisive in nature. The Talmud includes very negative condemnations of "scoffing" or "mocking" humor, even warning that those who engage in such activity will fall into *Gehinnom* (hell) (*Avodah Zarah* 18b).

Yet at the same time the Talmud contains many traditions that exhibit an extremely positive attitude toward joking. It is said of

Rabbah, one of the greatest talmudic Sages, "Before he commenced to teach the Rabbis he made a joking statement, and the Rabbis were mirthful. Then he sat reverently and began the lesson" (*Shabbat* 30b). Here Rabbah anticipates the advice routinely given to speakers and preachers today: begin with a joke to get the audience's attention before launching into the lecture. Another story relates that Rabbi Yehudah ha-Nasi promised forty measures of wheat to Bar Qappara, who was famous for his pranks and jokes, if the jokester did not make him laugh. Elsewhere we learn that Rabbi Yehudah ha-Nasi had suffered stomach ailments for thirteen years, during which time the Jewish people were spared divine punishment, and the Rabbi's painful suffering was seen as atoning vicariously for their sins. Rabbi Yehudah ha-Nasi apparently was concerned that laughing would signal the end of his travails and expose the people to punishment. The story continues:

Bar Qappara said to him, "But see—I can take the wheat in whatever measure I choose." He took a gigantic basket, smeared it with pitch, and placed it upside-down on his head. He went and said to him, "Measure me out the forty measures of wheat that I am entitled from you." Rabbi Yehudah ha-Nasi burst out laughing and said to him, "Did I not warn you not to make me laugh?" Bar Qappara said to him, "I'm just taking the wheat you owe me." (*Nedarim* 50b–51a)

The core idea in this odd story can be summarized fairly as, "One Rabbi makes another Rabbi crack up against his will." Minimally, we learn that some Sages joked and clowned around, and this behavior was not frowned upon, as the storyteller proffers no criticism of Bar Qappara. Indeed, by having him succeed and giving him the last word, the punch line, the story portrays Bar Qappara as a comic hero who triumphs over the staid opposition. This is the case despite the fact that a great deal seems to be at stake— whether the Jewish community will be forgiven for its sins since the great Rabbi ceased to suffer. The storytellers seem to be telling us that humor trumps all else: no matter how serious someone claims the situation to be, laughter and joking are appropriate.

Moreover, the vast number of humorous passages throughout the Talmud makes it clear that the talmudic editors had a very funny side to them—even granting the difficulty of cross-cultural humor, of figuring out whether what *we* judge to be funny today was intended as such by these ancient and distant authors. Consider the following vignette about the Prophet Elijah who featured in our story:

Rabbi Yosei expounded in Sepphoris: "Our Father Elijah [the Prophet] was a hothead." Now, Elijah had regularly visited Rabbi Yosei, but [after this] he concealed himself from him for three days and did not visit him.

When Elijah [eventually] visited, Rabbi Yosei said to him, "Why did you not visit earlier?" Elijah said to him, "Because you called me a hothead." He retorted, "But you, Sir, just showed us that you are hot-tempered!" (*Sanhedrin* 113a–b)

The humor of course lies in Elijah's ironically displaying the very character trait to which he takes exception. (Note, too, the intimacy between the Rabbi and Elijah, as marked by the latter's daily visits.) Or consider the following anecdote, which follows a discussion of why the Jewish people were exiled to Babylonia in particular. Various Rabbis offer answers, and then Rabbi Ulla states: "So that they might eat dates and occupy themselves with Torah." Dates were cheap in Babylonia, so Ulla means that the Rabbis could easily earn a living, or at least earn enough to eat, and still have time to devote themselves to full-time Torah study. It is hard to know whether Ulla means to be serious or humorous in proposing that "cheap dates" (the pun, alas, only works in English) are sufficient explanation for the exile to Babylonia. Ulla may have intended to give a serious answer, but the talmudic editors, who consumed a lot of those dates, judged it to be silly or disrespectful. For they follow Ulla's remark with the following story:

Ulla visited Pumbedita [a city in Babylonia]. They brought him a basket of dates. He said to them, "How many of these can one buy for a *zuz*?" They said to him, "Three for a *zuz*." He said, "A basket full of [date] honey for a *zuz*, and the Babylonian Rabbis don't occupy themselves with Torah?!"

At night, the dates caused him [stomach] pain. He said, "A basket full of the poison of death for a *zuz* in Babylonia, and yet the Babylonian Rabbis occupy themselves with Torah!"

(*Pesaḥim* 87b–88a)

Ulla journeys from the Land of Israel to Pumbedita, a Rabbinic center in Babylonia, to exchange words of Torah with his Babylonian colleagues. When he learns how inexpensive the dates are, and apparently how delicious, too (honey!), he reprimands his fellow Rabbis. With no need to work long hours to earn one's daily bread, how could the Babylonian Rabbis not devote themselves to full-time Torah study?

Ulla evidently helped himself to more than his share of dates that day. At night, he suffers terrible stomach cramps or diarrhea, the typical consequence of overindulgence in dates. In the morning he utters similar words with the complete opposite meaning: with dates so cheap, available, and, apparently, hard to resist, how impressive is it that the Babylonian Rabbis manage to study any Torah at all with the inevitable bowel pangs they must suffer! The humor does not depend on the scatological dimension, but that is always a nice touch when making fun: here we picture the learned—and pompous and judgmental—Rabbi running to the toilet throughout the night. The storyteller turns the Rabbi visiting from Israel into the butt (!) of a Babylonian joke.

Scholars debate why the Talmud contains so much humor. The sociologist Peter Berger theorizes: "The comic experience provides a distinctive diagnosis of the world. It sees through the facades of ideational and social order, and discloses other realities lurking behind the superficial ones."[10] In this respect humor functions in a similar way to many talmudic stories: by pointing to deeper truths that often contrast with superficial reality. Some scholars believe the humor provides a needed balance to the otherwise serious subject matter and intricate legal argumentation, a type of comic relief. Others see it as a psychological defense mechanism to cope with the suffering of exile and the historical experience of persecution. And some just try to treat talmudic humor in a humorous way, as one contemporary rabbi replied when asked if the Talmud contains jokes: "Yes, but they are all old!" Perhaps the ability to punctuate even the most significant of pursuits, namely the quest to understand the law of God, with humorous interludes reveals the healthy instinct not to take anything, including oneself, too seriously. To be able to laugh at oneself entails the potential to entertain other points of view, to tolerate other assessments of priorities, even those that undermine and poke fun at one's own deeply held commitments.

This tolerant attitude in turn limits the tendency to slide into a dogmatic and uncompromising obstinacy—always a positive trait in our complex and multidimensional world.

Divine Comedy

If the Talmud has a sense of humor, what does that say about God? Like the Bible, talmudic sources do not shy away from anthropomorphism but offer a vivid depiction of God's emotional life. Some stories even portray God laughing. For example, the "Oven of Akhnai" (*Bava Metzi'a* 59a–b) recounts that Rabbi Eli'ezer disagrees with his colleagues over whether an oven constructed in a certain way is susceptible to ritual impurity (an issue that would have been relevant only in Temple times). When the other Rabbis refuse to accept Rabbi Eli'ezer's legal arguments, he resorts to miracles—seemingly divine proof of his correct view. When Rabbi Eli'ezer calls on the water in the aqueduct, it proceeds to flow backward. To no avail—the Rabbis refuse to accept this and other such miraculous evidence. Finally, Rabbi Eli'ezer calls on "heaven" to support him—and indeed a heavenly voice declares, "What is it for you with Rabbi Eli'ezer,"—that is, why are you giving Rabbi Eli'ezer a hard time—"since the law follows him in every place?" Yet even now the Rabbis reject God's unambiguous declaration, stating, "It is not in heaven"—that is, God gave the Torah to humans to interpret and apply, rendering God's own testimony irrelevant.

This paradoxical human dismissal of the divine Author's explanation of the meaning of the Torah, God's own text, has intrigued literary theorists, philosophers, and legal scholars alike. Constitutional scholars, for example, debate whether the "original intent" of the founding fathers who drafted the U.S. Constitution determines the meaning of the text today or whether the text should be interpreted differently to remain relevant in our times. Similarly, do authors' explanations of what they intend their literary works to mean preclude other, different interpretations?

The talmudic storytellers, however, do not delve into the theoretical implications of the Rabbis "exiling" God from the house of study and seizing interpretive authority over the divine text. Rather, they want us to know how God reacted to this turn of events. When the Rabbis declare that the Torah "is not in heaven," is God—still very much in heaven—angry or annoyed, insulted or disgusted, dismissive or accepting? Knowing this will make an enormous difference in Rabbinic—and perhaps human—self-understanding. The story continues:

Rabbi Natan came upon Elijah the Prophet. He said to him,
　　"What was the Holy One, Blessed be He, doing at that time?"

Elijah said to him, "He laughed and smiled and said, 'My
　　children have defeated me, my children have defeated me.'"

(*Bava Metzi'a* 59b)

Functioning once again as a mediator, Elijah discloses to the Rabbis that God laughed at this bit of human chutzpah. Like parents who take great satisfaction when their children reach maturity and independence ("My children!"), God rejoices that the Rabbis assert their own interpretive authority. After all, it is God's Torah they are dedicating themselves to interpreting and applying, even if not exactly in the way God intended. This kind of "defeat" is in fact a victory in the long run, as the Rabbis accept the responsibility of keeping Revelation alive for future generations.

This exceedingly complex story, which cannot be analyzed fully here,[11] does not end on this happy note. Immediately it takes a dark turn. Because Rabbi Eli'ezer does not accept the majority decision, the Rabbis place him under a ban—a type of excommunication or ostracism. Rabbi Eli'ezer feels ashamed and disgraced to the point of tears; divine punishments for this harsh treatment ensue; and the story concludes with the death of Rabban Gamali'el, the Rabbinic leader who opposed Rabbi Eli'ezer. The miserable ending suggests that whatever humorous elements characterize the relationship between God and humans, however amused God may feel when God's "children" seemingly encroach upon Divine authority, there is absolutely nothing funny about insulting or rejecting another person. God will not tolerate shaming of other human beings.

More generally, the fact that the talmudic storytellers portrayed God laughing indicates that they believed God has a sense of humor. Perhaps this conclusion is already presupposed in Genesis 1:27, when God creates humanity in the divine image. If human beings have a sense of humor, then talmudic logic requires that God must have a sense of humor too. Indeed, some psychologists point to humor as a characteristic that distinguishes humans from all other animal species, which is precisely what Creation in the divine image means: God and humans share something unique to them. Different scholars have made diverse claims as to those shared qualities, but the most commonly cited characteristics are free will, moral agency, language, highly abstract thought, second-order desires (i.e., the desire to have specific desires, such as the desire to have a desire to quit smoking or go on a diet), and a sense of humor. To claim that God created humans in the divine image but that the divine image lacks a funny bone . . . well, that would be a very cruel joke.

After all, humor plays a vital role in the human (and perhaps divine) psyche. Throughout history, humor has helped the Jewish people defy oppression—providing a needed way of striking back and making the best of the worst circumstances. The refusenik Natan Sharansky resisted his Soviet persecutors with humor, explaining: "The sense of humor is one of the most important weapons by which you defend yourself."[12] The psychologist and

Holocaust survivor Viktor Frankl stated: "What helps people survive awful circumstances is their ability to detach and get beyond themselves. This is seen in heroism and humor."[13]

Frankl's insightful coupling of heroism and humor may point to another reason that the jesters appear in the same exalted company as the jailer in this talmudic story. As defiance, humor asserts that no matter how dire the situation, the spirit of the persecuted cannot be crushed by oppressors. As combat, humor undermines the power and honor of the tyrants by making them objects of ridicule. Many generations later—heroically risking imprisonment and death—Voltaire, Montesquieu, Diderot, and other Enlightenment authors employed satire to resist and expose the oppressive policies of eighteenth-century absolutist monarchs and their allies. In a similar way, talmudic humor frequently makes fun of Persian and Roman authorities, both to undermine their power and to assert the Jewish people's freedom. True heroism can be found in many guises, including civil disobedience and humor.

Part 3 The Individual, Society, and Power

11 Showdown in Court

Among the most dramatic biblical confrontations were those between kings and prophets. Like many ancient societies, biblical Israel was ruled by kings for much of its history, and these kings, who controlled the army, had almost no checks on their power. When the kings violated religious or moral law, few could effectively call them to account.

One exception was the prophets—those rare individuals God chose to serve as earthly mouthpieces, revealing the divine will when humans went astray. The Prophet Samuel rebuked King Saul for not carrying out God's instructions in his battle with the Amalekites and informed him that God was taking the monarchy from him (1 Sam. 13:10–15). When King David abused his powers by committing adultery with Bathsheba and engineering her husband's death, the Prophet Nathan made the king aware of his sin and disclosed the divine punishment to follow (2 Sam. 12:1–14).

Confronting those in power has always been a risky proposition, necessitating tremendous courage. Not all kings were as fundamentally pious as David, who reacted to Nathan's castigation with contrition and repentance. The Prophet Elijah, together with one hundred other prophets, hid from King Ahab and Queen Jezebel for years to avoid being put to death after denouncing their crimes (1 Kings 18–19). Once the Prophet Uriah criticized King Jehoiakim's policies, Uriah fled to Egypt in hopes of saving his life, to no avail; the king had him extradited and killed (Jer. 26:20–23).

The dynasties of biblical kings came to an end with the Babylonian conquest of the Israelites in 586 BCE and the "first exile." Interestingly, the era of prophecy ended soon thereafter: the Rabbis considered Zechariah, Malachi, and Haggai, who prophesied toward the end of the sixth century BCE after the Persians allowed the Jews to return to Judea, as the last of the prophets. With the cessation of prophecy, Rabbis and scribes inherited the prophets' role of disclosing the divine will through interpretation of the Torah, God's sacred text, if not through direct revelation. They also inherited the prophets' role as the critics of the excesses of political authorities.

Toward the end of the second century BCE, a new dynasty assumed the mantle of Jewish royalty. The Hasmonean dynasty, sometimes called the Maccabees, led the Jews in rebellion against the Syrian-Greek kingdom that ruled them after Alexander the Great had imposed Hellenistic rule throughout the Mediterranean. A priestly family, the Hasmoneans seized the high priesthood after the revolt and, several generations later, made themselves kings too. While Judah Maccabee and his brethren were undoubtedly the heroes of the Hanukkah festival, fighting for independence and purifying the Temple, some of their descendants did not live up to their predecessors' pious standards. As kings they were repeatedly embroiled in conflicts with the common people and reportedly even perpetrated a few massacres. At such times, it fell to the scribes, Pharisees, and Sages, as heirs to the prophets, to confront the Hasmonean kings. (Historically, there were no Rabbis in the time of the Hasmoneans. The Rabbis considered scribes and Pharisees as their predecessors and anachronistically gave them the title "Rabbi.")

The following story is set in the time of King Yannai, Judah Maccabee's grand-nephew, who ruled Judea from 103 to 76 BCE. The story recounts a judicial conflict between King Yannai (whom the historian Josephus and other Greek sources call Alexander or

Jannaeus) and one of the leading early Sages, Shimon ben Shetah, the head judge of the Rabbinic court. The Talmud adduces the story to justify a law in the Mishnah that prohibits a king from being tried in court. That is, the disaster resulting from Shimon ben Shetah's attempt to try King Yannai caused a change in the law that removed kings from the authority and purview of the judicial system. As such, the story raises important questions about the relationship between (what we now term) the executive and judicial branches of government and the difficulties of calling to account a sovereign who holds the reins of power. The nuances of these difficulties are more complex than may appear at first glance:

Why is a king of Israel "not judged" [*Mishnah Sanhedrin* 2:1]? Because of what once happened. For—

> the slave of King Yannai killed someone. Shimon ben Shetah said to the Sages, "Set your eyes upon him and let us judge him."

> They sent a message to [Yannai], "Your slave killed someone." Yannai sent [the slave] to them.

> They sent to him, "It is written, 'If that ox had been in the habit of goring, and its masters have been warned, and it kills a man or a woman, the ox shall be stoned and its master, too, shall be put to death' [Exod. 21:29]. The Torah stated, 'Let the master of the ox come and stand by his ox.'" Yannai came and sat down.

> Shimon ben Shetah said to him, "King Yannai! Stand on your feet and let them give testimony regarding you. You do not stand before us but before He-Who-Spoke-and-the-World-

Came-into-Being, as it says, 'The two parties to the dispute shall stand before the Lord, before the priests or magistrates in authority at the time' [Deut. 19:17]." Yannai said to him, "I will not act as you say but as your colleagues say."

He turned to his right, but they looked down to the ground. He turned to his left, but they looked down to the ground.

Shimon ben Shetaḥ said, "Are you preoccupied with your thoughts? Let the Master of Thoughts come and punish you." The angel Gabriel came and struck the Sages to the ground and they died.

At that time they said, "A king does not judge others and is not judged in court. He does not testify and is not testified against."

(*Sanhedrin* 19a–b)

The Talmud introduces the story by quoting part of the rule of *Mishnah Sanhedrin* 2:1, "a king is not judged," and concludes with the full quotation: "A king does not judge others and is not judged in court. He does not testify and is not testified against." The king cannot be a judge, litigant, or witness; his position places him outside of the judicial system. Why is this the case? Why should the courts be unable to put a king on trial or summon him as a witness?

There follows a narrative justification of this law rather than the more typical legal analysis with dialectical argumentation or a midrashic derivation anchoring the rule in biblical prooftexts. The Talmud tells us a story of what went wrong—more specifically, a story suggesting that the royal exemption from the judicial system is not the ideal, and was not always the law, but arose in light of a catastrophic event of the distant past.

A key question to ponder is: Does the storyteller see King Yannai as a villain? Does he portray the king negatively? When Shimon ben Shetaḥ informs Yannai of his slave's crime, Yannai dutifully sends the slave to trial. Yet the Rabbis of the court are not satisfied. They quote a biblical midrash, an interpretation of Exodus 21:29, "proving" that Yannai himself must appear. The interpretation turns on the phrase "its masters have been warned." When a dangerous ox causes damage, the master or owner stands in judgment along with his ox, as the master was himself negligent and bears responsibility. Applying the same principle to a slave, Shimon ben Shetaḥ notes that the master is responsible for the damage his slave causes and must stand trial. Therefore he summons King Yannai to court.

Whatever the merits of this analogy according to Rabbinic sensibilities, one could imagine a king respectfully insisting that an ox is an ox while a slave is a slave. The former acts according to animal instinct alone; the latter has free will to perpetrate evil or to resist his impulses. Hence the Rabbis may have their way with the slave but not with the king.

To this Shimon ben Shetaḥ might respond that slaves or "servants"—the Aramaic word admits either meaning—especially the slaves/servants of kings, typically carry out their masters' bidding. The slave may have done the deed, but are we seriously to believe that Yannai had nothing to do with it? Would a king's servant have the audacity and autonomy to commit murder without the king's tacit—or explicit—instruction? An owner of a dangerous beast that kills a human is negligent according to the biblical law and therefore stands trial along with his animal. How much more so should a murderous slave's owner, who may have been complicit or directly responsible, and not merely negligent, stand trial for the crime?

Were Yannai to counter by arguing that a human slave differs from a bestial ox insofar as he has personal autonomy and responsibility for his own actions, Shimon ben Shetaḥ would respond that this distinction applies only in theory. In reality, he would say, a king's slave may have little or no choice to act as he sees fit. With a sword pressed against his throat, with his back still bearing the scars of whippings due to previous acts of disobedience, the concept of free will becomes rather murky.

Yet the opposite view seems plausible. Here we have a court of Rabbis with power, apparently, to subpoena—and even try—the king. Had King Yannai ordered the slave to kill, couldn't the slave have come to this very court, informed the Sages, and requested asylum? Is it possible that he did not do so because he himself was complicit in the affair?

It also is possible that this slave had his own share of personal grievances and conflicts and that the murder resulted from some private squabble. In the Roman world many slaves of nobles and royalty owned property and even amassed considerable wealth. The storyteller does not begin his account, "King Yannai ordered his slave to kill someone," but only, "The slave of King Yannai killed someone." How frustrating the lack of information provided by the storyteller! Or is this precisely the point? Is Shimon ben Shetaḥ jumping to conclusions, immediately presuming King Yannai to be guilty when the Sages *first* should have interrogated and judged the slave before summoning the king?

In any event, Yannai acquiesces again. He comes to the Sages—apparently to the Rabbinic court—and sits down quietly. What more could be asked of a king? Many rulers, ancient and modern alike, would not think twice about refusing to appear, perhaps even sending in some soldiers to deliver the message with a little calculated violence. To show up in and of itself can be perceived as a humiliating submission to the authority of others.

King Yannai's presence, however, still does not satisfy Shimon ben Shetaḥ. Quoting another biblical verse, he commands the king to stand up—to honor the Rabbis not only by his appearance but by his posture. How are we to read his motives? Does Shimon ben Shetaḥ feel Yannai has insulted the court by refusing to abide by the standard protocol—standing—demanded of all other litigants? Or is this a power struggle, an effort to demonstrate to everyone in attendance who in this situation possesses the higher authority and status? Shimon ben Shetaḥ seems to disavow a personal stake in the conflict by declaring: "It is not before us that you stand, but before He-Who-Spoke-and-the-World-Came-into-Being." He insists on God's honor, not his own. Should we take this rhetoric seriously?

At this point King Yannai balks. Yet he does not refuse Shimon ben Shetaḥ outright, nor does he articulate a warning or a threat. He resists the Rabbi's authority, but he acknowledges, at least on the surface, the authority of the Sages, of Shimon ben Shetaḥ's colleagues, the Rabbis serving as judges of the court. He will defer to the institution but not to Shimon ben Shetaḥ, whom Yannai seems to think is on a power trip. Yannai appears to believe that this Rabbi wants everyone to see that he is superior to the king and that the king must obey his commands. This court case has become too personal. A test of wills. A power play. Yannai appeals to a more neutral judiciary.

"He turned to the right . . ." Who turned, Yannai or Shimon ben Shetaḥ? Does the pronoun refer to Shimon ben Shetaḥ—in other words, did Shimon ben Shetaḥ look to his colleagues for support, but they let him down? Or does the pronoun indicate Yannai, who looks to the Rabbis seated at Shimon ben Shetaḥ's sides, but they refuse to meet his imperious glance? Either way, how do we construe the Sages' averted eyes? Is this abject cowardice, a failure of nerve? Do they abandon their colleague when he most needs their support? Do they fear that the powerful King Yannai will suddenly call in the troops and take revenge on the Rabbis who tried to humiliate him? Or, do they feel Shimon ben Shetah has overstepped his authority? Do they think a king, even when tried in court, or at least when tried for an act he did not personally commit, retains his honor and need not stand? Shouldn't the ruler of the Jewish people be treated like a true king, with due honor and prerogative? Is not an insult to the king an insult to his people, too, just as if a Greek or Roman governor had summoned King Yannai and made him stand before that court? Has their colleague Shimon ben Shetah unfairly placed them in a most awkward position? Or again, are they simply caught in the middle, confused, bewildered, trying to weigh the different factors and figure out the appropriate response?

The miraculous divine intervention that follows suggests Shimon ben Shetah stands in the right. He invokes the axiom of divine justice, the measure-for-measure principle: are you "preoccupied with your thoughts"?—the Hebrew literally translates as "Are you masters of thoughts"?—then "let the [true] Master of Thoughts come and punish you."

This sharp rebuke plays ironically on the Sages' impotent retreat to the realm of thought to solve their predicament at the very time they need to act. Because they are immersed in thought— thinking too long, but not thinking straight—the divine "Master of Thoughts" summons his angelic messenger to strike them down. Turning their eyes to the ground out of fear of the king, the Sages are displaced from their seats on the court to that very ground. Having not "stood" up to Yannai, whom Shimon had ordered to stand, they are struck down prostrate, their reduced posture manifesting the loss of honor. Shimon ben Shetah calls on God with a sobriquet that emphasizes speech, "He-Who-*Spoke*-and-the-World-Came-into-Being," a pointed contrast to the Sages' silence. By not supporting Shimon and confronting Yannai, they failed in their capacity as leaders and judges.

Given their transgression, the punishment may seem draconian to us. Perhaps we should not take it literally but figuratively, in keeping with the exaggerated and dramatic talmudic narrative style. The storyteller means to inform us how disastrous such cowardice can be, so it is a disaster we get.

Concluding the story with the angel Gabriel killing the Sages may suggest that the slave at the story's beginning did indeed commit the murder at Yannai's behest. The storyteller may be inviting us to draw a parallel: just as Gabriel, God's angelic servant, acted on his Master's command (the "Master of Thoughts"), so the slave/servant killed someone at his master Yannai's order.

Yet despite this possibility and the Sages' punishment, we would be unwise to take the story as either a complete endorsement of Shimon ben Shetah's efforts or a consummate indictment of King Yannai. First, the Talmud does not conclude from the story that those particular Sages were particularly unworthy but rather that the structural dynamics of judging a king are inherently problematic. The Talmud does not offer a lesson about judges' qualifications—about only appointing to the judiciary those who display courage and bravery—but rather informs us that the law was changed so that kings would never be tried again. Second, Shimon ben Shetah's initial call to his colleagues—"Set your eyes upon him [Yannai] and let us judge him"—is a metaphoric use of vision anticipating King Yannai's imperious gaze at the Sages. Note this curious locution: the narrator could have had Shimon ben Shetah say, "Summon King Yannai," or "Call King Yannai to appear," or suchlike. The expression "set your eyes upon" generally has negative connotations, as we saw with the story of the pious jailer in the previous chapter. Likewise, the Talmud's story of the wicked King Herod relates that Herod "set his eyes on a maiden" of the Hasmonean family and proceeded to seize power and kill the entire Hasmonean clan (*Bava Batra* 3b–4a). That Shimon ben Shetah calls upon his colleagues to "set your eyes" upon

King Yannai suggests his motives are not pure, that he perhaps sees an opportunity for self-aggrandizement. He not only is interested in justice but in demonstrating the Sages' superiority and humiliating the king. Finally, however we view Shimon ben Shetah's motives—pure or impure, self-interested or selfless—many Sages die as a result of his actions.

For the Talmud, then, the story teaches a tragic lesson of the incompatibility of power and justice. It is extremely difficult to bring the powerful to justice because the very presence of power disrupts the system such that it cannot function. It has often been said that, in contrast to secular kings who were regularly considered to be the source of the law—"The king is the law"—in Judaism the king is like all other humans in being subject to God's law. While that may be true in theory, it cannot work in practice, at least not in a terrestrial court. At the same time, the story suggests that the problem is not only due to a sovereign's potential use of violence and to human weakness (the Sages' failure of nerve) but to the reflexive escalation that tends to result when judges seek to exert their own authority, as Shimon ben Shetah did.

The Law of the King

This talmudic passage about Shimon ben Shetah and King Yannai raises profound political and philosophical questions about the use, abuse, and regulation of power. In particular: should there be limits on the power of the sovereign, and if so, how can those limits be structured? If the sovereign is not above the law, but subject to law, yet oversees the very instruments of maintaining that order (police, army, etc.), how can the law force the sovereign to submit? Recall that our modern democratic systems, with their checks and balances as well as separation of executive, legislative, and judicial powers, are relatively recent developments. Throughout human history many political systems have included a king, despot, tyrant, or single sovereign. Checks and balances only originated in the political thought of the eighteenth-century Enlightenment, amidst efforts to reform powerful European monarchies. Moreover, even democracies and constitutional republics do not preclude abuses of the system. Hitler and his National Socialist German Workers' (Nazi) Party came to power through a democratic process and free elections—and then maneuvered to secure "emergency" plenary powers that granted almost unlimited authority and the right to act without parliamentary consent.

What is more, government by a sovereign still prevails today in many parts of the world. And indeed, for much of human history, the king or sovereign was considered a god—or at least a divine offspring of sorts. Whether that sovereign's power could be limited, and if so, how, are questions with a long pedigree in political thought.

The Torah itself weighs in on this question in a famous passage known as the "Law of the King" in Deuteronomy 17:14–20:

(14) If, after you have entered the land that the Lord your God has assigned to you, and taken possession of it and settled in it, you decide, "I will set a king over me, as do all the nations about me" (15) You shall be free to set a king over yourself, one chosen by the Lord your God . . . (16) Moreover, he will not keep many horses or send people back to Egypt to add his horses, since the Lord has warned you, "You must not go back that way again." (17) And he shall not have many wives, lest his heart go astray; nor shall he amass silver and gold to excess. (18) When he is seated on his royal throne, he shall write a copy of this Torah in the presence of the Levitical priests. (19) Let it remain with him and let him read in it all his life, so that he may learn to revere the Lord his God, to observe faithfully every word of this Torah as well as these laws. (20) Thus he will not act haughtily toward his fellows or deviate from the Instruction to the right or to the left, to the end that he and his descendants may reign in the midst of Israel.

The passage undermines and constrains the king's prestige and power in several ways. The Torah attributes the impulse to crown a king to the people, construing the monarchy as a political option or possibility, rather than an obligation or divine commandment. By biblical standards the motivation that might occasion such a request is suspect or negative: the desire to emulate the surrounding peoples. That God chooses the king in this context presumably means that God must approve of the people's choice or that God will select the occupant once the people request a sovereign—not that God desires such a political order.

A concession, rather than an ideal, the monarchy's powers are to be limited in several respects. The injunction that the king may not possess many horses restricts the size of his cavalry and army. Likewise curtailing his wealth naturally constrains the king's ability to indulge his whims for whatever he desires. The mandate not to have too many wives may be concerned with impeding them from influencing him to adopt their idolatrous religions, but the restriction also serves to close the gap between king and commoner, bringing the king closer to the level of other Israelites, who were generally monogamous, although polygamy was technically permitted. In these ways the Torah can be said to "disempower" the king. Most important, the command that the king produce a copy of the Torah in the presence of the priests expresses his subservience both to the rule of law and to its priestly interpreters.[1] The priests seem to be the caretakers of the Torah. They give the Torah to the King to copy and essentially supervise his efforts ("in their presence"), perhaps instructing him on what to do.

Earlier in Deuteronomy 17 judicial authority is explicitly granted to priests and magistrates:

(8) If a case is too baffling for you to decide, be it a controversy over homicide, civil law, or assault—matters of dispute in your courts—you shall promptly repair to the place that the Lord

your God will have chosen, (9) and appear before the Levitical priests or the magistrate in charge at the time, and present your problem. When they have announced to you the verdict in the case (10) you shall carry out the verdict . . . .

The juxtaposition of this passage delineating the judicial system (Deut. 17:8–13) just before the "Law of the King" (Deut. 17:14–20) suggests that they be read as a unit describing two separate and distinct institutions. In many cultures the king sits in judgment, speaking for God, administering the law, and functioning as a supreme court beyond appeal. By contrast, the Torah confers judicial authority on those beyond the royal circle. In this way the Torah implicitly ordains that the king not be involved in the judiciary, neither as judge nor as authorizer of judges. Thus we have a rudimentary attempt at delineating the "separation of powers" more than two millennia before philosophers and political theorists formulated the doctrine in Western thought.

That the judiciary must be independent of the king leaves open the question of whether the king is himself subject to the system or stands above and apart from it. Can the king be subpoenaed to the priestly courts? The implied subservience to the priests who direct the king to write out the Torah perhaps hints that this is the case, as these same priests administer the courts. But as with other biblical laws, the skeletal legislation of the Torah does not address every necessary question; rather, it leaves the door open to future interpreters to fill the gaps.

Against this background both the Mishnah, on the one hand, and the Talmud's story of King Yannai and Shimon ben Shetaḥ, on the other, may be seen as attempts to address this unanswered biblical question. In the Rabbinic era Sages were understood to be the equivalent of the biblical "priests and magistrates." The talmudic story pictures the court of Sages, the wise and rightful legal interpreters "in charge at that time," as possessing authority over the king, who must obey their demands that he hand over his slave and even heed their summons himself. Alas, this scenario results in catastrophe: a standoff between the authorities and the death of the judges. Conclusion: the king must stand apart from the judiciary, as the Mishnah rules: "A king does not judge others and is not judged in court."[2]

Judicial Review and Its Limitations

The story thus raises, but does not fully resolve, the question of the relationship between the judicial and executive branches of government. It calls for a separation of powers but does not tell us who, ultimately, has sovereignty: the judge or the king. When the king promulgates or acts upon a law rejected by the judiciary, or when the judges articulate a legal interpretation that the king disputes, who prevails? Indeed, the characters repeatedly sidestep the question, as if the storyteller wishes to avoid taking a position: King Yannai defers to the Sages, the Sages remain silent, and Shimon ben Shetah appeals to God. Certainly in the Rabbinic worldview God is the ultimate authority, judge, king, and sovereign, and the Rabbis would take some comfort in the depiction of a divine ruler willing and able to answer such a summons. But what of a time like ours when divine intervention appears to have become a feature of the past? Without supernatural intervention, we have a stalemate. Is violence our only recourse? In fact, even God's intercession in the story involves a good deal of violence, so are we supposed to conclude that no other possibility exists? In any event, in the story God's intervention only punishes the Sages but fails to resolve the ultimate question.

This larger question remains relevant in modern times. In America, for example, the founding fathers made great efforts to delineate in the Constitution the powers of each branch of government but could not anticipate or provide guidance for every future conflict. The famous case of *Marbury v. Madison,* routinely dubbed "the most important case in Supreme Court history," addressed precisely this issue. President John Adams, a federalist, appointed a large number of justices just before leaving office, but their commissions were not delivered when President Jefferson, of the new Democratic-Republican Party, took office in 1801. Jefferson ordered Secretary of State James Madison not to deliver the commissions, whereupon William Marbury, one of the appointed judges, petitioned the Supreme Court to intervene. On the one hand, Chief Justice John Marshall ruled that the refusal to grant Marbury his commission was illegal—in other words, Jefferson was not acting lawfully—and penned some harsh criticism of President Jefferson. On the other hand, Marshall ruled that the law according to which Marbury brought his claim to the Supreme Court was unconstitutional, and therefore the court could not order the president of the United States to honor the commissions. Marbury is thus credited with establishing the principle of "judicial review": judges decide when congressional laws and executive actions are unconstitutional, that is, judges are the highest interpretive authorities. In Marshall's words: "It is emphatically the province and duty of the judicial department to say what the law is."[3] Yet by deciding the case on what might be called a technicality and refusing to issue an order to President Jefferson, who many believed simply would have ignored it, Marshall nimbly sidestepped a showdown over authority. Nor did he address the issue of how the Supreme Court could enforce its decisions if Congress or the president rejected them. The ultimate question of what would happen when the judiciary and president dispute was therefore avoided—as in our talmudic story.

Marshall's claim of judiciary supremacy was met with resistance by various U.S. presidents, including Jefferson, Andrew Jackson, and Abraham Lincoln. Lincoln, for his part, espoused a theory known as "departmentalism": that the judicial, legislative, and executive branches of government, and not just the courts, all bore equal responsibility for constitutional interpretation. He rejected the Supreme Court's famous *Dred Scott* (1857) decision that African-Americans could never be citizens according to the Constitution. Lincoln's administration passed numerous measures that should have been prohibited by the court's ruling, such as granting passports to African Americans, and Lincoln wrote that he "never doubted the constitutional authority" to act in this way.[4]

Another famous example of conflict between the judiciary and president was the Judicial Procedures Reform Bill of 1937, also known as the "court-packing plan." President Franklin D. Roosevelt, frustrated that the Supreme Court had struck down some of his New Deal legislation as unconstitutional, proposed adding more justices to the Supreme Court. By "packing" the court with his appointees, Roosevelt could be assured that his legislative initiatives would be deemed lawful. Soon after he announced his plan, the Supreme Court decided by a 5–4 decision to support a New Deal minimum wage law and approved two related measures as well. Franklin did not succeed in having his packing bill voted into law, but one justice's retirement later that year rendered the situation less urgent, as did the retirement or death of four more justices over the next two years of Franklin's presidency. While the exact dynamics of this conflict were very complicated, in the final reckoning the threat of this type of assault on the Supreme Court allowed the president's laws to stand. As later Chief Justice William Rehnquist noted, "President Roosevelt lost the Court-packing battle, but he won the war for control of the Supreme Court."[5]

This issue resurfaced in the 2017 controversy between President Donald Trump and the U.S. Court of Appeals for the Ninth Circuit over the legality of Trump's executive order banning immigration from seven predominantly Muslim countries. When this appeals court affirmed a lower court's ruling that Trump had exceeded his authority, the Justice Department asserted that the president had "unreviewable authority" in this area of law. The president called the judicial proceedings "disgraceful," asserting that the "so-called judge" had issued a "ridiculous" ruling and predicting that he would "win the battle"[6]—which raised concerns about the separation of powers and the degree of judicial independence in America.

Some analysts characterized Trump's response as "aggressive attacks on the judiciary," "engaging in a rhetorical battle," "hostile," and "dangerous," in that his violent talk might spill over into real violence, if not by U.S. authorities then by his own supporters. Some readers recalling Trump's hostility at this juncture might picture a scene of Trump staring imperiously at the judge along the lines of the Yannai encounter, with thinly veiled threats hovering just below the surface.

Note, too, that in the Jefferson and Roosevelt disputes, like the Trump dispute, the parties on both sides of the conflicts permeated their speeches with "verbal violence": acrimonious charges, bitter criticism, and hostility. Rehnquist aptly described the Roosevelt conflict in terms of "battle" and "war." To this day, legal scholars continue to analyze, debate, and philosophize about the political and constitutional implications of the issues raised long ago by the talmudic story of Shimon ben Shetaḥ and King Yannai.[7]

12 Alexander the Great and the Faraway King

Alexander the Great, called "Alexander Macedon" (i.e., Alexander the Macedonian) by the Rabbis, featured in numerous legends and tales throughout the ancient world. Many of these stories were ultimately collected in a long text known as the *Alexander Romance*, written in Greek in the third century CE, with different versions produced in Latin, Armenian, Aramaic, and, by the Middle Ages, Arabic, French, English, and other European languages.

His image was extremely positive: heroic conqueror, fearless warrior, brilliant general, intrepid explorer, wise king. In particular, Alexander was heralded as a purveyor of Hellenistic culture to the barbarians: as he conquered each territory, he introduced philosophy, Greek literature, and other civilized arts to these alien peoples. Many episodes depict Alexander encountering foreign rulers or wise men and discussing vital issues in cross-cultural, philosophical dialogue.

At the same time, a more negative image of Alexander developed alongside these adulatory portrayals. After all, as one modern historian succinctly put it: "He spent much of his time killing and directing killing, and, arguably, killing was what he did best."[1] The peoples whom Alexander and his armies conquered, devastated, and dispossessed of their territory and independence recalled the "Great King" with acute bitterness. Ancient authors more impressed with piety and justice than world domination advanced a similar perspective. Augustine of Hippo, the prolific fourth-century bishop and theologian, noted: "Indeed, that was an apt and true reply which was given to Alexander the Great by a pirate who had been seized. For when that king had asked the man what he meant by keeping hostile possession of the sea, he answered with bold pride, 'What thou meanest by seizing the whole earth; but because I do it with a petty ship, I am called a robber, whilst thou who does it with a great fleet are styled emperor.'"[2]

The Talmuds contain several stories of Alexander the Great. Most derive from the *Alexander Romance,* or from popular oral versions of those accounts, and retain the glorified image of Alexander as a wise and powerful king. In one talmudic story, when various peoples sue the Jewish people in a quasi-ancient international Court of Justice, Alexander rules in favor of the Jews.

By contrast, the following story from the Jerusalem Talmud reflects that "minority" voice, the sober perspective that refuses to ignore the true motives of a world conqueror. A king who ranged over the earth with a massive army ultimately must have been moved by greed, megalomania, and a self-aggrandizing quest for personal glory, whatever his pretenses otherwise.

Alexander Macedon traveled to the Faraway King. The king showed him much gold. He showed him much silver. Alexander said, "I do not need your gold or your silver. Rather, I have come to observe your ways: how you do business, how you judge."

While the king was occupied with Alexander, a certain man approached, disputing with his fellow. He had bought a field, and while he was digging it up he found a treasure of gold coins.

The one who bought the field said, "I bought a field; I did not buy a treasure."

The one who sold it said, "I sold you a field and everything in it."

While they were arguing with one another the king said to one of them,

"Do you have a male child?" He said, "Yes."

He said to the other, "Do you have a female child?" He said, "Yes."

He said, "Marry them one to the other, and the treasure will go to both of them."

Alexander began to laugh. The king said to him, "Why do you laugh? Did I not judge well?" The king then said, "If this case had come before you, how would you have judged?" Alexander said, "We would kill both the one and the other, and the treasure would fall to the king."

The [Faraway] King said to him, "Then you love gold so much?!" He made Alexander a meal. He brought before him meat made from gold and fowl made from gold. Alexander said to him, "Do I eat gold?" He said to him, "Blast your bones! If you don't eat gold, then why do you love it so much?"

The king said to him, "Does the sun shine for you?"

Alexander said to him, "Yes."

"Does the rain fall for you?" "Yes."

He said to him, "Perhaps there is small cattle among you?" He said to him, "Yes."

The king said, "Blast your bones! You live solely on account of the small cattle, as it says, "You save man and beast, O Lord"

[Ps. 36:7, meaning, "you save man because of" or "on account of the beasts"].

(Jerusalem Talmud, *Bava Metzi'a* 2:5, 8c.)

Perfect Justice

Despite the laconic style necessitated by the oral nature of talmudic literature, our story displays features of the literary genre "legend": a protagonist travels to a distant land on a quest. This distance is evoked by the name of the king Alexander encounters, the "Faraway King." Typical of folktales, the name provides the essential characterization, much like "Snow White" or the "Wicked Witch of the West." Literally, the Aramaic word translated as "faraway" means "end" or "extreme": the king at the end of the earth.

So Alexander goes to the ends of the earth on a quest. A quest for . . . what? That is the key question.

The Faraway King produces silver and gold for him. Why else would Alexander go to so much trouble, traveling so far with a large army, if not for riches?

Surprisingly, Alexander spurns the proffered treasure. No, he insists, he has not come for wealth but for wisdom: he wishes to learn from the king and his people how they live, how they administer justice. Here the storyteller adopts the well-known portrayal of Alexander the Great as a type of cultural anthropologist and protophilosopher. As a student of Aristotle and champion of Hellenistic culture, Alexander has come not only to teach the "barbarians" about Greek wisdom, not only to be a cultural exporter, but to be an importer too—to learn other and better ways of running a society.

The litigants who enter provide Alexander with exactly what he claims to seek: the opportunity to observe this foreign culture

and their ways. And quite a court case it is! Two exceedingly virtuous citizens come before their king disavowing a plausible claim
to a fortune and requesting judgment in favor of their fellow. In
these circumstances the sagacious king dispenses wisdom, not
justice—a brilliant solution worthy of the supermorality of his
subjects: the citizens' children are to marry, enabling both families to retain the entire treasure that each was willing to forego.

In this "faraway," utopian land, Alexander thus observes a type
of supersociety characterized by virtue, wisdom, and—we should
surely infer—happiness, as two outstanding families celebrate
their union.

Alexander's derisive laughter now unmasks his true motives and
character, confirming the king's initial assessment of the reasons
the Macedonian undertook his journey. By mocking his host's
sage advice, Alexander reveals that the gold—not any aspiration
of crosscultural interchange—has brought him and his army to
the ends of the earth. A treasure without a clear owner affords an
immoral king opportunity to seize it for himself. To add insult to
injury, as it were, Alexander discloses he would even murder these
exemplary citizens, presumably to prevent attempts to reclaim
what was rightfully theirs.

This perfect injustice is an inverted mirror image of the perfect
wisdom dispensed by the Faraway King. Rather than uniting the
families in marriage and the happiness of new life, it would bond
them in death and misery.

The Faraway King proceeds to teach, or to try to teach, Alexander a lesson in self-awareness. In a play on the myth of another
Greek sovereign, King Midas, the Faraway King produces the gold
and silver he had initially offered Alexander.

Alexander again rejects it. This time, though, Alexander makes
no pretense to seek learning rather than riches but complains only
that the riches do not provide him sustenance. That, of course, is
precisely the point: Alexander should realize that his conquests

and other quests for wealth, even if successful, accomplish nothing other than wrecking destruction and misery. For the storyteller, Alexander should not be perceived as a purveyor of Greek culture and civilization to improve the lives of the "primitive" barbarians in his empire but an exporter of suffering and death. If Alexander has come to learn, let him learn that.

The final interchange provides a Rabbinic stamp and moral on a story that otherwise has little else to mark it as Rabbinic or even Jewish. The questions about the sun and rain evoke the common biblical idea that God punishes disobedience by disrupting the weather cycle such that crops will not grow. Deuteronomy 11:6, for example, from the second paragraph of the *Shema* prayer, warns that God will "close off the heavens, and there will be no rain." To explain why Alexander and his corrupt people have not received such punishment, the Faraway King adduces Psalms 36:7, "You [God] save man and beast," interpreting it as "You save man *because of* the beasts" or "*for the sake of* the beasts." Were it not for the animals in Alexander's kingdom, God would sweep away the wicked king and his followers, blocking out the sun's rays and denying the rain needed for life to flourish. The opening verses of this psalm, which the storyteller and his Rabbinic audience would have summoned to mind together with the verse he cites, are particularly apt:

(Ps. 36:1) I have a message from God in my heart
concerning the sinfulness of the wicked:
There is no fear of God
before their eyes.
(2) In their own eyes they flatter themselves
too much to detect or hate their sin.
(3) The words of their mouths are wicked and deceitful;
they fail to act wisely or do good.

The storyteller is thus indirectly relaying a strong moral message: Alexander and his admirers deceive themselves with a false self-image as seekers of learning, flatter themselves for their purported achievements while uttering "wicked and deceitful" words, and fail "to act wisely or do good." Their readiness to confiscate treasures and to murder the rightful owners show "no fear of God before their eyes." Only God's mercy, like that (and perhaps better understood) for innocent animals, can justify the lack of divine punishment for such wickedness.

By contrasting "Alexander the Great," a historical figure of towering fame, with the "Faraway King," a stock character beyond time and place, the storyteller invites us to ponder: Why was Alexander great? Was he in fact so great? Should we take the name "great" ironically? True, Alexander conquered more of the world than anyone before or after, building an empire that stretched from Greece to India, from Egypt to Persia. He also amassed more treasure, gold, riches, than any previous king—by means of a massive army, conquest, taxation, and enslavement. But what kind of society and what kind of people did he create? Would we rather live in his land or in that of the Faraway King?

Virtue, Treasure, and Happiness

At first glance the answer to the Faraway King's query "If you don't eat gold, then why do you love it so much?" is obvious: he takes the gold and purchases whatever he desires. Let Alexander answer him: one cannot eat the gold, but one need not eat the gold.

Of course the Faraway King knows this. He means to teach Alexander that one who desires gold to this extent can never buy all that he wants. Someone who thinks about obtaining money at all costs will always yearn for more than he has attained. If one's fingers always itch to hold more gold, one will always suffer the same pangs as King Midas. Wealth cannot buy the serenity of purpose bestowed by the virtuous life.

The "litigants" of the Faraway Kingdom possess this insight. In what may strike us in the modern west as somewhere between bizarre and insane, they behave with selflessness and generosity, each arguing on behalf of his fellow and eschewing the just and reasonable arguments he could make to claim the treasure for himself. These people, their king, and ostensibly the broader community of the Faraway Kingdom have built a meaningful and happy life without focusing on material goods. We might even say: because they did not focus on material goods.

The true treasure of the Faraway Kingdom is not the gold in the ground but the virtue of its citizens. That, the storyteller means us to understand, is the only treasure worth pursuing.

Buried Treasure: A Cross-Cultural View

To undermine the glorified image of Alexander the Great, the storyteller makes subversive and ironic use of Greco-Roman motifs. Historians generally consider Alexander's conquests the beginning of the "Hellenistic Age" of ancient history, which dates from his death in 323 BCE; our storyteller turns the trope of Alexander as purveyor of Hellenistic culture on its head to suggest Alexander was not motivated by such lofty ideals but by greed. He also employs the Greek myth of King Midas, who almost starved to death after the god Dionysus granted his wish that everything he touched turn to gold.

A third motif deriving from Greco-Roman culture is the king's confiscation of treasure discovered by citizens. In many countries throughout the ancient and medieval world the law specified that all "ownerless" treasures belonged to the king—an easy and convenient way for monarchs to enrich their coffers. While the Roman law of the "treasure trove" changed several times over the centuries, in some periods it stipulated that all treasures belonged to the emperor and at other times that half of all treasures had to be bestowed on the public treasury (the repository of public funds, including taxes and war spoils, controlled by the Senate), no matter where they were found.[3] According to the Talmud, Persian law ruled that all lost property belonged to the Persian king (*Bava Metzi'a* 28b). The Dutch lawyer and jurist Hugo Grotius (1583–1645) wrote that England, the German states, France, Spain, and Denmark followed the ancient Germanic law that all discovered treasure went to the prince—and this law continues in some countries to the present day.[4]

The talmudic storyteller embellishes the corruptness of such laws by adding that Alexander not only would claim the treasure but murder the litigants as well. This provision is unattested in antiquity. However, in the Middle Ages treasure hunting was associated with magic and witchcraft, as many attempted to locate lost treasures by such means, and was therefore considered a capital crime.[5] The notion that finders of a treasure trove be put to death is thus not all that far-fetched.

These laws contrast sharply with the Jewish teachings extolling the mitzvah of "returning a lost object" (*hashavat aveidah*), derived from Deuteronomy 22:1–3: "When you see your brother's ox or sheep gone astray, do not ignore it; you must take it back to your fellow . . . . So too shall you do with anything that your fellow loses and you find: you must not remain indifferent." Two chapters in the Mishnah and Talmud tractates *Bava Metzi'a* provide a detailed explication of this principle, requiring that great efforts be undertaken to identify the owners and return their possessions. For example, finders are directed to proclaim the lost articles they have found for as long as a year in some cases, and to inform all neighbors, acquaintances, and residents of the town (*Mishnah Bava Metzi'a* 2:6, Tosefta *Bava Metzi'a* 2:8). Codifying these talmudic rulings, the Shulḥan Arukh, the great medieval compendium of Jewish law, adds that discovered treasures are to belong to the finder or to the owner of the property depending on the circumstances (Shulḥan Arukh, *Ḥoshen Mishpat* 260:1).

Our chapter's story appears within these chapters in the Jerusalem Talmud discussing the laws and ethics of finding lost objects. By contextualizing the story in this way, the Rabbis invite us to compare and contrast the two societies—in particular, to appreciate the moral society delineated by the Talmud in light of the values of the surrounding cultures.

A Hypothetical Countertale

Let us consider, for a moment, a hypothetical countertale I invented about Alexander and the King of the North.

The King of the North visited King Alexander the Great. One day, while they were speaking together, two men entered and bowed low before Alexander:

"O King, we humbly come before you for judgment," they said.

"State your case," replied Alexander the Great.

One said: "I bought a field from this man for one hundred pieces of silver. One day, while I was digging, I found a treasure of gold buried in the earth. I bought the field, so the treasure is rightfully mine."

The other said: "I sold him a field, not a treasure. The treasure is mine."

They continued to argue for a short while, whereupon Alexander the Great spoke: "Take these greedy litigants out, whip them, and bring me the treasure."

The King of the North stared at Alexander the Great. "Why do you stare?" asked Alexander. "Did I not judge well? If this case had come before you, how would you have judged?"

Said the King of the North: "Had I been judge, I would have said: 'They both make a good argument. Let them split the treasure evenly.'"

Said Alexander the Great, "That is a judgment worthy of a tailor or washerwoman, but unworthy of a king."

In this alternative story, two greedy, selfish litigants stake their own claims to a fortune before a king who governs with injustice and cruelty. The citizens' lack of empathy for their fellow human being also trying to eke out a living is matched by Alexander's own lack of concern for their well-being. The buyer and the seller of the field each seek justice because they are not content to share their good fortune. They may not deserve the king's harsh verdict, but at first glance the story seems to imply that they don't deserve much better.

There is a more charitable reading of the story. Are the litigants who approach Alexander the Great truly greedy? Don't both of them have a just and valid claim? Granted they do not display the generosity of the citizens in the Faraway Kingdom, but does that make them evil? Neither means to steal from or harm the other. Suppose they had not come before Alexander but before the King of the North, who articulates a reasonably just verdict—wouldn't all be well? They could just split the fortune and go home.

Then again, is this more charitable reading tenable? Imagine that they in fact received the King of the North's judicious verdict. Dismissed, neither litigant is completely satisfied. Each bears resentment toward his neighbor and the king. Each ruminates on the loss of half the fortune he feels is rightfully his, nurses his anger, harbors hatred and ill will toward his fellow, and despises him in his heart. Perhaps this type of society would not self-destruct, but neither would it thrive and flourish. Nor would it provide security, happiness, and meaning for its citizens.

To frame this issue in other words: we tend to see the immorality of Alexander the Great as the core problem and thereby hold him responsible for the selfishness of his people. In this view the holders of power determine the ethos of the society they govern. Yet the reverse could also be true: Alexander the Great's ruthlessness might be a product of the type of people in his domain. If the wisdom of the Faraway King in the talmudic story can be seen as a response to the kindness and generosity of his citizenry, then the mean-spiritedness of Alexander's citizens in this story could be responsible for the king's ruling. Might virtuous subjects thus receive wise counsel and greedy subjects a harsh response?

In this view, the key to building a virtuous society resides with the people, especially where the government is relatively benevolent. Morality cannot be imposed from the top down but filters up from the bottom. It all begins when citizens distinguish true value from false treasure, even when the false treasure is real gold.

Didactic stories portray the extremes of character to accomplish their pedagogic purposes: consummately evil or benevolent rulers and exceedingly virtuous or selfish citizens. The reality is obviously more complex, as both leaders and subjects will typically exhibit a combination of positive and negative qualities and will also influence each other in various ways. These texts function as thought experiments, inviting the audience to examine themselves, their authorities, and their societies to reflect on where they fall on the continuum and to assess how they can move toward more salutary conditions. The utopian depictions are aspirational, pointing to an ideal that may be approached if never realized completely.

The Judgment of a King

What does Alexander mean by dismissing the verdict of the King of the North as the "judgment of a tailor or washerwoman"?[6]

In Alexander's eyes true sovereigns are extraordinary, and therefore all their deeds must be extraordinary. To suggest that the litigants split the treasure evenly is banal, routine, unexceptional, and unworthy of a great leader. When you are extraordinary, you must do extraordinary things.[7]

The Rabbis of the talmudic era lived under the political domination of the Romans in Palestine and the Persians in Mesopotamia. In the more than one thousand years from 586 BCE, when the Babylonians conquered Judah and destroyed the First Temple, until the end of the talmudic era, the Jews enjoyed only a brief period of political independence under the Hasmoneans (Maccabees). The Rabbis accordingly had a dark view of government, associating it mostly with conquest, taxation, and subjugation. They understood that even the most powerful kings were human, in contrast to the pretensions of many ancient societies that their rulers were extraordinary, having descended from the gods or being semi-divine themselves. Alexander the Great, in fact, was among history's leading offenders in this regard, claiming to be the son of Zeus, who had impregnated his mother through a lightning bolt. Even King David, King Solomon, and other virtuous biblical kings, in the Rabbinic view, were completely human, hence prone to error and sin. The Bible candidly reports that King David orchestrated the death of Uriah so he could marry Uriah's wife, Bathsheba, whom David had adulterously impregnated, prompting the Prophet Nathan to charge him, "Why then have you flouted the command of the Lord and done what displeases him?" (2 Sam. 12:9). King Solomon, for his part, had seven hundred wives, and "In his old age, his wives turned away Solomon's heart after other gods" (1 Kings 11:4).

The Rabbis taught that power and conquest should be directed within not without. We are to subjugate our own flaws not to subjugate other peoples: "[Shimon] ben Zoma taught: Who is mighty [*gibbor*]? One who conquers his [evil] inclination, as it says, 'Better to be forbearing than mighty, to have self-control than to conquer a city'" (Prov. 16:32) (*Mishnah Avot* 4:1). A medieval commentator elaborates: "To be a hero in war is not such a great achievement, as there are many others who also have power and strength and have taught themselves the arts of battle." By contrast "to conquer the evil inclination, the enemy that causes the loss of one's share in the next world, is the most exalted might and strength" (Commentary of Rabbeinu Yonah on *Mishnah Avot* 4:1).

Ben Zoma's teaching, which first appears in the Mishnah, is brilliantly incorporated into yet another of the Talmud's stories of Alexander the Great: Alexander travels to a distant region and there asks the "Elders of the South" ten questions about the cosmos and humanity, among them, "Who is called a mighty man?" The elders respond with an adaptation of Ben Zoma's words, "One who conquers his evil inclination" (*Tamid* 32a). When Alexander then asks, "What should a man do to make himself popular among other people?," they answer, "Let him hate authority and sovereignty." Alas, these words of wisdom do not seem to have made a deep impression on Alexander: he rewards the elders for their wise answers but then continues on his voyages of adventure and conquest. How fundamentally different are the values of Rabbinic and Greco-Roman societies!

13 The Carpenter and His Apprentice

The stories appearing throughout the Talmud are generally integrated smoothly within the back-and-forth of talmudic argumentation. Most stories relate in some way to the main legal topic of the larger talmudic passage. However, the Talmud also contains a few extensive compilations of ten or more stories that follow one another in a sustained collection, all oriented to the same basic topic. Among the longest of these compilations is a series of "stories of destruction" that tell of military conquests, subjugation to foreign powers, and national tragedies, especially the Romans' destruction of the Second Temple in 70 CE (*Gittin* 55b–58a). By means of these stories the Rabbis provide a multifaceted meditation on the causes, repercussions, and consequences of defeat and loss.

Talmudic stories pay little attention to military, economic, or political causes to explain the vicissitudes of war. Factors crucial to a modern military historian such as the size and quality of the respective armies, fiscal strength, the ability to mobilize resources, and the extent of political unity or disunity were of little concern to the Rabbis. After all, in 2 Kings 19 God's angel struck down the 185,000 Assyrian soldiers besieging Jerusalem in one night, forcing the Assyrian king to abandon his campaign—a demonstration of divine power proving to the Rabbis that no terrestrial force could stand against the Jewish people when they remained in God's favor. If the Babylonians, Greeks, Romans, or others triumphed over Jewish forces, it was only because God withdrew divine protection and delivered them into enemy hands.

What caused the loss of divine protection offered a perfect opening for didactic storytellers. In speaking of the past they were really addressing their contemporaries and looking to the future. Storytellers attributed morality and piety, or, conversely, sin and wickedness, as the driving forces determining national fortune. Often they targeted the moral failings of leaders, both because the leaders officially represented the people and also because it was presumed the leaders' sins were representative of the people's. In other cases storytellers told tales about ordinary folks, attempting to impart that immorality can also corrode society from the bottom up—each individual's conduct having a much larger impact than one might think.

The following story concludes the long collection of "stories of destruction." Its final line reads: "At that hour, the [heavenly] judgment [of destruction] was sealed." In other words, after these events, God finalized the divine decree that the Romans would triumph over the Jews and destroy the Temple.[1]

Underlying the story is the critical question: What was so terrible about this affair as to have pushed God over the edge irrevocably to doom his Temple and people?

Rav Yehudah said in the name of Rav: to what does this verse refer: "They defraud men of their households and people of their heritage" [Mic. 2:2]?

Once there was a certain man who set his eyes upon the wife of his master—he was a carpenter's apprentice.

At one point his master needed a loan.

The apprentice said to him: "Send your wife to me and I will give her the loan."

The master sent his wife to him. She stayed with him three days.

The master went ahead and came to the apprentice. He said to him, "Where is my wife whom I sent to you?"

He said to him, "I dismissed her immediately, and I heard that some youths abused her on the way home."

The master said to him, "What should I do?"

The apprentice said to him, "If you wish to listen to my advice— divorce her."

He said to him, "Her marriage settlement is great."

The apprentice said to him, "I will loan you [the money], so that you can pay her marriage settlement."

This one [the master] rose up and divorced her. He [the apprentice] went and married her.

When the time came and the master had no money to pay back the loan, the apprentice said to him, "Come and work for me to pay your debt."

So they [the apprentice and the wife] were sitting and eating and drinking, and the master was standing and serving them drinks. His tears were falling from his eyes into their cups.

At that moment, the heavenly judgment of destruction was sealed.

(*Gittin* 58a)

Rav, one of the leading early talmudic Rabbis, introduces his story by quoting a biblical verse: "They defraud men of their households and people of their heritage" (more on this later). The story proper begins with an ominous situation: an apprentice who has fallen in lust with his master's wife. The talmudic idiom "set one's eyes upon" always refers to illicit desire (see chapter 11).

Opportunity presents itself when the master requires a loan. That an apprentice would have funds at his disposal to lend his master is unusual, as we tend to think of apprentices as young and poor, earning minimal wages while learning a trade. However, in the Greco-Roman world wealthy families sometimes apprenticed their sons to talented artisans to learn a respectable occupation, and in such cases an apprentice's resources might exceed those of his master. Or this apprentice may simply be thrifty and crafty; knowing that his master routinely gets himself into monetary difficulties, he may carefully have saved his meager salary for just this occasion. In either case, the apprentice takes advantage of his master's current financial predicament by telling him to send his wife to pick up the money.

When his wife fails to return with the loan, the master "went ahead" to his apprentice's house to look into the delay. The phrasing "went ahead" or "preceded" is somewhat awkward, and probably should be taken ironically: the husband "went ahead" of his wife in that he set out to retrieve her "ahead" of her coming home herself. But what kind of husband waits three days before acting in a situation like this? What did he think was happening during this time? Presumably, given the small villages of that age, walking to the apprentice's home to pick up money and then walking back home should have taken no more than an hour or two.

Perhaps his lack of concern is another sign of his naïveté. Or maybe he legitimately cannot fathom that the apprentice he trusts would seduce his wife. Ostensibly the apprentice has shown good faith and generosity by offering him a loan. Yet surely something else could have happened to jeopardize his wife's safety. Indeed, he is aware of the perils of road travel—including molestation—as he accepts the apprentice's lie that she has been abused on the way home. And perhaps he had attributed her unexpected absence to positive reasons: maybe she had taken the opportunity to visit her family who lived close by.

When the master arrives at the apprentice's home, the scene of the crime, and the wily fellow springs the trap—lying that he dismissed the wife some time ago and heard that she was "abused" or raped on the way home—the naïve husband is at a loss about how to react. His confusion seems to result from a misplaced concern that his wife is somehow complicit in the sexual abuse she suffered, a kind of "blame the victim" mentality. As we know today, this perspective, however unjustified, was not uncommon. Nonetheless, according to Jewish law, if the wife was raped—the term "abused" is ambiguous—she should return to her husband and marriage without penalty. Only if she willingly committed adultery would Jewish law require the husband to divorce his wife (unless he is a *Kohen*—a "Priest"). Still, the master carpenter appears to feel that her violation—irrespective of her degree of responsibility—has debased his honor or his family's honor.

Proceeding with his diabolical plan, the apprentice now recommends divorce, and the master innocently consents. Yet once again his financial problems cause trouble. A provision of the marriage contract signed at a Jewish wedding stipulates that if a husband divorces his wife, he must pay her a sum of money known as the "marriage settlement" (*ketubah*). This payment functioned as protection for the wife, both in the sense of serving as a disincentive to divorce and guaranteeing that she would not be destitute if the husband insisted. Indeed, the "marriage settlement" would have functioned in precisely this way in our case . . . were it not for the nefarious machinations of the apprentice. But for a ready loan the master would not have been able to divorce his wife and, sooner or later, would probably have forgiven her (to the extent she needed forgiveness). With the apprentice's cash conveniently available, however, the master impulsively divorces his wife, inadvisably contracting another debt in the process.

The storyteller's careful choice of words contributes to the perversity of this plot. The husband "sends" (*shagger*) his wife to pick up the loan, while the apprentice informs the husband that he has "dismissed" or "released" (*petartiha*) the woman, not that he has "sent" her back home as we would expect. This same verb, "dismiss" or "release," also means "divorce."[2] Thus the verb foreshadows the husband's choice to divorce his wife and exposes a warped measure-for-measure causal nexus: the (false) dismissal of the wife by the apprentice leads to the ill-advised dismissal/divorce by the master. At the same time, the apprentice's words point to himself as the ultimate cause of the future dissolution of the marriage: "I dismissed her" functions as a double entendre for "I divorced her," that is, brought about the divorce.

The key transition is narrated with extreme economy and verbal balance, like two hemistichs of a line of poetry: "This one [the master] rose up and divorced her / He [the apprentice] went and married her." There are six words in the original Hebrew: four verbs and two pronominal subjects (in the Hebrew, the pronominal objects are attached to the verbs: divorced-her, married-her). The parallel set of two verbs in each half emphasizes both the premeditated relationship between the events and their immediacy: rose/divorced→went/married. The precipitous reaction is mirrored by calculated counterreaction: *as soon as* the one divorced her, the other married her. We might even picture a scribe finalizing the writing of the divorce document on behalf of the master and then proceeding directly to the next item of business on his desk: the new marriage contract on behalf of the apprentice.

Quickly the reversal of fortune hurtles toward its tragic conclusion. The hapless master cannot pay his debt, as the apprentice no doubt anticipated. He now adds the ultimate insult to injury: forcing the former teacher to serve his student and thus coercing a former husband to witness another man supping happily with his former wife. Surely at this point the victorious apprentice, having acquired the wife he had long desired, could now forgive the master's debt, or at least make some other repayment arrangement such as having the master work as a servant in any third-party's home and recompense the apprentice accordingly. Such an arrangement would have been infinitely preferable to servitude by the former husband—now impoverished, cuckolded, reduced to servitude, weeping bitter tears into the very cups the apprentice and wife raise to their lips in comfort and satisfaction.

The story begins when the apprentice "set his eyes" upon his master's wife and ends with tears dropping from the master's eyes. This heartrending situation moves God to doom his people and Temple.

The Cup of Tears

In the final scene, the two cups containing the master's bitter tears are powerful symbols of grief. In fact "tear cups" or "tear flasks" were common ritual objects in the ancient Mediterranean world. Mourners collected their tears in small containers, often in tear-shaped flasks, sealed them with wax, and gave them to relatives of the deceased to keep as memorials of grief for loved ones who had died. The fuller the cup, the more profound the grief, and the greater the honor for the departed. Such cups could be opened at sad occasions, such as anniversaries of the death, days of lamentation, and public fasts, to stimulate grief and further weeping. Psalm 56, a lament by a despondent and wretched man bemoaning his misery, pleads to God: "You keep count of my wanderings; put my tears in Your flask, into Your record" (Ps. 56:9). Here the Psalmist asks God to keep the flask of his tears to rouse God to compassion and mercy. A late midrash relates that when God removed his "holy spirit" from King David as punishment for his sin of adultery with Bathsheba, "Each and every day he [David] filled a cup with tears" due to his deep grief (*Midrash Yalqut Shimoni*, 2 Samuel, #165).

Some psalms incorporate the drinking of tears, a particularly poignant image, as the symbol of misery is not only exuded from the body but then ingested again, as if the body cannot free itself from despair. Psalms 102:9 laments: "For I have eaten ashes like bread, and mixed my drink with tears, because of Your wrath and Your fury." Similarly, Psalms 80:5–6 pleads: "O Lord, God of hosts, how long will You be wrathful toward the prayers of Your people? You have fed them tears as their daily bread, made them drink great measures of tears." Unremitting suffering pervades the Psalmist's experiences to the point that there is no respite even for mundane and necessary activities like eating and drinking.

The talmudic storyteller, however, provides a twist on this biblical imagery: Rather than the master drinking his own tears, the happy couple will drink them as they raise their cups to their lips. This grotesque gesture is to be taken as the ultimate expression of triumph, like warriors in some cultures consuming the heart or blood of their victims. The apprentice has taken away his former master's freedom, his wife, his financial resources, and now, in the most extreme form of physical dominance, he consumes his bodily secretions.

The cups also are symbolic of the wedding feast. In Jewish tradition, seven wedding blessings are recited over a cup of wine, which is then mixed with another cup of wine blessed during the *Birkat ha-Mazon* (Grace after Meals), and the blended wine is given to the bride and groom to drink together. The mixing of the wine symbolizes the joyous, shared life they now begin. While the meal described in our story is not the marriage feast (or the meals of the following week, which also include this special ceremony), the cups of a recently married couple supping together evoke this symbolism. Yet here their drinks are mixed with tears of the former spouse, symbols of suffering, making for an obscene mixture of mirth and sorrow. Not only has the one purchased his joy with the sadness of the other, but he forces the two into a shared space. The cosmos cannot abide such humiliation, the storyteller means us to understand: God seals the decree of destruction.

Prophecy of Disaster

The storyteller presents the account as an exemplification of a biblical verse—actually a biblical prophecy—quoted at the outset. In context the Prophet Micah (Mic. 2:1–4) warns the Israelites of an impending disaster:

(1) Ah, those who plan iniquity
   And design evil on their beds;
   When morning comes they do it,
   For they have the power.

(2) They covet fields and seize them;
   Houses, and take them away.
   They defraud men of their households;
   And people of their heritage.

(3) Assuredly, thus says the Lord: I am planning such a
   misfortune against this clan that you will not be able to free
   your necks from it. You will not be able to walk erect; it will
   be such a time of disaster.

(4) In that day,
   One shall recite a poem about you,
   And utter a bitter lament,

And shall say:
"My people's portion changes hands;
How it slips away from me!
Our field is allotted to a rebel.
We are utterly ravaged."

The first two verses denounce certain wicked people who perpetrate social abuses, and verses three and four delineate the impending punishment for the crimes. Notably the apprentice's machinations in the story match the offenses in the first two verses. He deviously "planned iniquity" and "designed evil," evidently possessing the "power to do so" (2) on account of his wealth. The storyteller probably understood "on their beds" to mean "about their beds," that is, about the beds of others; the apprentice seduces the wife from her rightful marriage bed. He "coveted" and "defrauded" a man of his "household," meaning his wife (in Rabbinic Hebrew the word for "house," *bayit,* means "wife" as well), and also defrauded him of his "heritage," that is, his livelihood and possessions, by impoverishing the master and requiring him to work as a servant to repay his debts.

God pays keen attention to such oppression, the prophet warns, and metes out a terrible punishment (3–4). More broadly, this can be understood to explicate the Temple's destruction and the Jewish people's defeat by the Romans. The "people's portion changes hand" when God favors their enemies rather than treating the Jewish people as the Chosen People, God's special "portion." The storyteller likely interpreted the "field allotted to a rebel" to allude to the Roman conquest of the Temple; in Rabbinic exegesis biblical references to a "field" commonly refer to the Jerusalem Temple. Finally, the "disaster" and "bitter lament" (3) proclaiming the people to be "utterly ravaged" (4) serve as an apt description for the Roman defeat and the destruction of both the Second Temple and Jerusalem.

If the events recounted in the story represent the realization of Micah's prophecy, then from the storyteller's perspective it follows that God sealed the decree of destruction "at that moment." Both the Rabbinic storytellers and the biblical prophets viewed social evils such as immoral interpersonal behavior as among the most heinous sins, often judging them worse than religious offenses. For example, another talmudic tradition states that despite the fact that the Jewish people were learning Torah, fulfilling the commandments, and performing acts of piety, God destroyed the Temple due to the "gratuitous hatred" (*Yoma* 9b) they showed one another. Elsewhere the Talmud observes, "Anyone who humiliates another person in public, it is as though he spilled his blood" (*Bava Metzi'a* 58b)—a condemnation rarely extended to other sins.

And so it is in our story: A premeditated "plan of iniquity" involving deception, seduction, prevarication, and impoverishment, culminating in a cruel reversal in which the former master must continually witness the wicked apprentice rejoicing in triumph with his ex-wife and household possessions— "at that moment" God draws the line and condemns the people to "disaster."

Story and Allegory

If the key to appreciating the outrage perpetrated by the apprentice devolves from the reversal in fortunes, then we might take the story more allegorically to refer to the Rabbinic perspective on the Jewish people's historical experience. In talmudic times, after the Temple's destruction, the Rabbis looked out at a topsy-turvy world: the wicked Romans prospered while the righteous Jewish people suffered. Descendants of Abraham, the bearers of God's Revelation, the Jewish people who studied Torah and observed the commandments ought to have been the most powerful nation in the world. The Romans—pagans, sinners, brigands—ought to have been subservient to the Jews. This much the Bible promised. Isaiah 60:10–12 proclaimed: "Aliens shall rebuild your walls; their kings shall wait upon you. Your gates shall always stay open; day and night they shall never be shut—To let in the wealth of nations, with their kings in procession. For the nation of the kingdom that does not serve you shall perish; such nations shall be destroyed." Deuteronomy 28:1 pronounced: "Now, if you obey the Lord your God, to observe faithfully all His commandments, which I enjoin upon you this day, the Lord your God will set you high above all the nations of the earth." For the Romans to have defeated the Jews and destroyed the Temple was an inversion of the biblical hierarchy, a reversal of the proper order of the cosmos.

Because Deuteronomy 28:1 and other such verses made the Jewish people's fortunes conditional upon their observing the commandments, the standard Rabbinic explanation for their defeat was sin (as discussed in chapter 5). Indeed, the apprentice's despicable crimes exemplified sinful behavior and its repercussions. Yet in concluding the passage with a story of reversal the Talmud simultaneously portrayed an upside-down society: a master serves his apprentice; a teacher waits on his student; a wife is deceitfully stolen from her rightful husband. This vision of a social order with its proper structure inverted paralleled the Rabbis' sense that the Roman conquest represented an upside-down world with its rightful political and social hierarchies reversed. The story thus functioned as a type of mirror image of the fallen world in which the Rabbis found themselves. For the Rabbis, telling the story of the apprentice was a way of telling their own story.

To advance this allegorical reading we can understand Micah 2:2 as referring to the sins of the Romans, not the Jews. The word for "household" or "house," *bayit*, also refers to God's house, the Jerusalem Temple, while the word translated as "heritage," *naḥalah*, also means "land" and often refers to Israel's heritage/land, the Land of Israel. The verse can thus be understood as a coded prophecy of the Rabbinic experience: "They [the Romans] oppressed men [the Jews] [through the destruction of] their Temple, and a people [through the destruction] of their Land [Israel]." Like the apprentice who despoiled the master by taking his wife and his position, the Romans destroyed the Temple and stole its treasures, took possession of the Land of Israel, and subjugated the Jewish people. The concluding line of the story should then be understood ironically: "At that moment the judgment was sealed?" That is, "Granted we Jews have sinned, but You, God, delivered us to the Romans for punishment? To the evil empire who conquered and killed peoples throughout the known world, enslaved entire populations, taxed the vanquished to the point of starvation? To this nation who seized our land and plundered our Temple?" The Rabbinic storyteller voices a protest: "What kind of a judgment is this?"

Another potential allegorical reading focuses on the fact that the master is identified as a carpenter. This datum appears to add nothing to the story, as the profession does not play a role in the plot. Had the story opened, "He was a weaver's (shoemaker's, blacksmith's, bricklayer's) apprentice," the analysis would be no different. In fact, several Talmud manuscripts lack this line, suggesting it was a later addition to an original version that did not specify the master's profession. As often happens, the incorporation of a later gloss produces an awkward text: "Once there was a certain man who set his eyes upon the wife of his master—he was a carpenter's apprentice." The story would read more smoothly as: "Once there was a carpenter's apprentice who set his eyes upon the wife of his master." What do we gain by learning that the master was a carpenter?

One possibility is that a carpenter's primary endeavor, namely building, contrasts with the story's purpose, namely to explain the destruction, the tearing down of the Temple. A carpenter builds houses, whereas God's terrestrial house, the Jerusalem Temple, has been razed. This contrast would reemphasize the cruel reversal in fortune marked by the Roman conquest. But there may be a deeper symbolism at work.

According to Christian tradition Jesus was a carpenter by trade. Mark 6:3 refers to Joseph, Jesus's father, as a *tekton*, a Greek word meaning "craftsman" or "carpenter." Later Christian authors assumed Jesus learned this trade too. Justin Martyr, a Christian writer of the second century CE, wrote: "He [Jesus] was deemed a carpenter, for he was in the habit of working among men, making ploughs and yokes; by which he taught the symbols of righteousness and an active life."[3]

For the Rabbis, the narrative of a carpenter supplanting and displacing his master could be interpreted as an allegory of Christianity's attempt to supersede Judaism. Christianity claimed to be the "true Israel," to hold the "new covenant" with God that replaced the "old covenant" with Abraham and his descendants. In the fourth century CE, a few decades after the Roman emperor Constantine converted to Christianity, it became the official religion of the Byzantine Empire. The Rabbis of the time were therefore experiencing a painful reversal whereby Christianity seemed to be displacing Judaism—and even appropriating Jewish identity itself, much like the appropriations of identity the apprentice perpetrates against his master.

Now this allegorical reading is imperfect as, for one, the symbolism of the wife is unclear. Does she represent the Torah/covenant that Christianity has seized from Judaism? Or God, who Christians claimed had severed ties with the Jews, "divorcing" them in favor of his new people? Or Jewish converts to Christianity?

Certainly the Rabbis believed that Christians tricked and deceived the Jews, seducing them to accept false theological claims much as the apprentice deceives and seduces the wife. The uncertainty regarding the symbolism of the wife notwithstanding, this reading has much to recommend it: Rabbinic allegories and parables rarely map perfectly onto that which they represent. Indubitably the master's tears at the end of the story poignantly express how the Rabbis must have felt as they were forced to witness the rise of Christianity.

Victim or Conspirator?

The story analysis thus far has pitted a wicked and cunning apprentice against his naïve and credulous master. However, might there be an alternative reading in which the master shares some culpability?

First, the master blithely sends his wife to pick up the loan, as the apprentice instructs, rather than go himself. Shouldn't he have questioned why the apprentice directs him to do so? Why couldn't the apprentice have delivered the loan when he arrived at the master's home or shop for work? In the Hellenistic world upper-class women or noblewomen would never walk unescorted in public, much less call at a bachelor's house.

Second, why does the master delay for three days before setting out in search of his wife? Even if he had conjectured a plausible explanation for her absence, shouldn't he at least have entertained the possibility that she encountered some trouble along the way and gone to investigate that first day? How could he sleep soundly that night, as if he were oblivious to her absence?

Third, why does the master immediately accept the apprentice's report of her abuse on the way home? Any man with sound judgment, on the one hand, and concern for his wife, on the other, would immediately question the apprentice's report that he had "heard" she was violated. How did he hear and when? Who told him—a respected, reliable individual or a known busybody who exaggerated chatter while circulating it? In short, was there any truth whatsoever to this report? And, most of all, where was his wife now?

Even more so, if his wife had been violated, shouldn't the master have reacted with dismay, shock, anger, compassion, or some combination thereof? Shouldn't he have continued to question the apprentice until he ascertained where his wife was, and then sprinted to meet up with her, comfort her, attempt to heal her pain?

Our protagonist does none of these. Instead, he solicits advice from the apprentice as to the best tactical response—the very apprentice who the master believes did nothing for three days despite hearing that his master's wife was abused after leaving his home—neither informing his teacher / her husband nor attempting to find and console the wife!

Finally, his decision to divorce his wife who was victimized by others—and this solely on hearsay—is flagrantly insensitive.

Perhaps the storyteller is even inviting us to entertain the possibility that the master was not simply negligent but complicit, at least early on in the affair. Could the apprentice have winked knowingly as he said to the master, "Send your wife to me and I will lend her the money"—the unspoken understanding, "I'll lend you the money—on condition that you let me have my way with your wife"? The master consents . . . but then three days go by. He believed the price was a single assignation. This has gone too far. People are beginning to talk. He determinedly sets out for the apprentice's house, but by the time he arrives, the dashing, resourceful apprentice has won the wife's affection—a conquest rendered surprisingly easy as she resented her husband for prostituting her. The two have concocted a plan: The apprentice remorsefully informs the master that he regrets his illicit requirement— and indeed in the final reckoning, he could not bring himself to commit adultery and dismissed the wife immediately. Alas (or so he heard), on her way home she enticed some youths who then accosted and abused her. The master, as he anticipates, now asks for his advice, and the foul scheme succeeds.[4]

Along these lines we might also consider the wife's behavior. To what degree should she be held responsible for the tragedy? For the most part she appears to be a pawn: ogled, coveted, and preyed upon by the apprentice; sent forth and then divorced by the master, presumably against her will. The transition line emphasizes her passivity, "This one [the master] rose up and divorced her. He [the apprentice] went and married her." She is the object of their actions, not an acting agent in her own right. This portrayal is in keeping with the frequent Rabbinic assessment that women, like children, lack full adult legal capacity. On the other hand, in many Rabbinic stories women are just as clever and crafty as the male protagonists, or more so.

The only action attributed to the wife in the story is the datum "She stayed with him three days." Need we even assume anything unseemly happened during those three days? It's possible that no sin occurred whatsoever. Or, maybe the apprentice raped her and locked her in the basement. Or did she willingly fornicate with an attractive, brilliant rival who she realized had more potential than her husband?

If in fact she was seduced into committing adultery, Jewish law required her husband to divorce her, in which case she might have decided to throw in her lot with her seducer for lack of a better option. In theory she would be forbidden to the adulterer too, but the false account of her abuse on the road may have obviated this problem.

Going even further: What if the wife participated in the plot from the outset? What if she returned the handsome young apprentice's lecherous gaze, and the two of them devised the scheme together?

To the extent that we blame the master and wife as well as the apprentice for the debacle, the story becomes less about the wicked oppressing the innocent and more about the corruption of society in general. In this case the story teaches that the destruction of the Temple was a response to a widespread breakdown of social mores. A society characterized by covetousness, seduction, infidelity, deception, and defrauding; a society replete with husbands who show no concern for their wives, husbands who unjustly divorce their wives, wives who betray their husbands, students who supplant their masters, rich men who impoverish poor men, victorious men who demean the men they have triumphed over just to extend the pleasure of gloating at their victims' expense— such societies cannot endure in a holy world.

14 Standing on One Leg

Among the most popular talmudic stories today is that of the potential convert to Judaism who approaches Hillel and Shammai with a strange proposition:

Once a gentile came before Shammai. He said to him, "I will convert to Judaism on the condition that you teach me the entire Torah while I stand on one leg [*regel*]."

Shammai drove him away with the builder's measuring stick that was in his hand.

He came before Hillel [with the same condition].

Hillel converted him. He said to him, "That which is hateful to you, do not do to your fellow. That is the entire Torah. The rest is its commentary. Go and learn it."

(*Shabbat* 31a)

Like other talmudic stories, this is a fictional tale that imparts an important didactic lesson: "That which is hateful to you, do not do to your fellow." On another level the story also addresses a significant practical question: How should one treat potential converts whose conviction appears to be less than optimal? Such gentiles might include those who become inquisitive after hearing some positive things about Judaism, who feel dissatisfied with their own religion, who wish to marry a Jewish spouse, and/or who are exploring religious options. The gentile in this story approaches the Rabbis with an inappropriate—even rude and offensive—stipulation: to be taught the entire Torah while standing on one leg. That is, clearly, an extremely brief amount of time, whereas the "entire Torah" encompasses a prodigious body of literature: the Written Torah (the Bible) and the Oral Torah (the Mishnah with its sixty-three tractates and 525 chapters), the Talmud (in its present form, with more than two-and-a half-million words, though it may have been shorter when the story was composed), midrash (biblical interpretation), liturgy, customs, theology, and more. The Rabbis refer to the Torah as "vaster than the ocean." How could one even begin to teach this entire corpus in such a minimal span?

Shammai treats the potential convert as a troublemaker—a provocateur intent upon annoying or confounding the Rabbis. After all, in Shammai's view, at best the questioner displays a shocking lack of seriousness: "I am not willing to put in the time and effort to observe, study, and train as I would to master an important skill. Give me the reward without the hard work." In a nice touch of characterization, the storyteller describes Shammai sending the man packing with a builder's measuring stick, the wooden rod "that was in his hand," suggesting the short-tempered Sage habitually carried this implement to be ready to deploy it against others.

Note that by the time of the Babylonian Talmud, Hillel had become a Rabbinic hero of legendary proportions and Shammai a kind of antihero. Hillel would model the proper course of action, while Shammai functioned as a negative role model by showing the behavior to avoid (similarly, see the House of Shammai's response to an ugly bride in chapter 8).

In this instance, Hillel, the model of humility and patience, adopts a different tack with the questioner. Perhaps, he considers, what appears to be impudence is in fact naïveté or ignorance: a lack of awareness of the depth of the Jewish religious tradition and way of life. He gives the man the benefit of the doubt and complies with the stipulation.

At first glance, Hillel's response is as straightforward and direct as the demand, but on deeper reflection it is complex and challenging. The initial statement offers a version of the "golden rule" found in many religions, "Do unto others as you would have done to yourself" or, as Hillel puts it, "That which is hateful to you, do not do to your fellow." But there is more. On the one hand, that is "the entire Torah"; on the other, there is "the rest," the "commentary"—which must be learned too. Hillel thus temporizes with an answer acceptable for the situation but which contains an implicit, quasi-stipulation of his own, as if saying: "This is the entire Torah *for now*, but there is more, much more, a massive commentary, *which you must also learn*."

In this way, Hillel exemplifies virtuous character traits—patience, humility, gentleness, understanding—and thus the story teaches us the proper manner of reaching out to interested proselytes. Indeed, the Talmud subsequently relates that the prospective convert felt eternally grateful that Hillel's gentleness "brought me under the Divine Presence," unlike Shammai's impatience, which had sought to "drive me from the world."

At the same time, the odd stipulation and paradoxical answer suggest an alternative way to approach the story's main point. What if the question itself is considered independently of its narrative setting? Is there an essence to the Torah? If so, what is that essence? What is Judaism's fundamental principle—observing the Sabbath, believing in one God, observing the Ten Commandments, performing good deeds? This then becomes a serious and difficult theological issue.

Framed more personally, the question might be: what is the minimum I must do to be pious? In other words, since it is virtually impossible to observe the entirety of Judaism—how much suffices?

The story ostensibly attributes such a query to a potential convert because he could plausibly pose it, given his unfamiliarity with the tradition. Yet there is a deeper reason to feature a gentile. When we ourselves are forced to confront and struggle with our own theological doubts, anxiety may foment within us. A safer tactic is to project such troubling questions on the "Other," as if the uncertainties originate from outsiders, not insiders, and certainly not from inside one's own psyche.

Why did the storyteller employ the image of "standing on one leg" rather than another method of indicating brevity, for example, "Teach me the entire Torah while I hold my breath" or ". . . while I count to twenty"? Scholars have suggested that this odd stipulation contains a wordplay. The Hebrew word for leg, *regel*, sounds like the Latin word *regula*, meaning "basic principle" or "rule" (as in English: "regulate, "regulation," "regular"). For this reason, too, the storyteller might have put the question in the mouth of a gentile who likely had studied Greek and Latin and would have been aware of these meanings. With the Latin-Hebrew pun in mind, we can understand the proposition slightly differently: "Teach me the entire Torah in one basic principle." The storyteller essentially asks, "Is there a basic principle that underlies the enormous, multifaceted, diverse aspects of Judaism?"

When Hillel answers both yes and no—formulating the fundamental principle but adding that the rest must be studied too— there is yet another wordplay. Besides meaning "rule," the Latin *regula* can also refer to a "ruler," a measuring-stick. While Shammai opposes the attempt to reduce the Torah to a basic *regula* (rule, principle) by means of his own *regula* (measuring stick), Hillel supplies the desired *regula* (principle).

Many retellings of this charming story focus on identifying the essence of Judaism. These storytellers typically omit the last line and conclude with Hillel's instruction: "That which is hateful to you, do not do to your fellow."

One recent paraphrase, for example, recounts that the Sages "tell of a man who wished to convert to Judaism and approached Hillel the Elder and requested that he teach him the whole of the Torah while standing on one foot. Hillel complied and told the man: 'That which is hateful to you, do not do unto your fellow.'"[1] The author subsequently explains: "What the convert was really asking Hillel the elder was, 'What kind of religion do you Jews have? Is it for the benefit of man, or does it involve idol-worship?'" Hillel's answer is understood as "conveying to him the message that a man must develop self-control, since, if he does not, he will eventually do harm to himself, as well as to others."[2] How this writer derived his explanation about a religion that benefits human beings as opposed to idolatry is difficult to understand. But it is clear he abbreviates the story and takes Hillel's principle alone as the response.

Alas, those abbreviated versions whereby Hillel provides the shortcut that eliminates the demands for further engagement ironically undermine Hillel's point and turn the story on its head. Our storyteller wants us to understand that there are no real shortcuts, there is no way to reduce the depth of a tradition to one idea, no way to avoid serious study and dedication because the "rest" must be internalized too.

A similar fate has afflicted Hillel's concluding line: "The rest is its commentary. Go and learn it." By entering our public discourse in an abbreviated fashion as "The rest is commentary" without "Go and learn it," its meaning becomes "the rest is less important" or even "the rest is unimportant."[3] Thus when the economist Steven E. Landsburg wrote, "Most of economics can be summarized in four words: 'People respond to incentives.' The rest is commentary,"[4] he meant that other economic principles are secondary and largely unnecessary to understanding economic theory in action. Similarly, "Zero Tolerance to Prejudice—the Rest Is Commentary," a Huffington Post column decrying an antisemitic incident at the London School of Economics,[5] conveyed that there are no excuses or justification for intolerance; any discussion beyond this fundamental principle is unnecessary. When the great science fiction writer Isaac Asimov opined, "All life is nucleic acid; the rest is commentary,"[6] he meant that DNA is the most important factor in determining the nature of any life form; everything else that contributes to life pales in significance. In some cases the authors even invoke the Talmud directly. Thus Dr. Abigail Zucker opened a 2006 *New York Times* column assessing the state of treatment for the AIDS virus: "Instinctively, the first thing we want to know about a disease is whether it is going to kill us. As the Talmud says, pretty much all the rest is commentary. Twenty-five years ago, this was the only question about AIDS we could answer with any certainty."[7] Here "commentary" clearly means "secondary," of lesser significance.

For the talmudic storyteller, by contrast, the two halves of Hillel's statement are interdependent and inextricably connected: the rest is (its) commentary, it is of crucial significance, and *therefore* one *must* learn it. Nothing in the original context indicates that "commentary" is any less significant than what is commented upon. Indeed, in Rabbinic terms "commentary" is equal to, if not more important than, the base text, because it explains how to understand that text. Likewise, the following mandate, "Go and learn it," far from minimizing the significance of the rest of the Torah rather emphasizes its indispensability.

#Shortcut@postmodern_age.com

These contemporary trends of abbreviating Hillel's instruction—either neglecting the directive to "Go and learn it" or employing "The rest is commentary" to minimize the importance of comprehensive study in favor of one overarching idea—conform to a widespread aspect of modernity in the digital age. We live in the era of the shortcut, the sound bite, the short attention span. We postmoderns approach just about everything like the gentile approaches Hillel, expecting that whatever we need to learn will be presented to us such that we can absorb it while standing on one leg. Researchers recently found that since the year 2000 human attention spans have dropped more than 30 percent, to about eight seconds. The study authors concluded: "The age of smartphones has left humans with such a short attention span even a goldfish can hold a thought for longer."[8] Similarly, studies have shown that if web pages do not load within two seconds, the user often will abandon them.[9] The editors of the *New York Times* redesigned the paper's second and third pages to provide article abstracts or "shortcuts" that avoid the "inefficient" task of having to read the full stories, explained its design director Tom Bodkin.[10] In *The Atlantic,* Nicholas Carr, a leading writer on technology and culture, bemoaned the influence of the internet: "Immersing myself in a book or a lengthy article used to be easy. My mind would get caught up in the narrative or the turns of the argument, and I'd spend hours strolling through long stretches of prose. That's rarely the case anymore. Now my concentration often starts to drift after two or three pages."[11]

The erosion of reading ability has in turn influenced the dissemination of knowledge. Book publishers now advise contemporary authors to write shorter books appropriate for the "shrinking reader attention span."[12] University professors are routinely pressured to reduce the number of readings assigned for their courses.[13] Dozens of websites— PinkMonkey, Shmoop, Grade-Saver, and the like—offer short summaries of assigned readings as well as essay topics, study questions, quizzes, and other such aids for abbreviated attention spans. *The Great American Bathroom Book*, now in three volumes, with more than one million copies sold, presents two-page summaries of classics such as Joyce's *Ulysses* and Homer's *The Odyssey*—making cursory knowledge of a work of high literature achievable in one "sitting." In *How to Talk about Books You Haven't Read* (2007), French professor of literature Pierre Bayard offers a plethora of strategies to accomplish this task, observing, "it is wholly unnecessary to have opened a book in order to deliver an enlightened opinion on it"; instructing, "the first condition for speaking about a book you haven't read is not to be ashamed"; and insisting, "reading any particular book is a waste of time compared to keeping our perspective about books overall."[14]

Perhaps nothing is more emblematic of the contemporary propensity for the shortcut than Twitter, where anything worth articulating must be radically limited to 140 (recently expanded to 280) characters. Indeed, a modern version of our story might read, "A gentile came before Shammai and Hillel and said: I will convert to Judaism if you tweet me the entire Torah in one Twitter post.'"

Stones and Waters

The Talmud story, in contrast, teaches us that there are no shortcuts to attaining wisdom. Anything worth learning, be it a meaningful way to lead one's life, a religious tradition, or a moral vision, requires patience (as modeled by Hillel), time, and perseverance.

In his bestseller *Outliers*, Malcolm Gladwell hypothesizes that many highly successful people did not achieve their greatness through brilliance or natural talents alone but required a great deal of practice—Gladwell estimates ten thousand hours. The same may be true of attaining the insight necessary to lead a meaningful life. Ancient civilizations imparted this wisdom: the slow, plodding tortoise in Aesop's fable prevails over the quick and frivolous hare.

Some Rabbinic stories about the great Rabbi Akiva transmit similar messages. According to one tradition, he had no education until he was forty years old. One day, beside a spring, he came upon a stone that had a natural hollow cut into it. When he asked, "Who hewed out this stone?" and was told that drops of water had worn it down little by little, Akiva inferred: if something as soft as water could wear away something as hard as stone, then "words of Torah can penetrate my heart, which is flesh and blood" (*Avot de-Rabbi Natan* 6:2). The Bible sometimes speaks negatively of those who have a "heart of stone," and Akiva may also have had this metaphor in mind, thinking that even a heart as (figuratively) hard as stone, as resistant to change, could be reshaped over the course of time. He resolved to study slowly and unremittingly, like the drops of water, until he became a great Sage. Thus this storyteller hoped to teach that it is never too late for us to start to acquire wisdom—yet at the same time, mastering a tradition is an arduous process, our progress measured little by little over years.

According to other traditions Akiva began with the Hebrew alphabet, studied the letters, then words, then biblical verses, then biblical interpretations, and then Rabbinic sayings and the rest of the commentaries until, more than twenty years later, he mastered the entire corpus of tradition.

This story also suggests that embarking on the pursuit of wisdom requires an inner spark. The vision of the water dripping on the stone transformed Akiva, altering his self-perception, allowing him to realize that he could change himself—he could accomplish what he yearned for if he devoted himself to that goal. Beholding the worn stone, he suddenly understood that despite his advanced age, he was not fated to be a shepherd for the rest of his life. He could fashion himself into a different person.

And so we return to stones. This book began with a story of an inconsiderate man tossing stones out of his yard into the public domain and eventually learning life lessons when he stumbled on those same stones. That story ends abruptly, but I would like to think that the protagonist, through his experience, internalized those truths and changed his perspective on life. His transformation, too, having begun with a self-inflicted wound, would require a great deal of effort to achieve a virtuous and moral character.

"All beginnings are difficult," observes the Talmud (*Ta'anit* 10b). It is tempting to counter with another saying the Talmud attributes to Hillel, "If not now, when?" (*Mishnah Avot* 1:14). But this adage, despite its straightforward truthfulness, seems rather simplistic. Study of talmudic stories teaches that the path to spiritual and moral growth is arduous and checkered. To appreciate the deeper truths behind superficial realities and to make them a part of one's life requires wisdom and experience—and the wisdom of experience. Nonetheless, the endeavor is by no means insurmountable—even the hardest rocks are worn away by persistent waters.

Notes

Introduction

1. MacIntyre, *After Virtue*, 201.
2. Quoted in Lewis, *The Undoing Project*, 250.
3. Amirtham, *Stories Make People*, vii–viii; Gottschall, *The Storytelling Animal*.
4. Wiesel, *The Gates of the Forest*, unpaginated first few pages.
5. Giddens, *Modernity and Self-Identity*, 188.
6. Weil, *The Need for Roots*, 41.
7. Mitchell, "The Homeless Modern," 13.
8. Kushner, *When All You've Ever Wanted Isn't Enough*, 156.

1. The Surreal Sleeper

1. Entis, "Chronic Loneliness."
2. Harris, "The Loneliness Epidemic."
3. Holt-Lunstad, "Loneliness and Social Isolation," 202.
4. "Seven Cultures that Celebrate Aging and Respect Their Elders."
5. For literature on this story, see Rubenstein, *Stories of the Babylonian Talmud*, 62–76, with additional bibliography; and Fraenkel, "Paronomasia in Aggadic Narratives." See also the references in Avery-Peck, "The Galilean Charismatic," 151–57.
6. Plato, *Critias* 11c, quoted in Sands, *Forestry*, 20. See also Hughes, *An Environmental History*, 64.
7. Lyons, "An Iroquois Perspective," 174.
8. Wood and Welker, "Tribes as Trustees," 374.
9. Wood and Welker, "Tribes as Trustees," 386.
10. Quote Investigator, accessed February 13, 2017, http://quoteinvestigator.com/2013/01/22/borrow-earth/.
11. Young, "Fallen from Time," 547–73.
12. Young, "Fallen from Time," 547.

2. What to Do with an Aged (and Annoying) Mother?

1. This is the way the Ten Commandments are divided in Jewish tradition. In some Christian traditions the commandments are divided differently, such that honoring parents is the Fourth Commandment.
2. Medieval Jewish tradition would take up many of the complexities of the commandment in great detail; see Blidstein, *Honor thy Father and Mother*.
3. Pillemer, *Thirty Lessons for Living*, 105.
4. My reading is indebted to Jay Rovner's masterful analysis of this story within "Rav Assi Had This Old Mother." For additional literature on the story, see Kosman, "'Internal Homeland' and 'External Homeland,'" 259–77; and Valler, *Woman and Womanhood*, 113–19.
5. See Rovner, "Rav Assi Had This Old Mother," 106–8.

3. Forbidden Fruit, or How Not to Seduce Your Husband

1. Dorff, "The Jewish Family in America," 223.
2. Feldman, *Marital Relations*, 75, 35.
3. In the printed versions of the Talmud a line has been added that Rabbi Ḥiyya fasted for the rest of his life (to atone for his sin) and died from the effects of fasting. This later addition attempts to avoid the tragic suicide. It does not appear in Talmud manuscripts and is not part of the original story.
4. For additional scholarship on this story see Naeh, "Freedom and Celibacy," 73–89; Fraenkel, "Remarkable Phenomena," 59–65.
5. Scheer, "The Playboy Interview: Jimmy Carter," 63–86.
6. *Qiddushin* 40a. The passage, however, is more complicated and deserves detailed analysis. There are also some areas of law in which intentions are considered tantamount to action, such as priests' intentions when performing sacrifices, when certain types of thoughts may disqualify the sacrifice. On this issue see Levinson, "From Narrative Practise," 345–68; and Rosen-Zvi, "The Mishnaic Mental Revolution," 36–58.
7. See McCarthy, *Rekindling Desire*, 5–6.
8. Out of respect for his fellow Rabbis, a talmudic storyteller would not have related a tale in which a Rabbi actually consorts with a prostitute or engages in extramarital sex; instead, this storyteller invented a brilliant plot that involved forbidden sex in a technically legal way.
9. Paik, Sanchagrin, and Heimer, "Broken Promises," 546–61.

4. Men Are from Babylonia, Women Are from the Land of Israel

1. This is the reading in the NJPS translation of the Bible. Others translate this as "Do not take the Lord's name in vain" and understand the verse to prohibit frivolous, casual mentions of God's name to no purpose. Some rabbinic interpretations apply the verse to "vain oaths," such as swearing that an apple is an apple or that an apple is a pear.
2. Kipling, *From Day to Day with Kipling*, 12.
3. Kahf, *E-mails from Scheherazad*, 51.
4. For additional analysis of this story, see Sperling, "Aramaic Spousal Misunderstanding," 205–10; and Faust, *Agadata*, 165–71. Sperling interprets the misunderstandings along slightly different lines than proposed here.
5. Garcia et al., "Polysemy," 51–57.
6. Chamberlain, "Women's Languages," 579–81.
7. Tannen, "You Just Don't Understand." See, too, Tannen, "Why Can't He Hear What I'm Saying?," 22.
8. Gray, *Men Are from Mars*, 5.
9. Cameron, *The Myth of Mars and Venus*, 180.
10. Link and Kreuz, "Do Men and Women Differ?," 153–82.
11. Twain, *Adventures of Huckleberry Finn*, v.
12. For detailed discussion, see Sewell, *Mark Twain's Languages*.
13. Twain, *Roughing It*, 2:63.
14. Some scholars explain this passage along slightly different lines.
15. Rabinovich, *The Yom Kippur War*, 229.

5. Sufferings! Not Them and Not Their Reward!

1. From the *Amidah* for the Musaf ("additional" service) on the Sabbath.
2. I have skipped over some of the passage. In the original the story does not follow immediately after these first two units.
3. See his commentary to *Berakhot* 5b.
4. For additional literature on this story, see Kraemer, *Responses to Suffering*, 193–99; and Jacobs, "The Sugya on Sufferings," 32–44.
5. Another interpretive possibility is that Rabbi Elazar exposes his arm and illuminates the room, and Rabbi Yohanan then weeps for Rabbi Elazar's beauty, which is about to die.
6. It also is possible that by "children" Rabbi Yohanan means that Rabbi Elazar also had children who died.

6. The Ugly Vessel

1. Printings of the Talmud here read "Rabbi Elazar son of Rabbi Shimon," but most manuscripts and text witnesses have "Rabbi Shimon son of Elazar."
2. See Fraenkel, "Paronomasia in Aggadic Narratives," 44.
3. For additional analysis of this story, see Fraenkel, "Paronomasia in Aggadic Narratives," 27–51; and Kosman, "R. Simeon ben Eleazar and the Offended Man," 106–15.
4. Waldenberg, *Responsa Tzitz Eliezer*, 11:41, 106.
5. "Antigone," lines 707–23, in *Sophocles I*, 188.
6. This analysis is indebted to the brilliant reading of Nussbaum, *The Fragility of Goodness*, 79–82.
7. "Antigone," lines 1024–29, in *Sophocles I*, 200.
8. "Antigone," lines 1090–99, 203.
9. On this story see Balberg, "The Emperor's Daughter's New Skin," 181–226.

7. An Arrow in Satan's Eye

1. For additional literature, see Kosman, "Pelimo and Satan," 3–13. Some commentators assume that Satan appeared at the door covered with boils, and for that reason Pelimo did not want to admit him to the house or seat him at the table.
2. The text of the Hebrew Bible has God make the pronouncement, but we should probably understand that the angel speaks for God rather than God speaking about God in the third person. Quite possibly the words "the angel of" dropped out of the text.
3. See, for example, Kass, "The Wisdom of Repugnance," 678–705.
4. Kelly, *Yuck!*, 101–36; Nussbaum, *From Disgust to Humanity*, 8–25.
5. Kelly, *Yuck!*, 43–60.
6. Miller, *The Anatomy of Disgust*, 158–59.
7. Bynum, *Holy Feast and Holy Fast*, 144, 182.
8. Miller, *The Anatomy of Disgust*, 136.
9. Miller, *The Anatomy of Disgust*, 134.
10. Curtis, "Why Disgust Matters," 347–90.
11. Orwell, *The Road to Wigan Pier*, 159–60.
12. Kahan, "*The Anatomy of Disgust* in Criminal Law," 1621; Belkin, "Texas Judge Eases Sentence," 8.

13. See Kahan, "*The Anatomy of Disgust* in Criminal Law," 1634, which suggests "hate crimes" themselves should be reconceptualized as "disgust crimes."
14. This tradition appears in the commentaries of Rashi and the Tosafists to *Nedarim* 50b.
15. Some versions read, "Their stench came upon me from carrion, non-kosher meat, and reptiles," that is, that the women had consumed these foods and still reeked of them.

8. The Land of Truth

1. Eliyahu Dessler, *Mikhtav Me'Eliyahu*, cited in Shapiro, *Changing the Immutable*, 239.
2. Quoted in Geary, "How to Spot a Liar."
3. *Daily Mail*, "Men Lie Six Times a Day," http://www.dailymail.co.uk/news /article-1213171/Men-lie-times-day-twice-women-study-finds.html.
4. Feldman, "Self Presentation and Verbal Deception," 163–70.
5. Bernstein, "A Guide to Little White Lies."
6. Bhattacharjee, "Why We Lie," 30–56.
7. For a comprehensive discussion of the Rabbinic ethics of truth and lying, see additional references in Shapiro, "Is the Truth Really That Important?" in *Changing the Immutable*, 239–85.
8. Yoma 47a.
9. A. J. Jacobs, "I Think You're Fat." A slightly longer version appears in his book *The Guinea Pig Diaries*, 41–60.
10. Jacobs, *The Guinea Pig Diaries*, 56.
11. Nyberg, *The Varnished Truth*, 25
12. Nyberg, *The Varnished Truth*, 32.

9. Torah for Richer or Poorer

1. The talmudic passage also includes a "wicked man," whom I have omitted.
2. For additional literature on these stories, see Rieser, *The Hillel Narratives*, 1–19; Telushkin, *Hillel*, 4–11; and Bar-On, "The Art of the Chain Novel."
3. For this point I am indebted to Bar-On, "The Art of the Chain Novel."
4. Bindley, "Overscheduled Kids."

5. See Lytton, *Kosher: Private Regulation in the Age of Industrial Food.*
6. Prager, "The Tuition Squeeze."
7. Wertheimer, "The High Cost of Jewish Living."

10. Heroism and Humor

1. It is admittedly not completely clear that the brothers are Jewish or attend to Jews. But the lack of a parallel comment about their gentile dress suggests they wore the normal garb of Jews and worked within Jewish circles. Otherwise we would expect the storyteller to have the Rabbi comment on their lack of a blue fringe too.
2. Bakhtin, *Rabelais and His World,* 73.
3. Cited in Morreall, *Comic Relief,* 42.
4. Adkin, "The Fathers on Laughter," 149–52.
5. Epictetus, *Enchiridion,* 33, cited in Morreall, *Comic Relief: A Comprehensive Philosophy of Humor,* 146.
6. Quoted in Holtzman, "Does God Really Laugh?," 190.
7. Abdul-Rahman, *Islam: Questions and Answers,* 17.
8. Plato, *Laws,* 11:935e.
9. Quoted in Lindvall, *God Mocks,* 38.
10. Berger, *Redeeming Laughter,* 34.
11. For extensive analysis see Rubenstein, *Talmudic Stories,* 34–63.
12. Shipler, "Shcharansky Skeptical on Soviet Rights Policy."
13. Quoted in Gregory, *Exploring Positive Psychology,* 94.

11. Showdown in Court

1. Some translations, including the NJPS, understand that the priests wrote out the Torah for kings. This would be directed toward the same ends. I borrow the term "disempower" from Yair Lorberbaum's fine book on this topic, *Disempowered King: Monarchy in Classical Jewish Literature.*
2. For additional literature on this story, see Kafir, "King Yannai," 85–97; and Lorberbaum, *Disempowered King,* 100–107.
3. Marbury v. Madison, 5 U.S. 137 (1803).
4. See Whittington, *Political Foundations of Judicial Supremacy,* 32–35.
5. Rehnquist, "Judicial Independence Dedicated to Chief Justice Harry L. Carrico," 595.
6. Davis, "Supreme Court Nominee Calls Trump's Attacks Demoralizing."
7. See, for example, Rudenstine, *The Age of Deference.*

12. Alexander the Great and the Faraway King

1. Bosworth, *Alexander and the East*, v.
2. Augustine of Hippo, *City of God*, 4:4.
3. See Hill, *Treasure Trove in Law and Practice*, 18–33.
4. Hill, *Treasure Trove in Law and Practice*, 49.
5. Dillinger, *Magical Treasure Hunting in Europe and North America*, 18–19.
6. For a version of this motif, see the story in Philostratus, *Life of Apollonius of Tyana*, 2:39.
7. A paraphrase of the lyrics of "Extraordinary" from *Pippin* by Stephen Schwartz.

13. The Carpenter and His Apprentice

1. Some scholars interpret this story as pertaining to the destruction of Bethar, not Jerusalem.
2. See *Gittin* 65b.
3. Justin Martyr, *Dialogue with Trypho*, chap. 88.
4. This reading is somewhat problematic in that the introduction presents the story as an exemplification of Micah 2:2, which condemns the unjust defrauding of the innocent, suggesting the master was the victim. Nevertheless, we might attribute to the master a share of the blame, albeit less than that of the apprentice.

14. Standing on One Leg

1. Sender, *The Commentators' Haggadah*, 305.
2. Sender, 306.
3. See Philologos, "The Rest of 'The Rest Is Commentary.'"
4. Landsburg, *The Armchair Economist*, 3.
5. Stoll, "Zero Tolerance to Prejudice—The Rest Is Commentary."
6. Asimov, "Science: Beginning with Bone," 138.
7. Zucker, "AIDS, at 25."
8. Watson, "Humans Have Shorter Attention Span than Goldfish."
9. Lohr, "Impatient Web Users."
10. Quoted in Carr, "Is Google Making Us Stupid?"
11. Carr, "Is Google Making Us Stupid?"
12. Briles, "Short Is the New Black."
13. Kingsleg, "The Art of Slow Reading."
14. Bayard, *How to Talk about Books You Haven't Read*, xii–xix.

Bibliography

Abdul-Rahman, Muhammed Saed. *Islam: Questions and Answers: Manners (Part 1)*. London: MSA, 2003.

Adkin, Neil. "The Fathers on Laughter." *Orpheus* 6 (1985): 149–52.

Amirtham, Samuel. *Stories Make People: Examples of Theological Work in Community*. Geneva: WCC, 1989.

Asimov, Isaac. "Science: Beginning with Bone." *Magazine of Fantasy and Science Fiction* 72 (1987): 128–37.

Augustine of Hippo. *City of God*. Translated by Marcus Dods. Peabody MA: Hendrickson, 2009.

Avery-Peck, Alan J. "The Galilean Charismatic and Rabbinic Piety: The Holy Man in Rabbinic Literature." In *The Historical Jesus in Context*, edited by A. J. Levine, Dale C. Ellison, and John Dominic Crossan, 149–65. Princeton NJ: Princeton University Press, 2006.

Bakhtin, Mikhail. *Rabelais and His World*. Translated by Helene Iswolsky. Bloomington: Indiana University Press, 1984.

Balberg, Mira. "The Emperor's Daughter's New Skin: Corporeal Identity in the Dialogues of Rabbi Yehoshua ben Hanania and the Emperor's Daughter." *Jewish Studies Quarterly* 19 (2012): 1812–26.

Bar-On, Shraga. "The Art of the Chain Novel in b. Yoma 35b: Reconsidering The Social Values of the Babylonian Yeshivot." *Hebrew Union College Annual* 88 (2017): 55–88.

Bayard, Pierre. *How to Talk About Books You Haven't Read*. Translated by Jeffrey Mehlman. New York: Bloomsbury, 2007.

Belkin, Lisa. "Texas Judge Eases Sentence for Killer of Two Homosexuals. *New York Times*, December 17, 1988.

Berger, Peter. *Redeeming Laughter: The Comic Dimension of Human Experience*. New York: Walter de Gruyter, 1997.

Bernstein, Elizabeth. "A Guide to Little White Lies." *Wall Street Journal*, June 6, 2017.

Bhattacharjee, Yudhijit. "Why We Lie: The Science Behind Our Complicated Relationship with the Truth." *National Geographic*, June 2017:
305–51.

Bindley, Katherine. "Overscheduled Kids: How Too Many Activities Affect
Moms and Dads." *Huffington Post*, August 29, 2011, http://www
.huffingtonpost.com/2011/08/29/overscheduled-kids-stressed-out
-parents_n_940481.html.

Blidstein, Gerald. *Honor thy Father and Mother: Filial Responsibility in Jewish Law and Ethics.* New York: Ktav, 1975.

Bosworth, A. B. *Alexander and the East: The Tragedy of Triumph.* Oxford
UK: Clarendon, 1996.

Boyarin, Daniel. *Carnal Israel: Reading Sex in Talmudic Culture.* Berkeley:
University of California Press, 1993.

———. *Socrates and the Fat Rabbis.* Chicago: University of Chicago
Press, 2009.

Briles, Judith. "Short Is the New Black: Your Shrinking Reader Attention Span," May 6, 2015, www.thebookdesigner.com, http://www
.thebookdesigner.com/2015/05/short-is-the-new-black-your
-shrinking-reader-attention-span/.

Bynum, Caroline Walker. *Holy Feast and Holy Fast: The Religious Significance of Food to Medieval Women.* Berkeley: University of California
Press, 1987.

Cameron, Deborah. *The Myth of Mars and Venus: Do Men and Women Really
Speak Different Languages?* Oxford: Oxford University Press, 2007.

Carr, Nicholas. "Is Google Making Us Stupid?" *Atlantic*, July/August, 2008.

CBS News. "Trump Attacks on Judiciary Raise Safety Concerns for Judges,"
February 11, 2017, http://www.cbsnews.com/news/trump-attacks
-judiciary-safety-concerns-judges/.

Chamberlain, Alexander. "Women's Languages." *American Anthropologist*
14 (1912): 579–81.

Chaviv, Yaakov Ibn. *Ein Yaakov: The Ethical and Inspirational Teachings of
the Talmud.* Translated by Avraham Yaakov Finkel. Northvale NJ: Jason
Aronson, 1999.

Coates, Jennifer. *Men Talk: Stories in the Making of Masculinities.* Oxford
UK: Blackwell, 2003.

———. *Women, Men, and Language: A Sociolinguistic Account of Gender
Differences in Language.* 3rd ed. Harlow UK: Pearson Longman, 2004.

———. *Women Talk: Conversation Between Women Friends.* Oxford UK:
Blackwell, 1996.

Curtis, Valerie. "Why Disgust Matters." *Philosophical Transactions of the Royal Society of London. Series B, Biological Sciences* 366 (2011): 347–90.

Davis, Julie Hirschfeld. "Supreme Court Nominee Calls Trump's Attacks Demoralizing." *New York Times*, February 9, 2017.

Dillinger, Johannes. *Magical Treasure Hunting in Europe and North America: A History*. Basingstoke, UK: Palgrave Macmillan, 2012.

Dorff, Elliot N. "The Jewish Family in America: Contemporary Challenges and Traditional Resources." In *Marriage, Sex, and Family in Judaism*, edited by Michael J. Broyde, 214–43. Lanham MD: Rowman & Littlefield, 2005.

Entis, Laura. "Chronic Loneliness Is a Modern-Day Epidemic." *Fortune*, June 22, 2016.

Faust, Shmuel. *Agadata: Stories of Talmudic Drama* [in Hebrew]. Tel Aviv: Dvir, 2011.

Feldman, David. *Marital Relations, Birth Control, and Abortion in Jewish Law*. New York: Schocken, 1968.

Feldman, Robert S., James A. Forrest, and Benjamin R. Happ. "Self-Presentation and Verbal Deception: Do Self-Presenters Lie More?" *Journal of Basic and Applied Social Psychology* 24 (2002): 163–70.

Ford, Matt. "Trump's Attack on a Judge for Staying His Travel Ban." *Atlantic*, February 4, 2017.

Fraenkel, Yonah. *The Aggadic Narrative: Harmony of Form and Content* [in Hebrew]. Tel Aviv: Hakibbbutz Hameuhad, 2001.

————. "Paronomasia in Aggadic Narratives." *Scripta Hierosolymitana* 27 (1978): 27–51.

————. "Remarkable Phenomena in the Text History of the Aggadic Stories [in Hebrew]." In *Proceedings of the Seventh World Congress of Jewish Studies. Studies in Talmud, Halachah, and Midrash* (1981): 456–9.

Garcia, Michael B., Lynne Geiser, Corrine McCawley, Alleen Pace Nilsen, and Elle Wolterbeek. "Polysemy: A Neglected Concept in Wordplay." *English Journal* 96 (2007): 51–57.

Geary, James. "How to Spot a Liar." *Time*, March 13, 2000.

Giddens, Anthony. *Modernity and Self-Identity: Self and Society in the Late Modern Age*. Stanford CA: Stanford University Press, 1991.

Ginzberg, Louis. *Legends of the Jews,* 7 vols. Philadelphia: Jewish Publication Society, 1909–38.

Gottschall, Jonathan. *The Storytelling Animal: How Stories Make Us Human.* Boston: Harcourt, 2012.

Gray, John. *Men Are from Mars, Women Are from Venus*. New York: Harper-Collins, 1992.

Gregory, Erik M., and Pamela B. Rutledge. *Exploring Positive Psychology: The Science of Happiness and Well-Being*. Santa Barbara CA: Greenwood, 2016.

Harris, Rebecca. "The Loneliness Epidemic: We're More Connected Than Ever—But Are We Feeling More Alone?" *Independent*, March 30, 2015, http://www.independent.co.uk/life-style/health-and-families /features/the-loneliness-epidemic-more-connected-than-ever-but -feeling-more-alone-10143206.html.

Hasan-Rokem, Galit. *Web of Life: Folklore and Midrash in Rabbinic Literature*. Translated by Batya Stein. Stanford CA: Stanford University Press, 2000.

Hezser, Catherine. *Form, Function, and Historical Significance of the Rabbinic Story in Yerushalmi Neziqin*. Tübingen, Germany: J. C. B. Mohr, 1993.

Hill, George. *Treasure Trove in Law and Practice from the Earliest Time to the Present Day*. Oxford UK: Clarendon, 1936.

Holt-Lunstad, Julianne, Timothy B. Smith, Mark Baker, Tyler Harris, and David Stephenson. "Loneliness and Social Isolation as Risk Factors for Mortality: A Meta-Analytic Review." *Perspectives on Psychological Science* 10 (2015): 227–37.

Holtzman, Livnat. "'Does God Really Laugh?'—Appropriate and Inappropriate Descriptions of God in Islamic Traditionalist Theology." In *Laughter in the Middle Ages and Early Modern Times*, edited by Albrecht Classen. Berlin: Walter de Gruyter, 2010.

Hughes, J. Donald. *An Environmental History of the World: Humankind's Changing Role in the Community of Life*. New York: Routledge, 2001.

Jacobs, A. J. *The Guinea Pig Diaries*. New York: Simon and Schuster, 2009.

———. "I Think You're Fat." *Esquire*, July 24, 2007.

Jacobs, Louis. *Structure and Form in the Babylonian Talmud*. Cambridge: Cambridge University Press, 1991.

———. "The Sugya on Sufferings." In *Studies in Aggadah, Targum and Jewish Liturgy in Memory of Joseph Heinemann*, edited by Jakob J. Petuchowski and Ezra Fleischer, 32–44. Jerusalem: Magnes, 1981.

Jellison, Jerald. *I'm Sorry, I Didn't Mean To, and Other Lies We Love to Tell*. Chicago: Contemporary, 1977.

Justin Martyr. *Dialogue with Trypho*. http://www.earlychristianwritings .com/text/justinmartyr-dialoguetrypho.html.

Kafir, Zivya. "King Yannai and Shimon ben Shetah [in Hebrew]." *Tura* 3 (1994): 85–97.

Kahan, Dan M. "*The Anatomy of Disgust* in Criminal Law." *Michigan Law Review* 96 (1998): 1621–57.

Kahf, Mohja. *E-mails from Scheherazad*. Gainesville: University Press of Florida, 2003.

Kass, Leon. "The Wisdom of Repugnance: Why We Should Ban the Cloning of Humans." *Valparaiso University Law Review* 32 (1998): 679–705.

Kelly, Daniel. *Yuck!: The Nature and Moral Significance of Disgust*. Cambridge MA: MIT Press, 2011.

Kim, Halla. *Kant and the Foundations of Morality*. Lanham MD: Lexington, 2015.

Kingsleg, Patrick. "The Art of Slow Reading." *Guardian*, July 15, 2010, https://www.theguardian.com/books/2010/jul/15/slow-reading.

Kipling, Rudyard. *From Day to Day with Kipling,* edited by Wallace and Frances Rice. New York: Barse & Hopkins, 1911.

Kosman, Admiel. "'Internal Homeland' and 'External Homeland': A Literary and Psychoanalytical Study of the Narrative of R. Assi and His Aged Mother." *Hebrew Studies* 46 (2005): 259–77.

———. *Men's World: Reading Masculinity in Jewish Stories in a Spiritual Context*. Translated by Edward Levin. Würzburg, Germany: Ergon Verlag, 2009.

———. "Pelimo and Satan: A Divine Lesson in the Public Latrine." *CCAR Journal* 57 (2010): 31–3.

———. "R. Simeon ben Eleazar and the Offended Man: The Ugliness of the Haughty Scholar." *European Judaism* 40 (2007): 116–25.

Kraemer, David C. *Responses to Suffering in Classical Rabbinic Literature*. New York: Oxford University Press, 1995.

Kushner, Harold. *When All You've Ever Wanted Isn't Enough*. New York: Kushner Enterprises, 2002.

Landsburg, Steven E. *The Armchair Economist: Economics and Everyday Life*. New York: Free Press, 2012.

Levinson, Joshua. "From Narrative Practise to Cultural Poetics: Literary Anthropology and the Rabbinic Sense of Self." In *Homer and the Bible in the Eyes of Ancient Interpreters,* edited by Maren R. Niehoff, 345–67. Leiden, Netherlands: Brill, 2012.

Lewis, Michael. *The Undoing Project: A Friendship that Changed the World*. New York: W. W. Norton, 2016.

Licht, Chaim. *Ten Legends of the Sages: The Image of the Sage in Rabbinic Literature*. Hoboken NJ: Ktav, 1991.

Locke, John L. *Duels and Duets: Why Men and Women Talk So Differently.* Cambridge: Cambridge University Press, 2011.

Lohr, Steve. "For Impatient Web Users, an Eye Blink Is Just Too Long to Wait." *New York Times,* March 1, 2012, A1.

Lorberbaum, Yair. *Disempowered King: Monarchy in Classical Jewish Literature.* New York: Continuum, 2011.

Lindvall, Terry. *God Mocks: A History of Religious Satire from the Hebrew Prophets to Stephen Colbert.* New York: NYU Press, 2015.

Link, Kristen E., and Roger J. Kreuz. "Do Men and Women Differ in Their Use of Nonliteral Language When They Talk about Emotions?" In *Figurative Language Comprehension,* edited by H. Colston and A. Katz, 153–80. Mahway NJ: Lawrence Erlbaum, 2005.

Lyons, O. "An Iroquois Perspective." In *American Indian Environments: Ecological Issues in Native American History,* edited by C. Vecsey and R. W. Venables, 171–74. New York: Syracuse University Press, 1980.

Lytton, Timothy. *Kosher: Private Regulation in the Age of Industrial Food.* Cambridge MA: Harvard University Press, 2013.

MacIntyre, Alasdair. *After Virtue.* Notre Dame IN: University of Notre Dame Press, 1981.

Marbury v. Madison, 5 U.S. 137 (1803).

McCarthy, Barry and Emily. *Rekindling Desire.* New York: Routledge, 2014.

Meir, Ofra. *Rabbi Judah the Patriarch: Palestinian and Babylonian Portrait of a Leader* [in Hebrew]. Tel Aviv: Hakibbutz Hameuhad, 1999.

"Men Lie Six Times a Day and Twice as Often as Women, Study Finds." Accessed March 7, 2017. http://www.dailymail.co.uk/news/article -1213171/Men-lie-times-day-twice-women-study-finds.html.

Miller, William Ian. *The Anatomy of Disgust.* Cambridge MA: Harvard University Press, 1998.

Mitchell, Mark T. "The Homeless Modern." *Intercollegiate Review* 41, no. 1 (Spring 2006): 13–22.

Morreall, John. *Comic Relief: A Comprehensive Philosophy of Humor.* Chichester, UK: Wiley-Blackwell, 2009.

Naeh, Shlomo. "Freedom and Celibacy: A Talmudic Variation on Tales of Temptation and Fall in Genesis and its Syrian Background." In *The Book of Genesis in Jewish and Oriental Christian Interpretation: A Collection of Essays,* edited by Judith Frishman and Lucas Van Rompay, 73–89. Lovanii, Belgium: Peeters, 1997.

Neusner, Jacob. *A History of the Jews in Babylonia.* Rpt: Chico CA: Scholars, 1984.

Nussbaum, Martha. *The Fragility of Goodness: Luck and Ethics in Greek Tragedy and Philosophy*. Rev. ed. Cambridge: Cambridge University Press, 1986.

————. *From Disgust to Humanity: Sexual Orientation and Constitutional Law*. New York: Oxford University Press, 2010.

Nyberg, David. *The Varnished Truth: Truth-Telling and Deceiving in Ordinary Life*. Chicago: University of Chicago Press, 1993.

Orwell, George. *The Road to Wigan Pier*. New York: Harcourt, Brace, 1958.

Paik, Anthony, Kenneth J. Sanchagrin, and Karen Heimer. "Broken Promises: Abstinence and Sexual and Reproductive Health." *Journal of Marriage and Sexuality* 78, no. 2 (2016): 546–61.

Pearl, Chaim. *Theology in Rabbinic Stories*. New York: Baker Academic, 1995.

Philologos. "The Rest of 'The Rest Is Commentary.'" *Jewish Forward*, September 24, 2008. http://forward.com/culture/14250/the-rest-of-the-rest-is-commentary-02564/.

Philostratus. *Life of Apollonius of Tyana*, https://archive.org/details/philostratusinho00philuoft.

Pillemer, Karl. *Thirty Lessons for Living: Tried and True Advice from the Wisest Americans*. New York: Penguin, 2011.

Plato. *Laws*. Translated by Benjamin Jowett. Mineola NY: Dover, 2006.

Prager, Yossi. "The Tuition Squeeze: Paying the Price for Jewish Education." *Jewish Action: The Magazine of the Orthodox Union*. October 18, 2005, https://www.ou.org/jewish_action/10/2005/tuition-squeeze-paying-price-jewish-education/.

Quote Investigator, accessed February 13, 2017, http://quoteinvestigator.com/2013/01/22/borrow-earth/.

Rabinovich, Abraham. *The Yom Kippur War: The Epic Encounter that Transformed the Middle East*. Rpt: New York: Schocken, 2005.

Rehnquist, William. "Judicial Independence Dedicated to Chief Justice Harry L. Carrico: Symposium Remarks." *University of Richmond Law Review* 38 (2004): 579–96.

Rieser, Louis. *The Hillel Narratives: What the Tales of the First Rabbis Can Teach Us about Our Judaism*. Teaneck NJ: Ben Yehuda, 2009.

Rosen-Zvi, Ishay. "The Mishnaic Mental Revolution: A Reassessment." *Journal of Jewish Studies* 46 (2015): 36–58.

Rovner, Jay. "'Rav Assi Had This Old Mother': The Structure, Meaning, and Formation of a Talmudic Story." In *Creation and Composition: The Contribution of the Bavli Redactors (Stammaim) to the Aggada,* edited by Jeffrey L. Rubenstein, 101–24. Tübingen, Germany: Mohr-Siebek, 2005.

Rubenstein, Jeffrey. *The Culture of the Babylonian Talmud*. Baltimore: Johns Hopkins University Press, 2003.

———. *Rabbinic Stories*. Mahwah NJ: Paulist, 2002.

———. *Stories of the Babylonian Talmud*. Baltimore: Johns Hopkins University Press, 2010.

———. *Talmudic Stories, Narrative Art, Composition, and Culture*. Baltimore: Johns Hopkins University Press, 1999.

Rudenstine, David. *The Age of Deference: The Supreme Court, National Security, and the Constitutional Order*. New York: Oxford University Press, 2016.

Sands, Robert. *Forestry in a Global Context*. 2nd ed. Boston: CABI, 2013.

Sender, Yitzchak. *The Commentators' Haggadah*. Jerusalem: Feldheim, 1991.

"Seven Cultures that Celebrate Aging and Respect Their Elders." *Huffington Post*, February 25, 2014, http://www.huffingtonpost.com/2014/02/25/what-other-cultures-can-teach_n_4834228.html.

Sewell, David. *Mark Twain's Languages: Discourse, Dialogue, and Linguistic Variety*. Berkeley: University of California Press, 1987.

Shapiro, Marc. *Changing the Immutable: How Orthodox Judaism Rewrites Its History*. Portland OR: Littman Library of Jewish Civilization, 2015.

Sheer, Robert. "The Playboy Interview: Jimmy Carter." *Playboy* 23:11 (November 1976): 63–86.

Shipler, David K. "Shcharansky Skeptical on Soviet Rights Policy." *New York Times,* February 17, 1986, https://www.nytimes.com/1986/02/17/world/shcharansky-skeptical-on-soviet-rights-policy.html.

Simon-Shoshan, Moshe. *Stories of the Law: Narrative Discourse and the Construction of Authority in the Mishnah*. New York: Oxford University Press, 2012.

Sophocles I. Translated by David Greene. Chicago: University of Chicago Press, 1991.

Sperling, David. "Aramaic Spousal Misunderstanding." *Journal of the American Oriental Society* 115 (1995): 205–9.

Stern, David. *Parables in Midrash: Narrative and Exegesis in Rabbinic Literature*. Cambridge MA: Harvard University Press, 1991.

Stoll, Jay. "Zero Tolerance to Prejudice—The Rest Is Commentary." http://www.huffingtonpost.co.uk/jay-stoll/prejudice-anti-semitism-zero-tolerance_b_1210491.html.

Tannen, Deborah. "Why Can't He Hear What I'm Saying?" *McCall's,* January, 1986: 20–24.

————. *You Just Don't Understand: Women and Men in Conversation*. New York: William Morrow, 1990.

Telushkin, Joseph. *Hillel: If Not Now, When?* New York: Schocken, 2010.

Twain, Mark. *Adventures of Huckleberry Finn, 1885*. Rpt: Mineola NY: Dover, 2005.

————. *Roughing It*. New York: Harper and Brothers, 1899.

Urbach, Ephraim. *The Sages: Their Concepts and Beliefs*. Translated by I. Abrahams. Jerusalem: Magnes, 1979.

Valler, Shulamit. *Woman and Womanhood in the Stories of the Babylonian Talmud*. Translated by Betty Rozen. Atlanta GA: Scholars, 1999.

Waldenberg, Eliezer Yehudah. *Responsa Tzitz Eliezer*. Jerusalem: Rav Kook, 1973.

Watson, Leon. "Humans Have Shorter Attention Span than Goldfish Thanks to Smartphones." *Telegraph*, May 15, 2105, http://www.telegraph.co.uk/science/2016/03/12/humans-have-shorter-attention-span-than-goldfish-thanks-to-smart/.

Weil, Simone. *The Need for Roots*. New York: Routledge, 1995.

Wertheimer, Jack. "The High Cost of Jewish Living." *Commentary*, March 1, 2010.

Whittington, Keith E. *Political Foundations of Judicial Supremacy*. Princeton NJ: Princeton University Press, 2007.

Wiesel, Elie. *The Gates of the Forest*. New York: Holt, Rinehart, and Winston, 1966.

Wimpfheimer, Barry S. *Narrating the Law—A Poetics of Talmudic Legal Stories*. Philadelphia: University of Pennsylvania Press, 2011.

Wood, Mary C., and Zach Welker. "Tribes as Trustees Again (Part 1): The Emerging Tribal Role in the Conservation Trust Movement." *Harvard Environmental Law Review* 32 (2008): 373–432.

Yassif, Eli. *The Hebrew Folktale: History, Genre, Meaning*. Translated by Jacqueline S. Teitelbaum. Bloomington: Indiana University Press, 1999.

Young, Phillip. "Fallen from Time: The Mythic Rip Van Winkle." *Kenyon Review* 22 (1960): 547–73.

Zucker, Abigil. "AIDS, at 25, Offers No Easy Answers." *New York Times*, June 6, 2006.

Subjects Index

law, Jewish (*halakhah*), xiv–xv, xxv–xxvii, 22, 46–47, 52, 108, 132, 146, 167, 207–8, 214, 240, 252, 266n6; authority and, 198–99; disgust and, 135–36; king and, 207–14, 218; of Levirate marriage, 43–44; of lost objects, 230–31; of oaths and vows, 57; of suicide, 20. *See also* intentions; kings: biblical law of; Sabbath

lentils, 53–56

Levi Yitzḥak of Berdichev, 91

Liar, Liar! (film), 156–57

lies and lying, 141–61, 240; Kantian ethic of, 153–55; vs. "modifying one's words," 148–50; studies of, 143–44; types of, 142–43, 146. *See also* truth

liminality, 123

lineage, 44, 95–96

literature, oral, xvi, xxv–xxvi, 38, 223

loneliness, 9–10, 86, 124

Maimonides, Moses, 81–82

Mar, son of Ravina, 193

Marbury v. Madison, 218–19. *See also* judicial review

market, 38, 56, 151, 182–87

marriage, xx, 33, 36, 50–51, 52–68, 96, 181, 185, 193, 225–26; contract/settlement (*ketuba*), 146, 238, 240–41; early, 121; Levirate, 43–44; seven wedding blessings of, 243–44. *See also* divorce

measure-for-measure principle, xii–xiii, 40, 59, 100, 212, 241

memento mori, 86–87. *See also* death

memorization , xvi, xxvi, 38, 166

menstruation, 132, 182–84, 188

Messianic Age, 45, 193

mezuzah, 110, 123

Middle Ages, xvi, xxiii, xxv, xxvii, 20, 41, 87–88, 122, 133, 138, 141, 222, 229–30, 266n2

midrash, xv, xxvii, 5, 75, 79, 107, 208–9, 243, 255. *See also* biblical interpretation

miracles, 3, 6, 19, 87–88, 186, 189, 198, 212

Mishnah, xiv, xxv–xxvii, 103, 136–37, 146, 185, 207, 217, 230, 235, 255

mitzvot. *See* commandments (mitzvot)

modernity, xvi–xvii, xxi–xxv, 10, 12, 20–21, 52, 69, 88, 135, 162, 260–61, 265n5; governments of, 214, 218–21

modesty, 48, 146–48, 150, 185

Moses, 11, 73–74, 155

murder, 47, 118–20, 135–36, 149, 152–55, 207–13, 226, 230

myths, xx, xxi, 160; Greek, xix, 14, 226, 229

Naḥman, Rav, 47

names, xvii, 64, 228; absence of, 36; of God, 57, 267n1; symbolic, xvi, 3, 120–21, 147, 225

Natan, Rabbi, 199

Native Americans, 13–14

next world. *See* world to come

Nyberg, David, 158–59

oaths and vows, 57–59, 63–65, 267n1

oven, 34–35, 40, 48; of Akhnai, 198–200

parents, honor of, 19, 21–32

peace, 59, 148–50, 183–84, 191; angel of, 159–60

Pelimo, 116–35

persecution, 47, 131, 183–84, 188–91, 197, 201

Persia and Persians, xvi, xx, xxvi, 184, 201, 206, 228, 233; emperor of, 185, 187, 230; law of, 230; in province of Ḥuzestan, 182, 185; religion of, 184. *See also* Babylonia

philosophy, 50–51, 73, 147, 225; Greek, 222; Kantian, 152–55; of radical honesty, 157; Stoic, 192. *See also* Aristotle; Plato

piety, 15, 25, 81, 105, 117, 119–26; cleanliness and, 103; disgust and, 133–34, 137. *See also* comandments (mitzvot); Torah

Plato, 12, 50, 192

pomegranate, 34, 39–41

poverty and the poor, 43, 85–86, 117–20, 124–26, 134, 162–69, 177–80, 253. *See also* charity; riches

prayer, xiv, xv, xxi–xxii, 3, 5, 26, 34–36, 49, 74, 91, 126, 162; that annuls persecutions, 183–84; for Day of Atonement, 11, 105–8, 116–17, 127; for death, 9, 20; for entering latrine, 128; of Musaf, 267n1; for the Sabbath, 169; *Shema*, 74, 187, 227; of supplication (*Taḥanun*), 36

presidents (U.S.), 45, 219–21; Donald Trump, 220–21

pride, 98–100, 110, 120, 137–38

privacy, 135, 146, 148, 150

prophets and prophecy, xx, 106, 111, 130, 186, 205–6, 244–47; cessation of, 206; Isaiah, 106, 116; Jeremiah, 106; Nathan, 234; Samuel, 149, 205. *See also* Elijah the Prophet

prostitutes, 38, 43–45, 189, 266n8

the public, 48, 56, 100, 122, 131, 135, 185, 242, 250; covering hair in, 146; domain, xi–xiv, 263; embarrassment in, 127, 152, 246; treasury, 229–30

Qushta (fictional place), 143–54, 159

Rabbah, 194

Rami bar Ḥama, 129

Rashi, 81, 114, 120

Rav, 237, 239

Rava, 4, 10, 78–83, 144–48

reality, deeper view of, xiii, 17, 20, 99, 188, 197

rebuke, 70, 80, 118–19, 126–27, 164, 205, 212; of Satan, 118–20, 130

reed, 96–97, 109–10

the Renaissance, 87

repentance, 74, 76, 79, 89, 116–17, 130, 205

riches, 84, 87, 128, 137–38, 164, 210, 216, 239, 253; Alexander the Great and, 223–28; Torah study and, 170–80. *See also* poverty and the poor; treasure

righteousness and the righteous, 34, 44, 116–17, 120, 128, 181, 183–91; angel of, 159–60; suffering of, 73–75, 81, 82, 87–90, 181–82. *See also* piety

Rip Van Winkle, 7, 14–15

Romans and Rome, xx, xxvi, 15, 75, 192, 201, 210–11, 229, 233–35; destruction of temple by, xxv, 236–47; emperor of, 15, 16–19;

Biblical and Rabbinic Sources Index